SSSP

Springer Series in Social Psychology

Advisory Editor:
Robert F. Kidd

Springer Series in Social Psychology

Advisory Editor: Robert F. Kidd

SSSP

The Ethics of Social Research
Surveys and
Experiments

Edited by
Joan E. Sieber

Springer-Verlag New York Heidelberg Berlin

Joan E. Sieber
Department of Psychology
California State University—Hayward
Hayward, California 94542
U.S.A.

Robert F. Kidd, *Advisory Editor*
Department of Psychology
Boston University
Boston, Massachusetts 02215
U.S.A.

Library of Congress Cataloging in Publication Data
Main entry under title:
The Ethics of social research.
  (Springer series in social psychology)
  Bibliography: v. 1, p.   ; v. 2, p.
  Includes indexes.
  Contents: [1] Surveys and experiments—[2] Fieldwork, regulation, and publication.
  1. Social psychology—Research—Moral and ethical aspects—Collected works. 2. Social
sciences—Research—Moral and ethical aspects—Collected works. I. Sieber, Joan E. II.
Series.
HM251.E76   174'.9301   82-5486
                    AACR2

Printed in the United States of America

9 8 7 6 5 4 3 2 1

ISBN 0-387-90687-8   Springer-Verlag   New York   Heidelberg   Berlin
ISBN 3-540-90687-8   Springer-Verlag   Berlin   Heidelberg   New York

Preface

Social scientists are unprepared for many of the ethical problems that arise in their research, and for criticisms of their ethics that seem to ignore such cherished scientific values as objectivity and freedom of inquiry. Yet, they possess methodological talent and insight into human nature that can be used to understand and resolve these problems. The contributors to this book demonstrate that criticism of the ethics of social research can stimulate constructive development of methodology.

Both volumes of *The Ethics of Social Research* were written for and by social scientists to show how ethical dilemmas arise in the day-to-day conduct of social research and how they can be resolved. The topics discussed in this book include ethical problems that arise in experiments and sample surveys; the companion volume deals with the ethical issues involved in fieldwork and in the regulation and publication of research. With candor and humor, many of the contributors describe lessons they have learned about themselves, their methods, and their research participants. Collectively, they illustrate that both humanists and determinists are likely to encounter ethical dilemmas in their research, albeit different ones, and that a blending of deterministic and humanistic approaches may be needed to solve these dilemmas.

The aim of this book is to assist investigators in preparing to meet some of the ethical problems that await the unwary. It offers perspectives, values, and guidelines for anticipating problems and devising solutions. Many of its chapters even offer specific methodological and procedural solutions to clearly defined problems. However, no ethical dilemma in social research is solved once and for all, and no procedure or value orientation, however broad and sophisticated, is acceptable to all or universally effective in confronting potential problems. Consequently, an equally important aim of this book is to provide role-models and a learning set that will enable investigators to effectively focus their moral sensitivity and scientific creativity on the unique problems that arise in their own research.

Appreciation is due various people who made this book possible. First, I acknowledge some intellectual debts: to Herbert Kelman, whose book, *A Time to*

Speak, compelled me to recognize that there is an important place in social science for conscience, humanism and social activism, along with intellect, determinism and objectivity; to Ian Mitroff and Ralph Kilmann, whose book, *The Methodologies of Social Science,* helped me to understand why social scientists find it hard to discuss the ethics of their research without getting upset (at one another and at society), and hard to agree on what their ethical problems are or how they should be handled; and to Donald Campbell and Robert Boruch who have been demonstrating for a long time that social scientists can use the tools of their trade to cope effectively with ethical problems in their research.

Second, I acknowledge my thanks to those who have worked with me: to the contributors for being so patient with my efforts; to my students and numerous colleagues who read chapters and commented on the organization of the book, especially my colleague, Conrad Taeuber, who kept me supplied with good ideas during the critical period of development of these volumes; to Diana Smith and LaVonne Dillian for their assistance with the preparation of this manuscript; and to the people at Springer-Verlag, who worked with speed, competence, and graciousness to transform a big box of paper into two attractive volumes.

Finally, I thank my long-term co-worker, my husband, Ben Zeitman, for his encouragement, and for the love and energy he has contributed to our creation of a two-career household in which activities such as book editing and wine making can exist side-by-side with a minimum of chaos.

Shenandoah Valley, California   Joan E. Sieber

Contents

Contributors

Robert F. Boruch, Department of Psychology, Northwestern University, Evanston, Illinois 60201, U.S.A.

Joe Shelby Cecil, Federal Judicial Center, 1520 H Street, Washington, D.C. 20005, U.S.A.

Ross F. Conner, Department of Social Ecology, University of California—Irvine, Irvine, California 92717, U.S.A.

Daniel M. Geller, TEAM Associates, Inc., Suite 510, 1625 I Street N.W., Washington, D.C. 20006, U.S.A.

Shirley Foster Hartley, Department of Sociology, California State University— Hayward, Hayward, California 94542, U.S.A.

Charles R. Knerr, Jr., Department of Political Science, University of Texas at Arlington, Arlington, Texas 76019, U.S.A.

Eleanor K. Levine, Department of Psychology, California State University— Hayward, Hayward, California 94542, U.S.A.

Chalsa M. Loo, Stevenson College, University of California—Santa Cruz, Santa Cruz, California 95064, U.S.A.

Philip H. Mirvis, School of Management, Boston University, 212 Bay State Road, Boston, Massachusetts 02215, U.S.A.

Stanley E. Seashore, Institute for Social Research, University of Michigan—Ann Arbor, Box 1248, Ann Arbor, Michigan 48106, U.S.A.

Joan E. Sieber, Department of Psychology, California State University—Hayward, Hayward, California 94542, U.S.A.

Anthony G. Turner, U.S. Department of Commerce, Bureau of the Census, 303 Scuderi, Washington, D.C. 20233, U.S.A.

Chapter 1

Ethical Dilemmas in Social Research

Joan E. Sieber

What kinds of ethical dilemmas arise in social research? This chapter describes the set of dilemmas that confronts investigators, and indicates how and why dilemmas arise and why social scientists are largely unprepared to solve them. The major ethical and scientific values that are available to guide social scientists are examined along with some of the characteristics of effective problem solving that underlie the work presented in subsequent chapters. Emphasis is placed on the creative use of alternative social science methods and value systems.

Ethical Dilemmas in Social Research

Ethical dilemmas in social research have become the subject of considerable concern during the last decade. Social scientists and their critics have raised many difficult questions such as the following:

1. Is it wrong to use deception? How can spontaneous private behavior be studied experimentally without using deception?
2. When does social science research violate individual interests in privacy? Can procedural solutions to these problems be found?
3. When investigators befriend persons in order to gather data (i.e., when investigators become participant observers), what obligation have they to respect and protect the privacy of the persons they study?

Case studies of ethical dilemmas in social research illustrate how problems arise and why it is difficult to find morally acceptable solutions. The case of sociologist Laud Humphreys' study (1970) of the "tearoom trade" provides a useful introduction to some of the kinds of ethical problems that this book's contributors have sought to solve:

The public, as well as law-enforcement authorities, tend to hold simplistic stereotypes about men who commit impersonal sexual acts in public restrooms. As a consequence, "tearoom sex," as fellatio in public rest rooms is called, accounts for the majority of homosexual arrests in the United States. Laud Humphreys, then a doctoral candidate in sociology in Washington University, sought to learn what kinds of men seek quick, impersonal sexual gratification and what motivates them to do so.

Humphreys gathered some of his data by stationing himself in "tearooms" and assuming the role of "watchqueen," the individual who keeps watch and coughs when a police car stops nearby or a stranger approaches. He played that role faithfully while observing hundreds of acts of fellatio. He gained the confidence of some of the men he observed, disclosed to them his role as a scientist, and persuaded them to tell him about the rest of their lives and about their motives for engaging in tearoom trade. Those who were willing to talk openly with him tended to be among the better educated members of the tearoom trade. To avoid socioeconomic class bias, Humphreys secretly followed some of the other men he observed and recorded the license numbers of their cars. A year later, and carefully disguised, Humphreys appeared at their homes and claimed to be a health service interviewer. He interviewed them about their marital status, employment, and so on. Most of these interviews developed into quite personal discussions in which the men disclosed a great deal. Humphreys was aware that his data could have been subpoenaed, which probably would have led to the arrest of his subjects; he claims to have guarded the data with great care.

Humphreys' findings destroy stereotypes: Fifty-four percent of his subjects were married and lived with their wives; superficial analysis would suggest that they were exemplary citizens who had satisfactory marriages. Most of these married men did not think of themselves either as bisexual or as homosexual. The marriages of these men were important to them but were marked with tension. Most of these men or their wives were Catholic and since the birth of their last child, conjugal relations had been rare, in some cases for reasons connected with family planning. Their alternative source of sexual gratification had to be quick, inexpensive, and impersonal. It could not entail involvement that would threaten their already unstable marriage, or jeopardize their most important asset, their standing as father of their children. They wanted some form of orgasm-producing action that was less lonely than masturbation and less involving than a love relationship. The 62% of Humphreys' subjects who seemed to be bisexual or homosexual included successful professional men, business men, generally unsuccessful men, and unemployed men. Only about 14% of Humphreys' subjects were members of the gay community and interested primarily in homosexual relations (Humphreys, 1970).

The gay community praised Humphreys' research for dispelling myths and stereotypes. Police departments in some cities responded to the knowledge he produced by ceasing to raid tearooms. Many social scientists have applauded Humphreys' research. The Society for the Study of Social Problems chose Humphreys' book for its highly prestigious annual C. Wright Mills Award. But others were outraged. Journalist Nicholas von Hoffman (1970) wrote the following commentary in *The Washington Post*:

> We're so preoccupied with defending our privacy against insurance investigators, dope sleuths, counter-espionage men, divorce detectives and credit checkers that we overlook the social scientists behind the hunting blinds

who're also peeping into what we thought were our most private and secret lives. But there they are, studying us, taking notes, getting to know us, as indifferent as everybody else to the feeling that to be a complete human involves having an aspect of ourselves that's unknown.

There was professional outrage as well. Some faculty members in the Sociology Department of Washington University who were not on Humphreys' dissertation committee and who learned of the research after it was completed were outraged at the methods he had employed and demanded that his doctoral degree be rescinded.

Humphreys' research raises a host of ethical questions: Is it ever justified to act contrary to the interests of subjects in order to obtain valuable knowledge? Does the importance of Humphreys' research justify spying on people and later visiting their homes and families and interviewing them under false pretexts? Did he endanger the social standing of his subjects? Would it be justifiable to replicate the study? Should student researchers be allowed to spy on subjects or to study illegal behavior? Are there scientifically valid ways to investigate behavior such as this without incurring the risks that Humphreys took?

Cases such as these compel one to puzzle over the seeming impossibility of studying some kinds of behavior in a way that is both scientifically valid and respectful to those who are studied. They provide material for philosophers, discouragement for scientists who can find no satisfactory way out of such dilemmas, and challenge for scientists who can envision possible solutions.

The Purpose of the Book

This book developed in response to such dilemmas, and out of concern for investigators who become embroiled in dilemmas that they cannot solve satisfactorily. In the ensuing chapters, examples are presented in which social scientists move beyond the recognition of dilemmas to their effective resolution. Each of these contributions illustrates the recognition of a dilemma and its ramifications, development of criteria for selecting a more ethical approach, development of procedural or methodological alternatives that meet these criteria, and ultimately a decision that the investigator can live with.

This book is intended to give social scientists (1) a greater awareness of some kinds of research problems that require ethical awareness and decision making, (2) a sense of the range of decision criteria and choice alternatives that a social scientist might consider, (3) evidence that a concerted effort to place the problem in appropriate perspective and to create and evaluate viable choice alternatives can lead to sound solutions, and (4) effective role models. The authors of subsequent chapters demonstrate the enormous creativity and productivity with which the methods of social science may be used to do valid research ethically. (In the final part of this chapter, the four major social science methods and their relevance to ethical choice are discussed.)

The chapters that follow contrast with much that has been said about conflict between the interests of scientists in freedom of inquiry and the interest of society in individual self-determination, privacy, and safety. It has been suggested that the conflict is unresolvable, and hence that we must take sides. In contrast, the position taken by the authors in this book does not presume an irresolvable or irreducible conflict and is not one of advocacy for one side. It is that the interests of both science and society can be served as new methodological and procedural alternatives become available for use in solving ethical problems, and that these interests may then become complementary. Ethical dilemmas in certain areas of research are inevitable. For example, the scientist's interest in studying private behavior is in conflict with the individual's interest in protecting privacy. However, it is precisely within the context of such conflicts that social scientists' ethical sensitivity coupled with persistent search for good solutions can lead to the development of methods and procedures that both serve the interests of research participants and increase scientists' power to obtain valid, sensitive data. (See, for example, Chapters 2, 3, 4, 5, 6, 8, 9, and 10, this volume, and Chapters 3, 4, 5, 6, and 7, companion volume.)

In one sense, the basic ethical problem that we address is as old as man's political and scientific activities: How can one observe and intervene in the lives of others without inflicting harm or wronging persons? (For a discussion of the distinction between inflicting harm and doing wrong, see Cassell, Chapter 1, companion volume.) But, in another sense the problem is new, or at least social scientists have failed to recognize it until about 1970. The dominant social science methodology stresses objectivity, accuracy, and understanding of social processes. Accordingly, it was widely assumed that social science, by its nature, is value free and that social scientists have better developed social consciences and greater awareness of the interests and needs of others than most, and hence are well-prepared to make the ethical judgments required by their work.

Mindful of the obligations of social scientists to remain objective and to respect the privacy of those whose lives are studied, some professional associations undertook early to develop ethical codes reflecting these obligations. The American Psychological Association began to develop a code in 1938, and the American Sociological Association in 1945. However, it was not until 1953 and 1969, respectively, that these two associations approved and published their first codes. Those codes were quite general, uncontroversial, and largely unenforceable. In short,[1] explicit concern about the ethics of social research at one time seemed unnecessary.

But since about 1970, the view that scientists' personal standards of morality largely suffice to deal with the ethical issues that may arise in their research has been vigorously challenged.[2] The emphasis on social conscience that arose during the late 1960s brought about both a press for "relevant" social research and many new laws that protect the rights of the individual.

---

[1] For a detailed discussion of the history and politics of the development of ethical concern and ethical codes within social science professional associations, see Orlans, H. *Contracting for knowledge*. San Francisco: Jossey-Bass, 1973; and Dalglish, T. *Protecting human subjects in social and behavioral research: Ethics, law and the DHEW rules: A critique* (Working Papers in Management Science). Center for Research in Management Science, University of California, Berkeley, May 1976.

With the press for "relevance" in social research, urgent social problems such as drug abuse, violence, crime, overpopulation, the aged, minority issues, and racial conflict became the object of much social research. But, the traditional training of social scientists was not adequate to their new roles. Scientists ventured into sub-cultures about which they knew far less than they realized concerning values, norms, and relationships with the larger culture. For example, much research on aging has been conducted without awareness of either the socioeconomic class stratification among persons born around 1900, or the corresponding stratification of interests, needs, norms, and abilities of that group (see Levine, Chapter 6). Similarly, scientists' understanding of what comprises risk and effective informed consent in ethnic minority community studies (see Loo, Chapter 5) or in work organizations (see

---

[2] Some of the political impetus for federal regulation and ethical review of social and behavioral research came about indirectly because of the extensive use of human research in biomedicine and because of some well-publicized cases of ethical abuse and misuse of human beings in biomedical research. This concern led to the issuance by the United States Department of Health, Education and Welfare of regulations that deal specifically with protection of the rights and welfare of human subjects in research, and prescribed establishment (as a condition of receiving DHEW and other federal agency research funds) of peer review boards at each institution engaged in human research. See the introduction to Part I (this volume) for a dis-cussion of the way in which current regulations pertaining to informed consent grew out of a biomedical model of the ethics of human research. Chapter 5 (com-panion volume) contains a discussion from the perspective of social scientists on some specific aspects of the regulatory process, and Chapter 6 (companion volume) contains a discussion of the role of peer review boards (Institutional Review Boards). However, the major focus of this book is not on the regulation of social science research, but on the development of scientifically based methods and procedures of ethical problem solving within the social sciences. For more comprehensive infor-mation on the federal regulation of human research the reader is referred to other sources: The origins of political concern about the use of human subjects in research are documented by Jay Katz in *Experimentation with human beings: The authority of the investigator, subject, professions and state in the human experi-mentation process.* New York: Russell Sage Foundation, 1972. This book provides a detailed historical and case study account beginning with cases of human experi-mentation in Nazi Germany which led to the Nuremberg trials and formulation of an international code governing research on humans. The sociology of the biomedi-cal professions as it pertains to the problems of social conflict and control of research is developed in Barber, B., Lally, J. J., Makarushka, J. L., & Sullivan, D. *Research on human subjects: Problems of social control in medical experimentation.* New York: Russell Sage Foundation, 1973. The development and implementation of federal regulations is discussed in Frankel, M. S. *The Public Health Service guide-lines governing research involving human subjects: An analysis of the policy-making process* (Monograph No. 18). Washington, D.C.: Program of Policy Studies in Sci-ence and Technology, George Washington University, February 1972, and in Dalglish, *op. cit.* Papers discussing the impact of federal regulations on the conduct of social science research are presented in Wax, M., & Cassell, J. (Eds.) *Federal regu-lations: Ethical issues and social research.* Boulder, Colo.: Westview Press, 1979.

Mirvis and Seashore, Chapter 4) has rarely been adequate to the tasks they have undertaken.

The second major effect of the new social conscience was on legislation and norms concerning the rights of the individual. For example, laws were enacted and vigorous action ensued to protect individual privacy, to protect the consumer, and to make public information freely accessible to the citizen. An integral part of this movement was the 1975 enactment by the United States Department of Health, Education and Welfare (HEW, later renamed Health and Human Services, HHS) of regulations designed to protect the rights and welfare of human subjects in research. These federal regulations prescribed establishment of peer review boards at each institution engaged in human research (as a condition of receiving research funds from DHEW, later HHS, and other federal agencies). While these changes promised to improve the quality of life in some respects, they conflicted with our accustomed ways of solving other problems. The conflict arises when we are unable to translate these values into action without jeopardizing other valued interests. New regulations mandate actions designed to solve a given set of social problems, but do not necessarily mesh smoothly with existing practices for solving other sets of problems, e.g., existing methods of social research.

Social scientists have encountered considerable difficulty in meeting the requirements of science on one hand, and of federal regulations, new professional codes of ethics, and ethical peer review on the other. They have been slow to recognize and resolve the emerging dilemmas, since their training has left them largely unprepared for the manifold problems raised by new legal and ethical perceptions of the rights of research participants and other members of society. Consider the following problems, some solutions to which are presented in subsequent chapters as indicated:

1. How can a social psychologist whose expertise lies in the design of deception research respond to the legal requirement that voluntary informed consent be obtained prior to research? (Geller, Chapter 2)
2. How can a sociologist who studies criminal behavior offer informants assurance of confidentiality as required by law, when the law does not necessarily shield research data from subpoena? (Knerr, Chapter 9)
3. How can a public policy researcher justify social experiments in which random assignment of clients to social programs may deprive needy families of valued services? (Conner, Chapter 3)
4. How can an anthropologist obtain voluntary informed consent to do research among members of a culture in which social science is unknown and in which tribal leaders do not grant their followers the autonomy to consent for themselves? (Wax, Chapter 2, companion volume)
5. How does the population researcher *locate* samples of interest without first delving into the private records of potential subjects to determine what samples are available? (Hartley, Chapter 8)
6. How can a survey researcher respect privacy while asking sensitive personal questions? (Boruch & Cecil, Chapter 10)

If social scientists had only a fixed set of traditional concepts, methods, and procedures with which to work, their professional interests and the interests of science would indeed be in grave jeopardy. Fortunately, this is not the case. Creative social scientists have begun to apply their scholarship and research abilities to the ethical problems in their research, and are bringing scientific and ethical requirements into alignment, so that one requirement is not met at the expense of the other. The work of such scientists is presented in this book.

This book focuses on some of the problems that arise when social scientists seek to mesh scientific requirements with the ethical requirement that they protect the interests and welfare of those who participate in their research. It emphasizes ways in which empirical and methodological ingenuity on the part of social scientists has contributed to explicating and resolving some of these problems, and it outlines some of the problems that remain unsolved.

What Does It Mean to Solve Ethical Dilemmas in Social Research?

To solve problems and make decisions effectively, certain clearly defined activities are required. Janis and Mann (1977) define effective decisions as those that are made with enough diligence and thoroughness that one is satisfied with them in the long run. This means that, in the case of problems that have satisfactory potential solutions, the decision maker is diligent enough to discover an excellent solution, and to recognize why it is superior to other possible solutions. But when none of the possible solutions is without serious pitfalls, one must seek the least unsatisfactory alternative, and anticipate any likely shocks, disadvantages, or discomforts, so that it is possible to live with that best of various unpleasant alternatives.

To illustrate the effective solution of ethical problems in social research, let us consider an example of each of these two kinds of problems: (1) The problem of protecting privacy in direct inquiry is one that yielded to an ingeniously tidy solution. (2) The dirty hands problem did not yield to an easy or perfect solution but it was so diligently examined that the scientist can live with the solution that was chosen.

1. *The problem of protecting privacy in direct inquiry.* There are many questions about the demography of crime which the survey researcher would like to ask, but cannot for ethical reasons. As examples of such questions:

Have you struck your child in anger this week?

Did you evade income tax this year?

Have you bought illegal drugs this month?

Serious legal, scientific and moral problems arise when the investigator asks questions such as these: (1) Legally, can investigators assure confidentiality and protect respondents from harm given that such data might be subpoenaed in connection with criminal investigations? (2) Scientifically, will the responses be valid or will respondents who have engaged in criminal behavior lie to the investigator? And (3) morally, has an investigator the right to ask strangers such personal questions? The social scientist is faced with a three-pronged dilemma, and a seemingly hopeless one, except in the hands of persistent problem solvers.

To keep the data from subpoena, the investigator might use any of the tactics discussed by Charles R. Knerr, Jr., in Chapter 9: mail the data out of the country,

obtain a legal shield, prove that the data are irrelevant to the needs of legal authorities, or go to jail. But none of these alternatives will make respondents more candid in their responses or entitle the investigator to ask such personal questions in
the first place. To get honest answers in direct inquiry and to circumvent the immorality or inappropriateness of asking deeply personal questions of a stranger, it
would be necessary that the investigator be in no position to know what the subject's response meant, and that the subject understand that this is so. For economist and algebraist Stanley Warner (1965) therein lay the kernel of a brilliant creative idea—the idea of the randomized response method.

The randomized response method circumvents the legal, scientific, and moral
problems raised earlier. Many variations of the method have been developed,
enabling the investigator to gather various kinds of data, as described in Chapter 10
by Boruch and Cecil. The following simple example is given here for illustrative
purposes:

> An investigator wishes to estimate the percent of parents in a given
> country who abuse their children, and plans to base the estimate on a sam-
> ple of 400. She selects 600 subjects, and creates a jar containing 600 beads,
> 400 of which are red, 100 white, and 100 blue. Each subject is asked to
> draw a bead, privately observe its color and replace it. The subject is then
> to answer the question "Have you struck your child in anger this week?"
> Subjects who draw a red bead are to give the true answer to the question;
> those who draw a white bead are to say "Yes" arbitrarily; and those who
> draw a blue bead are to say "No" arbitrarily. Thus, there will be 400 true
> answers and 100 false "Yes" responses. To compute the proportion of par-
> ents who have abused their child in the last week, the researcher would
> subtract 100 from the total number of "Yes" responses and divide by 400.

As discussed in Chapter 10, in Boruch and Cecil (1979) and in Warner (1979),
the randomized response method yields a higher percent of socially undesirable
responses (hence presumably more honest responses) to sensitive questions than
does the direct method. The problem of demonstrating to poorly educated persons
that the method is valid and not a trick has been resolved by methods of group discussion: a large group of potential subjects is given an opportunity to discuss the
method, see how it works, and to recognize that it offers a genuine means of safe-
guarding their privacy while enabling the researcher to discover important generalizations about a population as a whole.

As shown in the chapters by Boruch and Cecil (Chapter 10), Turner (Chapter 7),
Hartley (Chapter 8), and Knerr (Chapter 9), problems of privacy and confidentiality have yielded to the persistent efforts of social scientists, statisticians, and law
makers. The solutions have tended to be tidy, technical, and logical. So much so, in
fact, that they may give us a false sense of security about the possibility of banish-
ing ethical dilemmas from social science. The more difficult problems are ones in
which the social scientist must persistently seek the most moral way to live with
problems that will not go away.

2. *The problem of dirty hands.* This problem arises in areas of social research
where one must use "dirty" means in order to achieve good ends. A good example

of ethical decision making and the dirty hands problem is found in the writing of Klockars (1979).

Carl Klockars, a sociologist of criminal justice, has asked, and answered, some penetrating and painful questions about the "dirty hands problem" involved in fieldwork with deviant behavior:

1. Can persons who do fieldwork with deviant subjects do so without running the risk of using morally dubious or dangerous means?
2. Must they be willing to pay a price for using "dirty" means?
3. By what means can moral sensitivity be retained by fieldworkers despite their dirty hands?

By the nature of fieldwork on deviant behavior, the social scientist risks stepping into situations where one cannot emerge innocent of wrong doing. This is the "dirty hands" problem: in order to achieve a good end, dirty means *must* be employed. By "a good end" Klockars refers to an end that is unquestionably good and that it is morally offensive *not* to pursue, such as discovery of the conditions that precipitate police brutality. This would entail development of rapport with police who are noted for their crudeness, incompetence, racism, or liking for violence, then arranging to be deputized and accompanying such a policeman in his daily work. The fieldwork may involve such dirty means as (1) observing the policeman brutalize an innocent person boastfully to impress his new deputy (oneself) with his power, (2) participating in the set up and arrest of persons whom one considers harmless, and (3) having to forcefully subjugate persons to prevent their being injured in a fight with police.

The ethics of fieldwork demands that fieldworkers promise to remain in their agreed on role and play it competently, in return for the confidence and access that is granted them by their informants. Thus, for example, fieldworkers whose informants are shoplifters agree to play the role of shopper and to maintain that role even if store security guards accuse them of being a lookout for the informant, in return for the informant's agreement to let the fieldworker watch. To put it another way, whether the informant is a pickpocket, a shoplifter, or a brutal policeman, the fieldworker must begin the relationship with a sincere promise not to blow the whistle, and with assurances that that promise can and will be kept. To be a good fieldworker, then, one must do things that a good human being ordinarily would not do.

The answer to Klockars' first question, then, is Yes, fieldwork with deviant informants involves the risk of using morally dubious or dangerous means. Thus, Klockars has confronted a real moral dilemma and found that no tidy solutions are forthcoming; he goes on to consider the implications. To make a sound decision about whether to do fieldwork on deviant behavior, one must confront the moral, emotional, intellectual, behavioral, and legal consequences that are involved. The major issues that Klockars raises are the following:

1. Situations calling for brutal action tend to arise suddenly, leaving the fieldworker little time to puzzle over whether the brutality is truly necessary to achieve his or her end (the true dirty hands problem) or whether another less brutal course of action might serve as well. Thus, even after having accepted the dirty hands prob-

lem as part of one's work, one may make regrettable, painful, and even legally disastrous errors. No amount of experience or discussion with fellow fieldworkers can prepare one to make sound judgments as to when brutal action is absolutely necessary.

2. A utilitarian question continually arises regarding the justification of "dirty hands": Granting the long-term good of sound scientific research on deviant behavior, how valuable is one's particular research project likely to be to society? How often should this question be reopened, as one's hands get dirtier? How objectively can fieldworkers evaluate their own research?

3. Dirty hands problems tend to engender romantic fascination and enthusiasm on the part of new fieldworkers who avoid the pain of guilt by identifying with the informant. In this way, morally decent persons turned fieldworkers can deceive themselves for a while by "going native" in the process of trying to become a good fieldworker. When the romance of fieldwork begins to wear thin, the illusion of innocence can still be maintained by certain defenses such as denial of responsibility and injury, condemning the condemners, and appeals to higher motives. Klockars shows that these techniques for avoidance of guilt and suffering are morally and scientifically unacceptable. They are morally unacceptable because it is beneath the dignity of a mature person to have dirty hands and not know it. It is scientifically irresponsible because the fieldworkers who "go native" take the deviant's world view as their own; they become unobjective and sentimental in their glorification of deviant informants. Their field notes become caricatures and they lose the broader perspective that they set out to clarify and understand. But even more serious than these moral and scientific problems with "going native" is the tendency of those who accept dirty means without guilt and concern to jump to dirty means too quickly. Moreover, they tend to overestimate their competence at dirty means and take on field roles that are needlessly dirty.

Thus, Klockars' answer to the second question is also Yes: Competent fieldworkers who get their hands dirty must pay the price of guilt and concern; they must remain ever vigilant to avoid unnecessary dirty hands and to maintain the moral perspective necessary to serve the good scientific and social ends they set out to serve.

Klockars goes on to explore why fieldworkers and policemen who "go native" may become hardened and never recover their moral senses. Since there are severe legal sanctions (especially against policemen) for having "dirty hands," one learns to hide dirty deeds and to lie. All talk of dirty hands is suppressed. Candid moral discourse about "dirty hands problems" is impossible to generate in such a setting. This suggests the answer to Klockars' third question.

Fieldworkers and others who are exposed to such situations can be helped to maintain their moral concern about their dirty hands through seminars with colleagues and outsiders. This discussion might occur in formal or in informal settings, in groups of two to twenty, in person, or in print. It should focus on the morality of fieldwork in deviant behavior: "such talk remains the only way we know of developing moral maturity, the *willing* suffering of moral criticism" (Klockars, 1979, p. 279).

Ineffective Ethical Decision Making

As Janis and Mann (1977) point out, poor decisions often come about because of a lack of thoroughness and persistence at one or more of the various stages of the decision process:

1. One may avoid conflict and decision making entirely by failing to heed information bearing on the inadvisability of the current course of action. For example, as Knerr (Chapter 9) points out, most social scientists whose data are subpoenaed tend to respond with surprise and without an effective coping strategy, having never imagined that their data might be subpoenaed.

2. One may recognize the inadvisability of the current course of action, and impulsively adopt the first alternative that suggests itself or that an "expert" suggests, proceed without concern for the consequences, and be surprised to learn that that alternative leads to some undesirable outcomes.

3. One may note alternatives, be aware of their drawbacks, despair of finding better alternatives, and hence select a poor alternative without further consideration. As Janis and Mann have observed, a part of this style is to ignore subsequent information that would indicate that the decision should be reversed. As an example, Geller (Chapter 2) observes that many justify the use of unwarranted deception on grounds that some suggested alternatives to deception have proved invalid.

4. Or, one may generate reasonable alternatives, but run out of time evaluating them. Ethical dilemmas need to be resolved before the research is begun, or before binding deadlines are created. Frantic and undiscriminating last minute searches for information are likely to result in choices that are hard to live with and perhaps not the best choices in any case.

To make effective decisions, social scientists must be (1) sensitive to potential ethical problems in the research context, (2) sensitive to relevant values and personal concerns of the parties involved, (3) hopeful or persistent in the pursuit of good solutions, and (4) able to recognize a good solution when it becomes available. This kind of sensitivity does not occur in a vacuum. There needs to be discussion with colleagues who have struggled effectively with similar problems and an openness to alternative social science methodologies. Effective professional communication and openness to alternative methodologies sensitize the scientist to what might occur and what alternatives are available, *before the dilemma takes on catastrophic proportions*, and it helps to sustain persistent search for good solutions.

How Ethical Problems Arise in Social Science Research

The kinds of ethical problems examined in this book are problems that ensnare well-meaning investigators—problems having to do with harmful, unintended effects of research, rather than acts such as fudging data or claiming credit for the work of others which are intentional. The difficult and interesting ethical problems with which social scientists need to be concerned are ones in which important scientific, moral, or social values are in conflict. A typical ethical problem in research is one in which the investigator has identified a socially or scientifically important question and a valid method for investigating it, but where the method involves risk of harm or failure to respect participants as persons. Ethical problems of this kind may arise in various ways:

1. An ethical problem that arises in social research may be unforeseen by the investigator. As an example of the unforeseen, an investigator of the demography of radical college students may learn that some colleges may use the obtained demographic information to select out applicants who are likely to become radical students. A more subtle, but perhaps more common version of this problem involves harms that are never identified; for example, an investigator of effects of aging may assume that methods appropriate for the study of college students and adults are also appropriate for the study of the aged, and consequently may obtain and publish invalid data. (In Chapter 6, Levine examines a complex of ideological and methodological problems in the study of the aged, and presents theory and data that illustrate and resolve the ethical problems that she raises.)

2. An ethical problem may be inadequately anticipated. The nature or magnitude of the problem may be underestimated or the cost of taking precautions may be deemed too great, and consequently safeguards may not be employed. For example, an investigator may consider taking steps to render individual data anonymous but fail to carry out such plans because of uncertainty about the necessity, appropriateness, or possibility of doing so. (In Chapters 9 and 10, Charles R. Knerr, Jr., and Robert Boruch and Joe Cecil, respectively, discuss this dilemma and effective solutions.)

3. An ethical problem may be foreseen by the investigator and there may be no apparent way to avoid the problem. For example, since it seemed impossible to do controlled research on naturally occurring conformity, Asch (1956) devised a simple laboratory procedure in which subjects are asked to judge the length of lines in a setting where confederates, who purport to be other subjects, give unanimous judgments. Asch justified his use of deception on grounds that the social importance of this research problem warranted the necessary use of deception. This is the "dirty hands" problem in which the only apparent way in which a scientist can validly pursue a morally good research end is by using means that might ordinarily offend the moral sensibilities of decent persons. (In Chapter 2, companion volume, Murray L. Wax examines a host of cross-cultural "dirty hands" problems that arise in ethnographic fieldwork. In Chapter 2, Daniel M. Geller examines some scientific and ethical issues connected with the use of deception in social psychology and offers alternatives, but concludes that some forms of behavior cannot validly be studied without deception or concealment.)

4. A more complex version of the fully anticipated ethical problem is that in which it is unclear what one should do because it is unclear what the consequences of one's possible actions might be. Suppose, for example, that an investigator knows that grave harm may befall subjects if their data are disclosed to certain other people, and therefore takes every precaution to assure confidentiality. Should the investigator assure subjects that these steps have been taken? The investigator does not know whether subjects will respond to the assurance by feeling secure or

by worrying needlessly about why such confidentiality might be necessary. (In Chapter 7, Anthony Turner presents such a dilemma and reports research that provides some empirical answers.) To take a different kind of example of this problem, suppose an investigator made a revolutionary discovery about the effects of nutrition on hyperactivity. Clearly, mass media dissemination of these findings would maximize their value *if* the findings were responsibly reported. However, the investigator does not know whether the mass media reporting of the findings will be accurate and reasonable. (In Chapter 7, companion volume, S. Holly Stocking and Sharon L. Dunwoody present evidence and guidelines concerning the use of the mass media to disseminate scientific findings.)

5. Perhaps the most complex kind of ethical problem is that in which one's current moral outlook is simply inadequate to the problem, and a new approach is needed. This kind of problem is examplified in Chapter 4; Philip H. Mirvis and Stanley E. Seashore demonstrate that ethical organizational research lies not in the application of prescription but in the building and maintaining of relationships in which one may address and moderate ethical dilemmas that cannot be covered by prescription.

6. Finally, perhaps the most distressing kind of ethical problem that confronts the social scientist is a sociological and bureaucratic one, that of responding to regulations that jeopardize the interests of social science. While care has been taken to devise flexible federal regulations, the enforcement of those regulations has not always been flexible (Gray, 1979); the DHEW regulations of 1977 created dissatisfaction among social scientists. Numerous social scientists have shown that those federal regulations and the policy recommendations of the National Commission for the Protection of Human Subjects of Biomedical and Behavioral Research (1978) create very serious problems for the social sciences, forcing either the abandonment of certain important areas of social research, or "going underground" with the concomitant hazards of knowingly violating the law (see especially Reiss, 1979, and O'Connor, 1979). Subsequent federal regulations, which were issued in January 1981 by HHS and became effective July 1981, have proved more acceptable to social researchers.

Because regulation goes beyond the ethical "ought" to the legal "must," it may appear to leave little room for creative research and scholarship. However, creativity abounds in Chapters 5 and 6, companion volume, where Joe S. Cecil and Donald T. Campbell, and Elizabeth and Tony Tanke, respectively, provide insights for optimizing the effects of regulations on science, individual subjects, and society. Work such as theirs led to the 1981 revisions in HHS regulations and transcends any particular set of formal regulations.

What Values Should Guide the Resolution of Ethical Dilemmas?

The National Commission for the Protection of Human Subjects of Biomedical and Behavioral Research (1978) considered this question and concluded that the values that should guide human research can be derived from principles of beneficence, respect, and justice.

Beneficence means the avoidance of unnecessary suffering, injury or other harm and the maximization of good outcomes. In the example of the tearoom trade study (pp. 1-3), the good outcomes of the research, new knowledge and more enlightened social policy, are quite impressive, but there has been considerable debate about whether Humphreys took all reasonable precautions to prevent harm to those whom he observed and interviewed.[3] *Respect* means concern for the autonomy of persons. In the tearoom trade example, respect for persons is largely what is at issue: Humphreys observed people, traced them to their homes by surreptitious means, and interviewed them in their homes under a false pretext. Is it ever justifiable for investigators to lie to subjects or to involve them without their knowing that they are participating in research? *Justice* means equitable distribution of social benefits and costs. A highly desirable aspect of the tearoom trade study is that the population that benefitted from the research included as a subset those who bore the risk of disclosure.

The principles of beneficence, respect, and justice are extremely broad and pertain to human relations in general, as well as to social science. To focus these principles accordingly, the National Commission then identified six values or norms that pertain to research on human beings, each of which embodies at least one of the three basic principles just discussed.

Validity of Research Design

A valid research design is one that takes into account relevant theory, and prior findings and methods. The design employs the appropriate type of subjects and only as many subjects as are required to obtain informative, valid results. Valid research design is dictated by the basic values of respect (that subjects not be used frivolously) and beneficence (that valid results be obtained at minimal cost to society). Invalid research is unethical; it is neither beneficent nor respectful. For example, Hartley (Chapter 8) illustrates harms that are due to improper sampling and use of wrong conclusions.

Competence of Investigators

Even well-designed research may yield invalid results or cause harm if the investigators are insufficiently qualified or inadequately supervised. The meaning of "investigator competence" varies, of course, with the nature of the research. Kinds of competence required for given kinds of investigations are discussed in many of the following chapters. For example, Mirvis and Seashore (Chapter 4) illustrate the importance of the researcher's knowledge and use of organizational theory and role theory in the conduct of organizational research.

Identification of Consequences

The investigator should evaluate possible risks and benefits of the research and provide to research participants honest and adequate information about the procedure and its likely consequences. The investigator is also responsible for arranging to keep all promises made to participants, such as promises to maintain confidentiality of information received, and for taking all reasonable steps to minimize the risk of harm to them. The sponsoring institution and the funding agency are responsible for preserving legitimate opportunities for research, hence for scrutinizing the research they sponsor or fund.

Most undesirable consequences of research in social sciences arise indirectly, due to the context in which data are gathered or disseminated. For example, harm to reputation or to self-esteem are more likely than physical harm. Each area of research in the social sciences involves contexts that may generate harmful outcomes. Most of the chapters in this book explore possible sources of harm and benefit in relation to the nature of the research setting.

Selection of Subjects

The choice of research participants and populations should be dictated by sound science and justice. The sampling procedure should be such that the investigator can explore anticipated sources of variance and generalize the results in useful ways. The burdens and benefits of research should be distributed equitably; if possible, the population that is to benefit from the research should be the same as the population from which subjects are drawn, and persons having very limited power or autonomy should not be used as subjects.

Voluntary Informed Consent

The most basic rule of human research, derived from the values of respect and beneficence, is that the researcher obtain the voluntary informed consent of subjects beforehand. Since a detailed discussion of informed consent is presented in the Introduction to Part I, only a brief definition is offered here: *Voluntary* means freely, and without threat or promise of some valuable but undue inducement for consenting. *Informed* means that the subject knows all that a reasonable person in that situation would want to know before giving consent—the facts and judgments or probabilities that would affect a reasonable person's decision whether to participate. This information should be conveyed in terms that the subject is certain to understand. *Consent* means explicit agreement to participate. All of these elements imply possession of the legal and mental capacity to give consent. Informed consent serves primarily as a means of respecting persons, and secondarily as a means of protecting them from risk. The concept of consent is difficult to interpret and apply in some research settings, as illustrated in the case of the tearoom trade study. Various aspects of these difficulties are examined in the chapters that follow.

Compensation for Injury

In 1976, the National Commission recommended that subjects be compensated on a no-fault basis for injury incurred in biomedical research. The Brookings Panel on Social Experimentation (Rivlin & Timpane, 1975) recommend that there be com-

---

[3] The enlarged edition of *Tearoom Trade* (1970) includes all of the major critiques and rebuttals of Humphreys' research design and procedure.

pensation for harm done to subjects by social research as well. However, they point to the difficulty of attributing specific harm to social research procedures and recommend that great risks be avoided in the first place. They foresaw that some important social research may involve very large but rare risks, and recommended that provision for compensation be made through insurance. Clearly, compensation for injuries would serve all three of the basic principles discussed above. Some of the subsequent chapters contribute significantly toward our understanding of kinds of harm that might result from research in social science, but little has been done as yet to determine how an amount or procedure of compensation would be decided in the case of social research.

Some Broader Value Issues in Social Science

While the main focus of this book is on ethical issues that pertain to the relationship between the social scientist and the research participant, other broader value issues pertaining to social science are interwoven. These issues range across a spectrum from the value implications of *conceptions* (e.g., ideas about nature, purpose, and approach) of social science to the value implications of *applications* of social science.

Some examples of these broader value issues are:

1. Whether the scientist employs a deterministic model that views people as objects, buffeted about by external or internal forces beyond their control, or a humanistic model that views people as choosing agents and as ends in themselves.
2. Whether the scientist takes the purpose of science to be the generation of theory and knowledge per se, or the generation of theory and knowledge that is intended to be useful to society.
3. Whether the scientist takes a role in applying the knowledge that is generated by his or her research.
4. Whether the scientist considers facts and truth as absolutes found in the external world, or as distinctions made by the human mind that are relative to the context or perspective from which they are viewed.
5. Whether the scientist considers that valid and objective scientific knowledge about people is increased by distancing oneself from those being studied (e.g., by unilateral planning of research and interpretation of findings, and use of impersonal research techniques) or by more personal processes of generating knowledge (e.g., by planning in which those studied have a role in defining the research problem and in interpreting the findings, and use of more personal research approaches such as participant observation or mutual self-disclosure).

The various parts of this spectrum—those pertaining to scientific conceptions, research procedures, and research applications—tend to be interrelated, both logically and ethically. As Kelman (1968) points out, the kind of research that is done and the kind of applications likely to result are integrally related to the original conception that gave rise to the research and development. Also, the value implications of scientific conceptions arise precisely because given scientific conceptions lead to corresponding research activities and applications in society. To summarize, there are diverse models or methodologies of social science and these attach to corresponding value systems and kinds of applications.

This is not to imply that there necessarily are good and bad methodologies. Kelman (1968) and Mitroff and Kilmann (1978) consider the diversity of models or systems within social science to be both inevitable and desirable: such diverse models as humanism and determinism must both exist (inevitably in tension with one another) if social science is to make valuable contributions to humanity.

However, discussions of alternative systems in science often are written somewhat *in defense* of the more humanistically oriented systems (e.g., Kelman, 1968; Mitroff and Kilmann, 1978). This is not because determinism is not valued, but because it classically has been valued to the exclusion of humanism. The reader will note that a tendency to defend humanism is expressed in this book. That is, the various contributors to this book each recommend, to varying degrees, the incorporation of humanistic models and procedures. As we shall see in the subsequent examination of Mitroff and Kilmann's typology of methodologies, however, it is not accurate to equate ethical research conduct with humanism. Rather, being an ethical researcher might better be characterized as having an awareness of the alternative models of social science, and sensitivity to the normative or moral issues on which each model focuses. Thus, one is able to adopt whatever approach is required to anticipate and resolve a given ethical dilemma in research, e.g., a more humanistic, or analytical, or cognitively complex or particularistic (individualistic) approach, or some combination thereof.

For example, in their discussion of ethical dilemmas in organizational research, Mirvis and Seashore (Chapter 4) recommend the use of a variety of approaches: They recommend a limited form of humanism (e.g., giving those studied considerable autonomy—via staff meetings and interviews—to express their views and thereby to contribute to the definition of the research problem and to the formulation of research procedures). They recommend that the investigator use role theory to develop the cognitive complexity required to anticipate and interact effectively with the diverse roles and points of view that arise in organizations. They also implicitly recommend the use of sensitivity and personal authenticity needed to sense and communicate about issues that would otherwise remain hidden. Thus, for example, Mirvis and Seashore treat informed consent not as a formal and legal procedure, but as an open, multilateral, and ongoing relationship and process of communication. Their research procedures and ethical decisions do not follow strictly from any given model of man or of science. Rather their procedures and decisions follow from an openness to humanistic as well as deterministic models.

But are humanistic and other nondeterministic models consonant with, or a legitimate part of, social science? What is social science and what are its basic values? Is humanism not antithetical to "real" science?

According to many accounts found in the philosophy of science and in social science textbooks, social science is defined as deterministic, value free, apolitical, cumulative, autonomous impersonal, disinterested, precise, reliable, valid, reductionistic, causal, public, unambiguous, realistic, and pursued for the sake of knowledge itself. And, the social scientist is described as logical, unbiased, impersonal, precise, skeptical, exact, methodical, and employs controlled experimental methods that are reliable, valid, and rigorous and maintain distance between scientist and subjects.

But what about the action researcher and the participant observer who work immersed in the culture and viewpoint of those studied? For these investigators, research may be personal and concerned with humanity; it may involve intimate communication and cooperation between scientist and subject; the key concern may not be to generate knowledge, but to foster human growth and welfare. A broad range of innovative concepts, rather than a single reductionistic theory, may guide the research.

Even further off the proverbial "deep end" are the growing number of transpersonal psychologists who do not give their science a special position at all, but subordinate it to mysticism and other older ways of knowing. Tools such as meditation provide some of the kinds of intense personal knowledge and experience that these investigators deem necessary for obtaining true knowledge. Their focus is not on general, public, deterministic, or universal knowledge at all, at least not in the sense in which "hard" social scientists use these words. Rather, their purpose is to know an individual person and to enable that person to achieve her or his own goals.

We note that these differing conceptions of science have correspondingly different ethical implications. The "hard" social scientist who seeks knowledge for its own sake may readily believe that deception or other minor abuse to subjects is a reasonable price to pay for knowledge. The action researcher whose purpose is to foster human growth and welfare is likely to disagree. The transpersonal psychologist, whose concern is with the unique individual and with fostering that person's powers of self-determination, could never justify deception or personal abuse, unless it were done in the manner of the great teacher who tricks students into dropping their defenses and gaining greater self-insight. We also note that the three kinds of scientists we have described differ greatly in the extent of their relationship with their subjects and in their degree of exposure to facets of the relationship that would arouse ethical sensitivity. Also, their views on the nature of science (e.g., whether it is political, subjective, value laden) are likely to influence whether they believe they are responsible for the uses of the knowledge they generate.

Which of these is the real social science? We cannot safely dismiss the softer versions on grounds that they do not have the defining characteristics of science. Everything that the philosophy of science has asserted as characteristic of "real" science has been denied by the history and sociology of science (Mitroff & Kilmann, 1978). For example, the philosophy of science has stressed the logical, cumulative, public, and objective character of science. In contrast, the history and sociology of science have stressed the illogical or alogical character of actual scientific practice: historians such as Kuhn (1962) have stressed the noncumulative nature of science; Holton (1973, 1974) has stressed the interaction between "public" and "private" science; Westfall (1973) has discussed the role of "fudging" in theory testing; Feyerabend (1975) has emphasized the irrational, anarchistic, subjective and idiosyncratic aspects of science; Lakatos (1970) has noted the dynamic character of scientific schools and their indifference to empirical refutation; Crane (1972) has discussed the "invisible colleges" that convey and control scientific knowledge;

Hanson (1965, 1969) has discussed the lack of separation between observations and theories; and Mitroff and Chubin (1978) have discussed ways in which the old-boy network acts to favor some scientists and their ideas, while innovative ideas fare less well.

What, then, is the nature of social science? One could as well ask this question of physical science. But the question is more interesting in the case of social science which takes as its subject matter the social nature of ourselves: social science more readily lends itself to reflexive, subjective, or humanistic approaches in opposition to the "harder," more objective, distanced, and amoral approach that is espoused as the ideal. Accordingly, a large number of social scientists have felt intellectually, emotionally, or morally compelled to deviate, knowingly and purposively, from "ideal" social science. For example, in anthropology there is the research commune, in sociology, professional meetings are incomplete without papers on radical sociology, and in psychology, the various humanistic psychologies are well represented even in research circles.

Thus, a single, prestigious, idealized definition of social science gives way to various definitions of its place in humanity's intellectual and practical activities, its methods, its models of humanity, and its implications for the behavior of the scientist. These definitions are stratified into a hierarchy, not necessarily according to their correctness or to the degree to which they are actually practiced (as opposed to espoused), but according to the status and power of those who hold them.

Fortunately, this bewildering diversity of definitions and values has been systematized. We turn to Mitroff and Kilmann's typology for an elucidation of the broader value systems that exist in social science and the corresponding contexts in which social scientists define and resolve ethical dilemmas. The Mitroff and Kilmann typology provides a useful framework for understanding the subsequent chapters in the following five ways:

1. The Mitroff and Kilmann typology contrasts the more limited set of scientific values typically used with the possible broader set of scientific values from which ethical awareness and effective problem solving might derive. Warwick (1980) has described the limited value perspectives of many social scientists in his characterization of four ways in which they tend to deal with the tension between social science and values:

a. By claiming that talk of values represents semantic confusion.
b. By taking one's values from *prevailing* social norms and not examining the specific values of science.
c. By focusing extensively on a particular value issue such as scientific freedom or problems of social repression, and ignoring the broader matrix of values and value conflict in which science operates.
d. By asserting that science contributes to human welfare without examining whether this is indeed so.

2. The Mitroff-Kilmann typology of value systems presented subsequently explains this strange state of affairs, places it into a broader context and provides rich alternatives.

3. The Mitroff-Kilmann typology suggests ways of understanding some of the disproportionate amount of conflict, emotion, and controversy that often surrounds discussion of ethics in social research. Their examination of the basic conceptions and methodologies of social science reveals enormous differences among social scientists in their ways of perceiving their work and their world. It is not surprising, in view of these differences, that there is much heated disagreement among well-meaning individuals about the range and nature of the ethical concerns that are real or that pertain to social science, and about the correctness of given norms, prescriptions, or solutions pertaining to these problems.

4. The Mitroff-Kilmann typology shows that ethical treatment of research participants arises not simply from a sense of etiquette, but also from a system of beliefs about the role of science and the relationship between society and science. It also shows that disagreement among scientists about the breadth of interpretation to be accorded to ethical principles governing social research may be attributable to differences in these beliefs about the nature of social science, including its relationship to society.

5. The Mitroff-Kilmann typology suggests the possibility of regarding each model as *a model* rather than as *the reality* of science, and of regarding each as a conceptual tool from which insight and procedures may be selected in the service of ethical decision making in social research.

Following the discussion of the Mitroff and Kilmann typology, its ethical implications are examined. It is concluded that the link between social science and social values can be made irrespective of whether this link is acknowledged in one's own preferred model of social science. Each model shapes social values in certain ways and promotes certain social goals, irrespective of whether the model acknowledges that it does so. It is further concluded that social science might make the most valuable contribution to society if the goals, methods, and values of social science are informed by all four of the models of science that Mitroff and Kilmann discuss.

The Mitroff-Kilmann Typology of Methodologies in Social Science

In a provocative book entitled *Methodological Approaches to Social Science*, Ian Mitroff and Ralph Kilmann (1978) describe psychological styles and value systems of social scientists and corresponding scientific methodologies. Their taxonomy is based on Jungian typology and divides scientists into four types:

1. *The Analytic Scientist*, Jung's Sensing Thinking individual, is a convergent thinker, who focuses on impersonal external facts that are observed with certainty, and tests theory using classical logic. This scientist regards facts as separable both from values and from theories or ideas, and regards science as disinterested, impersonal, value free, precise, reliable, accurate, valid, reductionistic, causal, apolitical, cumulative, and progressive. According to this point of view, science contains clear standards for judgment, is realistic, antimystical, unambiguous, and exact. Inquiry proceeds by means of the controlled experiment. Knowledge is of value for its own sake, and the application of knowledge is not the scientist's concern.

Ethically, the overriding values are scientific freedom and validity of research (in the sense of whether the design follows classical logical principles). Informed consent may be regarded as a legal formality that offers no possibility for increasing the validity of the research, but that seems likely to decrease validity by letting the subject in on the point of the study. Given the Analytic Scientist's distance from subjects, a narrow range of possible harm to subjects is likely to be perceived. Experimenter competence would refer more to factual, technical, and logical mastery than to interpersonal sensitivity.

2. *The Conceptual Theorist*, Jung's Intuitive Thinking individual, is a divergent thinker whose forte is not the observation of external facts, but the creation of interesting alternative explanations of phenomena. This scientist is capable of seeing phenomena in diverse new ways. What formerly was regarded as changing is reconceptualized by the Conceptual Theorist as unchanging; what was seen as local is recognized as general; adaptive functions are found in phenomena formerly believed to be maladaptive; latent structure is found in phenomena that were believed to be unstructured. Because of this ability to recast ideas and thereby to perceive the world in new ways, it is patently obvious to the Conceptual Theorist that what one looks for and what one sees (i.e., theory and data) are highly interdependent, and that entire bodies of "knowledge" may become immaterial as a result of one sweeping theoretical insight. For the Conceptual Theorist, science is impersonal, value free, disinterested, and apolitical, but also holistic, imaginative, and marked by multiple causation, purposeful ambiguity, and uncertainty.

Ethically, the Conceptual Theorist judges the value of scientific work by how much it opens up possible new ways of viewing the world. The Conceptual Theorist's own cognitive complexity may provide heightened ethical sensitivity to the diverse interests, viewpoints, and vulnerabilities of others. For example, informed consent is likely to involve perceptive communication and to engender good rapport. However, this informed consent process is not necessarily an ongoing process aimed at making the research experience useful to the subject, for the point of research is to be interesting not useful. The competence of a researcher is, from the Conceptual Theorist's perspective, determined by the researcher's imaginativeness and the benefit of research lies in the intellectual complexity, stimulation, and enlightenment it provides.

3. *The Conceptual Humanist*, Jung's Intuitive Feeling individual, is a divergent thinker also, but in addition to having alternative conceptions or theories about the external world, the Conceptual Humanist "thinks" via experience of self. Mitroff and Kilmann borrow Rowan's (1976) conception of the research cycle to describe how the Conceptual Humanist thinks about research: For this scientist, the research process is a cycle consisting of five phases, each in a dialectical relationship (i.e., both denying and affirming) to previous stages. The phase are (1) being, (2) thinking, (3) project, (4) encounter, and (5) communication.

For the Conceptual Humanist, a problem is defined in relation to one's personal being: (1) When resting in one's *being*, one may sense that there is a problem: e.g., Do I know what I think I know about this field? Am I aware of my motives for doing this research? Can I listen to, fully accept and sincerely care for my research subjects as people? Am I a racist researcher? (2) One *thinks* by forming new theoretical possibilities that are challenging: e.g., Can I break this problem down into researchable parts? Can I separate my research from my other values? Can I change my role relationship with others? Can I discover and give up my paternalistic atti-tudes? (3) One tests one's thoughts and risks failure by creating a *project*: e.g., dis-covering whether I can design the implied study, whether I can interact in an open fashion with subjects, or whether the research design maximizes the potential for serendipity, and analyzing the political implications of the research design. (4) One then completes the *encounter*, and examines what has happened: e.g., Did I achieve validity of research design, authenticity in my interaction with subjects, trust, growth and self-determination on the part of subjects, justice in political outcomes of the research, freedom from oppressive role structures, or greater conceptual complexity regarding the matter under study? Finally, (5) one *communicates* about the process: e.g., I write up the research in a form others can understand and check, I make the results part of my life, and help others to benefit from the findings. The Conceptual Humanist then enters another cycle.

The Conceptual Humanist's research is experiential and dialectic; both the researcher and the subject strive to make full use of their thoughts, feelings, experi-ences, and intuitions to learn about themselves and each other. Examples of the Conceptual Humanist are the action researcher and the organizational development researcher who question whether much can be learned by peering at subjects through a controlled, unilateral, manipulative experiment. Argyris (1973) typifies the position of the Conceptual Humanist in his argument that rigorous experiments tend to set up conditions that cause subjects to withdraw psychologically, to be covertly hostile to the experimenter, and to fail to provide any insight into the more positive and constructive processes of human behavior. Subsequent chapters by Geller (Chapter 2), Mirvis and Seashore (Chapter 3), and Glazer (Chapter 3, companion volume) convey related Conceptual Humanist perspectives.

The Conceptual Humanist does not distinguish clearly between research and application, and is likely to focus on long-term projects in which the research par-ticipants learn to observe their own behavior and become more effective persons. Thus, the Conceptual Humanist would interpret the National Commission's ethical principles of beneficence and respect more broadly than would the Analytic Scien-tist or the Conceptual Theorist. Beneficence and respect for subjects of research would mean to the Conceptual Humanist their benefitting personally from partici-pation by gaining in self-understanding and personal effectiveness. Informed con-sent would be a natural part of an ongoing, open communication process out of which this benefit would evolve.

In short, Conceptual Humanists define scientific knowledge as personal, inter-ested, holistic, political, imaginative, concerned with humanity, and characterized by multiple causation and uncertainty. They are quick to admit and know their own biases and are highly personal in their approach to research.

4. *The Particular Humanist*, Jung's Sensing Feeling individual, is psychologically most opposite to the Analytic Scientist. Although a convergent thinker, the Particu-lar Humanist's thinking converges on a single individual rather than on a single idea. This convergence is applied in an inward, nonlogical way, producing a subjective and totally personal approach that can embrace mysticism and a host of other phe-nomena considered by many to be outside of the realm of science. The Particular

Humanist believes in none of the sociological norms of hard science. The Particular Humanist:

a. Has faith in the moral virtue of nonrationality as well as rationality.
b. Believes that emotional commitment is essential to the achievement of rational thinking.
c. Believes that the value of a claim is dependent on who made the claim.
d. Believes that the scientist is utterly responsible for the use of the knowledge created and hence may believe that some scientific knowledge should be kept secret.
e. Believes in serving one's own community of interest.
f. Believes in doubting the work of others while working with utter conviction on one's own ideas.

The Particular Humanist is concerned to discover the uniqueness of each individual and considers it both impossible and undesirable to develop general theories of human behavior. Of tantamount importance is the capturing of the total sense of an individual. Since the typical research method is the in-depth case study, one of the Particular Humanist's major ethical dilemmas in research has to do with protecting privacy and confidentiality. Since the Particular Humanist considers life and work inseparable, informed consent would involve extreme mutual self-disclosure in an ongoing personal relationship with research participants. The Particular Humanist does not believe the myth of impersonal or disinterested objectivity in science, but rather believes that objectivity consists of the exposing of the scientist's own interests in or motives for doing the study.

Ethical Implications of the Mitroff-Kilmann Typology

Earlier, it was stated that a tie exists between social science and social values, and that the use of diverse models of social science is more likely to enhance the value of science to mankind than is the use of a single model alone. We are now in a position to elaborate these ideas.

The link between social scientific ideas and social values is multifaceted. Philosopher William McKay (1981) describes one facet of the link as follows: An *is* can become an *ought*: Institutionalized facts come to entail values and obligations. (*Institutionalized facts* refers to society's inventions for structuring events and solving problems; a simple example would be our monetary system and its entailment of obligations to pay for goods and services received.) Effective scientific ideas and social interventions may become obligatory ways of perceiving or solving problems. For example, the scientific observation that infantile sexuality is a normal stage of development entails an obligation to perceive masturbation as normal in young children. Similarly, the perception that behavior modification techniques are the most effective means known for enabling mentally retarded children to learn skills of self-maintenance may entail an obligation to incorporate these techniques into educational programs for the mentally retarded.

Herbert Kelman (1968) describes a more complex, close, and continual tie between scientific ideas and social values: On the one hand, social research influences the values we hold and achieve: it may contribute to forces favorable to some values and unfavorable to others, and it may contribute to our understanding of the way in which values are manifested and shape our society. On the other hand, values affect the research that is done and the way in which it is done. (See also Weber, 1949, for an early and forceful statement of this point.) Significant social research cannot be carried out unaffected by the values of the investigator.

This linkage between social science and social values is not acknowledged in all areas of the social sciences. However, it is interesting to note, historically, that the all-too-human mind of the scientist makes intuitive leaps from social science fact to social value irrespective of whether the scientist's model of social science would permit this. For example, claiming all the while to have no room for ethics and other forms of unscientific philosophizing, John B. Watson wrote: "Give me a dozen healthy infants, well-formed, and my own specified world to bring them up in and I'll guarantee to take any one at random and train him to become any type of specialist I might select:—doctor, lawyer, artist, merchant-chief and, yes, even beggar-man and thief, regardless of his talents, penchants, tendencies, abilities, vocations, and race of his ancestors" (1962, p. 104).

Since social science and social values are linked so that social attitudes, values, and actions *do* follow from social scientific ideas and results, and vice versa, it is appropriate for scientists to examine how that linkage might work, to the good or detriment of society. Bermant, Kelman, and Warwick (1979) point out four value problems inherent in the linkage. These are problems that cannot adequately be resolved through sole reliance on the Analytic Scientist model that is dominant in our scientific culture. They call for the use of other models as well, as we shall see:

1. How a problem is defined depends on the perspective and values of those who are doing the defining. For example, from the perspective of a middle class social scientist, it is easy to regard the victim of a social problem as the cause of the problem, and to fail to explicate the factors that would give the individual viable choices in life or to seek to understand the problem from the perspective of its victim. Other equally middle class social scientists of a radical persuasion attribute the miseries of the poor to the success of the affluent. Neither of these mind sets prepares an observer to deal responsibly with ethical actualities. Multilateral research planning permits the persons who have the problem to define it in collaboration with the social scientist, and empowers these persons to help create a solution that would increase their power and autonomy. Creation of multiple definitions of a problem requires a Conceptual Theorist orientation, and creation of collaboration and empowerment requires a Humanistic orientation.

2. Whatever the research topic, there is some choice of goals that the social scientist chooses to foster. To be ethical, social scientists need to be aware of the goals of the persons whom they seek to study and to assist. This requires a Conceptual Humanist's ability to embrace the goals of persons from other subcultures, perhaps coupled with the Particular Humanist's ability to perceive and respect extreme diversity of personalities within subcultures.

3. There is a choice of means used to implement the solution to the problem. Is the subject coerced, manipulated, persuaded, or "helped" to accept and participate

in the "solution"? Or, are steps taken to reduce the power differential in the relationship between researcher and subject, and to facilitate individuals in making as autonomous a choice as possible? In other words, can the scientist be humanist enough to give individuals the freedom to choose their own goals?

4. The research is intended to benefit someone, somehow. But in the quest to be ethical, the scientist needs to answer these questions: Who benefits in the long and short run from the knowledge that was gained and from any social intervention that resulted? Who suffers? How does the change affect the distribution of power, the physical environment, and social values? Does it create lasting dependencies? What are its long- and short-term effects on the personalities of those involved? The imagination of the Conceptual Theorist and the research approaches of the humanists are needed to answer these questions responsibly.

Clearly, sole reliance on an Analytic Scientist model of social science does not yield solutions to these four value problems that Bermant, Kelman, and Warwick have raised. All four models in the Mitroff-Kilmann typology are required. The Analytic Scientist or deterministic models may be employed seemingly to provide all good things for all people, but they are inescapably paternalistic and dehumanizing when applied without some blending of humanistic considerations. The dangers of reliance solely on the Analytic Scientist model or on other deterministic models are well illustrated by Kelman (1968) in a profound and delightful essay entitled "From Dystopia to Utopia." There, Kelman shows that deterministic utopian models carry the seeds of dehumanization, failing to promote in humanity its highest potential. They are characterized by:

1. Attempts at total environmental control, e.g., the tendency to predetermine what is right for the individual and to train her or him to select that.
2. Emphasis on psychological manipulation, e.g., emphasis on the use of psychological techniques that enable persons to perform their required social roles, without concern for the development of mechanisms that enable people to seek freedom.
3. The search for panaceas, for simple routes to self-esteem and salvation, rather than the opportunity for each individual to try to work out the good life for herself or himself.
4. The avoidance of commitment through overuse of methods that might properly be employed to handle overwhelming stress or disabling emotions, e.g., detachment and self-observation are substituted for having strong commitments to basic values and deep involvements with others.
5. Denial of responsibility, since, in a deterministic model of the world, one's nature is outside of one's own control.

Kelman's point was not that the use of behavioristic or deterministic models is necessarily unethical. Rather, his aim was to challenge social scientists to use their entire range of models and methods. And that is my point also. Although a scientist may operate most comfortably from a given quadrant of the Mitroff-Kilmann typology, most social scientists have occupied more than one quadrant in the course of their career, and many are capable of moving from one quadrant to another depending on the way in which they wish to focus on a particular problem in social science. The ability to change perspectives or methodologies can enable social scientists to recognize and resolve ethical problems more effectively. The case for this assertion is presented in the chapters that follow.

The chapters in Part I focus on experimental and allied behavioral methods typical of social psychological research, for example, the use of various logical design and measurement approaches, control groups, and the research laboratory. In most cases, the subject is in a relatively low power status relative to the researcher. Informed consent is a key issue in these cases precisely because the subject otherwise has so little control over the research context. Issues of deception, coercion, researcher misperception of what is problematic in the subjects' lives, random assignment of subjects to treatment conditions, emotional harm deriving from experimental treatments, and subject duplicity as a defense against the researcher's power are among the problems considered in Part I.

Mitroff and Kilmann's taxonomy helps to explain and clarify the directions taken in these five chapters. Classically, psychological research tends to be based on the Analytic Scientist model, where logical and rigorous research prevails, and where experimenters characteristically design research without consulting those studied. Not surprisingly, the authors of all five chapters acknowledge certain advantages of rigorous design and show that these are not necessarily incompatible with ethical requirements, thus pointing to those aspects of the Analytic Scientist model that are of value. However, these authors then proceed to broaden the methodology in their fields by adding humanistic elements. Each indicates certain kinds of scientific as well as ethical problems that arise when researchers depend on logical design without considering that subjects' have perspectives, problems, and agendas of their own. Geller, for example, discusses problems in deception research where there may be more naive researchers than naive subjects, since most subjects of laboratory research have come to expect to be deceived and hence respond with some deception of their own, contrary to the assumptions of the researchers. The emphasis in each of these chapters is on the use of more imaginative assessment of subjects' perspectives, and more authentic, collaborative communication in which, true to the spirit of informed consent, participants are treated as ends rather than as means.

Part II focuses on survey research, which is a method of choice among sociologists. Here, the researched tend to be called respondents and the researcher takes the role of interviewer. The two tend to meet for brief encounters on relatively neutral territory. For example, they may communicate by phone or mail, or meet in public places or at the respondent's doorstep. Because the respondent typically is in a powerful position to refuse or to end the interview, informed consent is not the key issue. Rather, privacy and confidentiality are the major issues. In turn, these issues give rise to the necessity of the investigator's learning about the ways in which privacy and confidentiality may be at issue for the respondent. For example, is there danger to the respondent of embarrassment, blackmail, subpoena of data and criminal prosecution, or of loss of some valuable status or service? What steps are required to protect privacy and confidentiality in ways that are important? How can respondents' fears effectively be allayed? How can the investigator be sure the the promises of privacy and confidentiality that were made can actually be kept? In what other ways must the investigator be concerned to understand and deal effectively with respondents' point of view in the matter?

Certain tenets of rigorous design are defended, such as valid inference, stratified random sampling, and avoidance of confounding. And again, this rigorous, logical methodology is broadened with the humanistic perspectives that are required to deal effectively and ethically with the issues of privacy and confidentiality.

The chapters in Part I of the companion volume focus on ethnographic fieldwork, which is the method of choice of cultural anthropologists and is now used widely throughout the social sciences. The fieldworker performs ethnographic studies in the custody, or on the turf, of the persons being studied—the informants. Rigorous design and measurement are not a part of fieldwork; rather, the fieldworker comes to know the culture of those studied by participating in and experiencing it and by relating as a friend to members of that culture.

Unlike experimentalists or survey researchers, most fieldworkers would wish to be regarded as humanists (in the sense in which Mitroff and Kilmann use the term) and not as Analytic Scientists. Not surprisingly, then, we find that the ethical problems examined in Part I are those that arise when Particular Humanist methodology is employed. To recognize and deal with these ethical problems, the fieldworker must be prepared to move in the *analytic* direction. This is done not by ignoring humanistic considerations but by recognizing that there is more distance between fieldworker and informants than meets the eye, and that this hidden distance brings with it hidden dangers especially to the informants but also to the fieldworker. For example, one must recognize that fieldwork is not the same as friendship, that friendly intimacy of fieldwork must be blended with intelligent detachment and examination, so that critical scholarly examination of the host culture can occur, and so that the hidden dangers of fieldwork can be recognized and reduced. In addition, the information that was gathered from a Particular Humanist perspective must be made general and impersonal enough to protect the privacy of those whose lives are being described in publications.

In Part II of the other volume, we examine three professional roles that the ethical researcher needs to consider: the role of consultant to agencies that regulate social research, the role of research review board member or of the researcher in relating to review board members, and the role of social scientist who chooses to disseminate scientific knowledge via the mass media. Each of these roles is fraught with role conflicts that are understandable consequences of the conflicting scientific roles that Mitroff and Kilmann describe.

Campbell and Cecil, in their analysis and recommendations of safeguards to the rights and interests of research participants, illustrate the difficulty of pleasing both the determinists and the humanists who evaluate their work. The accompanying criticisms by Bradburn and House confirm this difficulty! Tanke and Tanke, in their analysis of the functioning of institutional review boards, examine some of the problems of review that inevitably arise when there are among those who propose regulations, serve on those boards, and have their research reviewed, persons having widely divergent methdological orientations. Not surprisingly, Tanke and Tanke stress the value of informal communication between investigators and board members. Finally, Stocking and Dunwoody discuss concerns that social scientists have about using the mass media to disseminate scientific information. One concern is that the scientist will be accused by peers of behaving in an unscientific manner, a concern that is warranted in view of the tenets of the Analytic Scientist model. Interestingly, we learn there that scientists can escape peer criticism for talking to the press only when they are senior and well known, if then. The other major risk of "going public" has to do with the very real possibility of irresponsible journalism. This problem has received little attention from social scientists until now precisely because the Analytic Scientist has no reason to worry about this problem in the first place!

Summary

The resolution of ethical dilemmas in social research is defined as the creative and persistent search for research approaches that provide the most valid scientific results and that anticipate and circumvent or minimize ethical dilemmas. This involves a willingness to embrace various models of social science and humanism and to apply social theory and methodology in creative new ways. The examples of ethical problem solving contained in the chapters that follow are offered with the intention of challenging social scientists to incorporate ethical problem solving strategies into their research methodologies.

References

Argyris, C. *Intervention theory and method*. Reading, Mass.: Addison-Wesley, 1973.
Asch, S. Studies of independence and conformity: A minority of one against a unanimous majority. *Psychological Monographs*, 1956, *70* (9, Whole No. 416).
Bermant, G., Kelman, H., & Warwick, D. *The ethics of social intervention*. Washington, D.C.: Hemisphere, 1978.
Boruch, R., & Cecil, J. *Methods for assuring confidentiality of social research data*. Philadelphia: University of Pennsylvania Press, 1979.
Crane, D. *Invisible colleges*. Chicago: University of Chicago Press, 1972.
Feyerabend, P. *Against methodology: Outline of an anarchistic theory of knowledge*. London: NLB, 1975.
Gray, B. The regulatory context of social research: The work of the National Commission for the Protection of Human Subjects. In C. B. Klockars & F. W. O'Connor (Eds.), *Deviance and decency: The ethics of research with human subjects*. Beverly Hills, Calif.: Sage, 1979.
Hanson, N. R. *Patterns of discovery*. Cambridge, England: University of Cambridge Press, 1965.
Hanson, N. R. *Perception and discovery*. San Francisco: Freeman, 1969.
Holton, G. *Thematic origins of scientific thought, Kepler to Einstein*. Cambridge: Harvard University Press, 1973.
Holton, G. On being caught between dionysians and apollonians. In G. Holton (Ed.), *Science and its public: The changing relationship*. Boston: Daedalus, 1974.

Humphreys, L. *Tearoom trade: Impersonal sex in public places*. Chicago: Aldine, 1970.

Janis, I., & Mann, L. *Decision making*. New York: Free Press, 1977.

Kelman, H. C. *A time to speak: On human values and social research*. San Francisco: Jossey-Bass, 1968.

Klockars, C. B., & O'Connor, F. W. (Eds.). *Deviance and decency: The ethics of research with human subjects*. Beverly Hills, Calif.: Sage, 1979.

Klockars, C. B. Dirty hands and deviant subjects. In C. B. Klockars & F. W. O'Connor (Eds.), *Deviance and decency: The ethics of research with human subjects*. Beverly Hills, Calif.: age, 1979.

Kuhn, T. S. *The structure of scientific revolutions*. Chicago: University of Chicago Press, 1962.

Lakatos, I. Falsification and the methodology of scientific research programmes. In I. Lakatos & A. E. Musgrave (Eds.), *Criticism and the growth of knowledge*. New York: Cambridge University Press, 1970.

McKay, W. Can an is become an ought? Paper given at California Polytechnic Institute, Pomona Faculty Retreat, June 17, 1981.

Mitroff, I. I., & Kilmann, R. H. *Methodological approaches to social science*. San Francisco: Jossey-Bass, 1978.

Mitroff, I. I., & Chubin, D. E. Peer review: A dialectical policy analysis. Unpublished paper, 1978.

National Commission for the Protection of Human Subjects of Biomedical and Behavioral Research. *The Belmont report: Ethical principles and guidelines for the protection of human subjects of research* (DHEW Publication No. (OS) 78-0012). Washington, D.C.: U.S. Government Printing Office, 1978.

O'Connor, F. W. The ethical demands of the Belmont Report. In C. Klockars & F. W. O'Connor (Eds.), *Deviance and decency: The ethics of research with human subjects*. Beverly Hills, Calif.: Sage, 1979.

Reiss, A. J. Governmental regulation of scientific inquiry: Some paradoxical consequences. In C. B. Klockars & F. W. O'Connor (Eds.), *Deviance and decency: The ethics of research with human subjects*. Beverly Hills, Calif.: Sage, 1979.

Rivlin, A. M., & Timpane, P. M. Introduction and summary. In A. M. Rivlin & P. M. Timpane (Eds.), *Ethical and legal issues of social experimentation*. Washington, D.C.: Brookings Institution, 1975.

Rowan, J. *Ordinary ecstasy: Humanistic psychology in action*. London: Routledge & Kegan Paul, 1976.

von Hoffman, N. Sociological snoopers. *The Washington Post*, January 30, 1970, pp. B1; B9.

Warner, S. L. Randomized response: A survey technique for eliminating evasive answer bias. *Journal of the American Statistical Association*, 1965, *60*, 63-69.

Warner, S. The randomized response method. In R. Boruch, J. Ross, & J. Cecil (Eds.), *Proceedings and background papers: Conference on ethical and legal problems in applied social research*. Northwestern University, 1979.

Warwick, D. P. *The teaching of ethics in social sciences*. Hastings-on-Hudson, N.Y.: The Hastings Center, 1980.

Watson, J. B. *Behaviorism* (Rev. ed.). Chicago: University of Chicago Press, 1962.

Weber, M. *Max Weber on the methodology of the social sciences*. (E. Shils & H. A. Finch, Eds. and trans.) Glencoe, Ill.: Free Press, 1949. (Originally published in three parts in 1904, 1905, and 1917.)

Westfall, R. S. Newton and the fudge factor. *Science*, 1973, *179*, 751-756.

Part I

Experimental Social Research and Respect for the Individual

The experimental method and the orientation of the Analytic Scientist have been hallmarks of rigorous psychological research for many decades. As experimentally trained social scientists accept the challenge to study significant social phenomena, parts of the experimental method are adapted to social research. For example, the social experimenter may employ complex research designs and go to considerable length to manipulate and control the research setting and the perceptions and beliefs of those who are studied. Such adaptation of experimental methods to social research raises manifold ethical issues.

The pivotal ethical issue raised by social experimentation is respect for the autonomy of the individual. Surrounding issues include protection from harm and wrong, validity and value of the research, concern for the privacy of those studied, guarantee of confidentiality of the data that are obtained, and empowerment of those studied so that wrongs do not arise from the power differential between the experimenter and the subject. Ideally, potential subjects should be placed in a position to decide voluntarily whether to participate in the experiment. Such a consent process should involve clear communication between the experimenter and subjects. There should be adequate analysis of the risks and benefits of the research, and adequate safeguards should be provided. The communication process should be so constituted that subjects can question, discuss, comprehend and believe what they are told and be given adequate opportunity to weigh the relevant factors in deciding for themselves whether to participate in the experiment. Thus, in addition to being respectful of individual autonomy and providing some mechanisms for protecting persons from risk, a well-designed consent process may even create elements of a Conceptual Humanist relationship between subjects and the experimenter. In addition to improving the quality of the informed consent process, the humanistic elements are likely to enhance the validity and value of the research (Geller, Chapter 2, Argyris, 1973).

However, two major problems arise in the pursuit of such an ideal relationship: (1) The Analytic Scientist orientation of the experimentalist does not involve a humanistic relationship between investigator and subjects. Moreover, it is likely to involve the use of concealment, deception, random assignment, and procedures of measurement that are highly inconsistent with humanist orientations; and these powerful procedures may be used in applied settings to determine the fate of individuals in significant ways: e.g., to evaluate performance in educational and employment settings, to determine whether an experimental public policy should be implemented more broadly, or to determine whether given social conditions (e.g., noise, crowding) are harmful. (2) Legal and philosophical concepts of informed consent have evolved in ways that are somewhat infelicitous both to analytic and humanistic approaches to social experimentation.

The ethical problems raised by the Analytic Scientist orientation are discussed in Chapter 1. As an introduction to Part I, we focus primarily on the second problem: the historical circumstances which brought about the current legal and philosophical concepts of informed consent. Then, some approaches that are respectful of individual autonomy and serve the interests of social science as well are summarized here and presented in detail in Chapters 2 through 6.

Most discussions of the ethical importance of voluntary informed consent in experimental research can be traced, historically, to a few well-known cases such as the involuntary participation of persons in experiments in Nazi concentration camps (Katz, 1972), the Tuskegee study of syphilis (Jones, 1981), and the Milgram study of obedience (Milgram, 1974). These three cases, in particular, provide a useful background for understanding why a somewhat inappropriate model of informed consent has been thrust on experimental social scientists.

The experimentation in concentration camps resulted in pain and death for many and is noteworthy here because it achieved international attention and resulted in the definition of a concept of informed consent that is still reflected in the regulation of human research today. The Nuremberg Military Tribunal's decision in the case of the United States v. Karl Brandt et al. includes the Nuremberg Code, which delimits permissible medical experimentation on human subjects. The Nuremberg Code holds that experimentation on humans is justified only if its results benefit society and if it is conducted according to principles that satisfy moral, ethical, and legal concepts. The code holds that the voluntary consent of the human subject is essential, and defines consent as follows:

> This means that the person involved should have legal capacity to give consent; should be so situated as to be able to exercise free power of choice, without the intervention of any element of force, fraud, deceit, duress, over-reaching, or other ulterior form of constraint of coercion; and should have sufficient knowledge and comprehension of the elements of the subject matter involved as to enable him to make an understanding and enlightened decision. This latter element requires that before the acceptance of an affirmative decision by the experimental subject there should be made known to him the nature, duration, and purpose of the experiment; the method and means by which it is to be conducted; all incon-

veniences and hazards reasonably to be expected; and the effects upon his health or person which may possibly come from his participation in the experiment. (*Permissible medical experiments.* Trials of War Criminals before the Nuremberg Military Tribunals under Control Council Law No. 10: Nuremberg October 1946-April 1949. Washington, D.C.: U.S. Government Printing Office (n.d.), Vol. 2, pp. 181-182)

The Tuskegee study, which first became known to the public in 1972, is noteworthy because it illustrated the need for federal regulation of human research (including regulation of the administration of informed consent) in the United States. In 1932, the U.S. Public Health Service undertook an experiment of 399 semiliterate, syphilitic black men in Macon County, Alabama. The purpose of the experiment was to study the effects of untreated syphilis. To encourage participation, subjects were led to believe that they were being treated. Their symptoms were studied during periodic examinations and autopsies were performed when they died. Although penicillin became available for treatment of syphilis in the 1940s, the experiment was continued. Treatment was still being withheld from those subjects who had not yet died when the study became known to the public in 1972. Public anger at this experiment played a major role in bringing about the development of strict federal regulation of research on human subjects.

There are no known abuses in social science experimentation that begin to approach these two cases in seriousness. However, in the early seventies, the stage was set for public advocates to seek abuses in social research. Consequently, cases were identified in which informed consent was not obtained, deception was employed, and there was possible (if not actual) risk of harm to subjects. One such case, which did not involve strict experimentation, was the Humphreys study of the "tearoom trade" which is described in Chapter 1. Another is the Milgram obedience experiment which is described in detail by Daniel Geller in Chapter 2.

Briefly, Stanley Milgram, an experimental social psychologist at Yale University, ran newspaper ads inviting the public to participate in a learning experiment. Volunteers were told they would be divided by lot into learners and teachers. Actually, the aim was to study obedience, not learning, and all of the volunteers found themselves in the role of teacher, where they were instructed to teach lists of words to learners, and to give learners increasingly severe electric shocks at every mistake. Unbeknownst to the teachers, the "learners" were not really wired to the shock apparatus and were paid confederates who feigned both failure to learn and pain at being "shocked." At the end of each session, the actual purpose and procedure was explained to the subject and subjects who had obediently delivered "severe shock" were assured that obedience under these conditions was not unusual.

A one year follow-up was carried out to determine whether participation in the study had detrimental effects. The majority of the participants were grateful at the insight that their participation had provided, and only 1.3% of subjects indicated that they wished they had not participated (Milgram, 1974).

The nonscientific public first learned of Milgram's experiment via the publication of his book *Obedience to Authority* in 1974. Although most social psychologists regarded Milgram's experiment as an important contribution to science, the general public responded with anger. It has been argued that some of this anger was provoked merely because of the unpleasant light that the Milgram study casts on human nature. But clearly part of the anger was due to Milgram's use of deception that resulted in persons' feeling psychological discomfort at the behavior that they had engaged in under duress and solely to please the experimenter.

Many social scientists defend the Milgram study as one of such importance that the knowledge it provides justifies the procedures that were employed. Nevertheless, it is research such as Milgram's that contributed to the public sense that social as well as biomedical research on humans should be regulated.

In response to the press for federal regulation of human research, a series of federal regulations were enacted (see footnote 1, Chapter 1). The regulations which are current at this writing (i.e., which became effective July 27, 1981) define the elements of informed consent as follows:

1. A statement that the study involves research, an explanation of the purposes of the research and the expected duration of the subject's participation, a description of the procedures to be followed, and identification of any procedures which are experimental;

2. A description of any reasonably foreseeable risks of discomforts to the subject;

3. A description of any benefits to the subject or to others which may reasonably be expected from the research;

4. A disclosure of appropriate alternative procedures or courses of treatment, if any, that might be advantageous to the subject;

5. A statement describing the extent, if any, to which confidentiality of records identifying the subject will be maintained;

6. For research involving more than minimal risk[1] an explanation as to whether any compensation and an explanation as to whether any medical treatments are available if injury occurs and, if so, what they consist of, or where further information may be obtained;

7. An explanation of whom to contact for answers to pertinent questions about the research and research subjects' rights, and whom to contact in the event of a research-related injury to the subject; and

8. A statement that participation is voluntary, refusal to participate will involve no penalty or loss of benefits to which the subject is otherwise entitled, and the subject may discontinue participation at any time without penalty or loss of benefits to which the subject is otherwise entitled. (*Federal Register*, Vol. 46, No. 16, Monday, January 26, 1981/Rules and Regulations, p. 8389)

The 1981 Federal Regulations recognize that not all social research can be conducted with informed consent. An Institutional Review Board (IRB) may approve a consent procedure which does not include or which alters some or all of the elements of informed consent if the research could not practicably be carried out without the waiver or alternation, provided that:

---

[1] Minimal risk means that the risks of harm anticipated in the proposed research are not greater, considering probability and magnitude, than those ordinarily encountered in daily life or during the performance of routine physical or psychological examinations or tests.

1. The research involves no more than minimal risk to the subjects.
2. The waiver or alteration will not adversely affect the rights and welfare of the subjects.
3. Whenever appropriate, the subjects will be provided with additional pertinent information after participation.

Moreover, the 1981 Federal Regulations exempt from IRB review many categories of social research, including: all research not funded by the U.S. Department of Health and Human Services, research on "normal educational practices," which is conducted in schools; research involving the use of cognitive, diagnostic, aptitude, and achievement tests or the collection or study of existing data if data are obtained in a manner which makes the identification of individual subjects impossible; survey and interview research, *except* where individual subjects can be identified, their responses, if known outside the research could place subjects at risk, and the research deals with sensitive aspects of the subject's own behavior.

Thus, we see that the legal definition of informed consent is incompatible with requirements for deception and concealment in social research, but that the Federal Regulations governing informed consent do not entirely rule out the use of deception and concealment. On the other hand, the legal definition of informed consent is also incompatible with a humanistic relationship between the investigator and the subject. And, while current regulations do not prohibit such a relationship, they do little or nothing to foster the emergence of full and trusting two-way communication between the investigator and the subject.

We may conclude that government regulation of social research has stimulated in social scientists an awareness that some form of informed consent and respect for the autonomy of subjects is required. However, most social research is somewhat incompatible with the model of informed consent that has been developed for regulatory purposes. Consequently, it must fall to social scientists, themselves, to create appropriate ways to respect the autonomy of subjects in experimental social research. The purpose of Part I is to present the work of social scientists who have done so, and to stimulate further methodological inquiry in this area. There are a variety of specific dilemmas in experimental research that revolve around problems of respect for autonomy and informed consent. In Part I, several of these dilemmas are identified by investigators who are trained in Analytic Scientist methodology, but who employ other methods of science as well in the service of understanding and resolving dilemmas in experimental social science.

In Chapter 2, Daniel M. Geller, a social psychologist, discusses issues of deception research from a scientific perspective and concludes that deception may be more difficult to justify (on scientific grounds) than social scientists have tended to assume. He reminds us at the outset that there are many kinds of deception and that simple generalizations about the value or harm of deception research are not forthcoming. The normally unexamined asumptions on which deception research is based are then examined and a critique of some forms of deception research is given.

Geller offers provocative evidence to indicate that some deception research is more harmful to research assistants who administer it than to subjects who are the object of the deception, and that the stress of administering deception research is likely to alter the way in which the deception occurs and hence to alter the nature and validity of the findings. Other questions about the scientific validity of deception research are raised also. The alternatives to deception research are described and evaluated, and some are shown to be more promising than has generally been acknowledged, although some of the alternatives raise ethical problems as well. Geller's own research on the validity of alternatives to deception, which is summarized in Chapter 2, provides a powerful incentive to social scientists to test, empirically, the validity of methodological alternatives to deception. Not surprisingly, many of the more collaborative approaches that have been rejected by those solely dedicated to the Analytic Scientist model turn out to have more merit than previously assumed.

In Chapter 3, Ross Conner defends the field experimental use of the Analytic Scientist's most rigorous tool for making valid statistical inference, the random assignment of subjects to experimental conditions. He shows that without this powerful device, it is quite easy for society to make incorrect inferences about the effectiveness of experimental social programs. Then, using insights that typify the humanist, Conner discusses various matters pertinent to random assignment that may concern those who serve as subjects of field experiments. We see that there are a variety of ways in which control groups in the field differ from those in the laboratory and that field control groups need not deprive subjects of goods and services they ordinarily would expect to receive. Conner also illustrates a variety of methods that may be employed to use random assignment ethically, with fully informed consent, in sensitive cases in which persons choose not to be randomly assigned. Conner provides an excellent example in a context (evaluation research) in which the investigator scarcely can afford to ignore either humanistic or deterministic ideologies in the design and administration of social research.

While Conner illustrates the virtues of embracing more than one ideology in evaluation research, Philip H. Mirvis and Stanley E. Seashore, in Chapter 4, illustrate the need for total ideological or methodological flexibility in organizational research. They demonstrate the use of all four of the perspectives discussed in Mitroff and Kilmann (1978) and in Chapter 1. Mirvis and Seashore, both psychologists and organizational researchers, present compelling and intriguing accounts of unintended and disastrous outcomes of organizational research to illustrate that good moral intentions and adherence to professional codes of ethics are inadequate to prevent ethical dilemmas in organizational research. Despite careful attention to "normal" ethical considerations, the organizational researcher is likely to become entangled in a set of multiple roles and in the ambiguous and conflicting expectations deriving from these roles. Since the investigator typically lacks final authority to make decisions affecting others in organizational settings, he or she may be powerless to prevent harm to subjects or to carry out the research as planned. In other words, at the heart of the problem of protecting subjects and respecting their autonomy in organizational research is not the researcher's overwhelming power, but rather lack of power within a much larger and more powerful context. Mirvis and Seashore propose the use of role theory as a means for understanding the ethical dilemmas in organizational research and for guiding the development of research relationships with subjects in which to address and moderate these ethical dilemmas. They propose the establishment of research guidelines and training designed to help investigators establish ways to deal with dilemmas for which there are no ethical solutions except those deriving from the ad hoc consent of all parties involved.

It is interesting to contrast Mirvis and Seashore's ethical problem solving approaches with those described in Wax (Chapter 2, other volume) and Glazer (Chapter 3, other volume). While organizational research may involve many of the methods of testing and observation derived from experimental psychology, it closely resembles ethnographic fieldwork in that the investigator is a relatively low-powered newcomer to an intact culture, and it involves both reciprocity and the serious risks entailed in disclosure of personal information to a stranger. However, because the modern organization is a more hierarchical and complex system of relationships than typically is found in fieldwork, it calls for a special system of reciprocities, a system rendered understandable through the use of role theory.

Chapters 5 and 6 focus on ethical dilemmas that confront experimentally oriented investigators when (1) their standard mode of rigorous research may be less appropriate than a more collaborative approach for ethical reasons, and (2) they come from backgrounds that are different from those of their subjects, and hence do not necessarily understand their subjects' perspective. Often, the experimentally oriented social scientist who is skilled in the use of a given method may assume that the method may be generalized validly to another subject population. However, failure to observe, understand, and empathize with members of vulnerable populations may result in the disrespectful or invalid use of procedures that would be entirely appropriate to use on other populations.

In Chapter 5, Chalsa M. Loo, a clinical, environmental, and cross-cultural social psychologist, reviews studies of crowding in vulnerable populations to illustrate problems that are likely to arise when generalizing various methods of social research to the study of the effects of stress on vulnerable persons. The inappropriate generalization of procedures, the failure to use culturally sensitive measures, and the failure to make culturally appropriate interpretations of data can cause direct harm to individuals and can produce harmful, invalid conclusions about entire populations. Yet, problems of stress and coping among vulnerable populations such as the poor, minorities, and the psychologically disadvantaged should not be ignored by investigators. Loo offers guidelines to social scientists for heightening their sensitivity to sources of possible disrespect and harm deriving from application of experimental research procedures to vulnerable populations and offers suggestions for circumventing or reducing these potential problems.

In Chapter 6, Eleanor K. Levine, a developmental psychologist and linguist, summarizes current research on the elderly and documents major erroneous assumptions that have been made by investigators and that characterize much of the research in this area. For example, inappropriate normative assumptions are made about healthy adaptation of the elderly; behavior is attributed to chronological age that can more parsimoniously be attributed to other factors such as social class, sex, ethnicity/race, and social context. Disrespectful and inappropriate (invalid) research procedures invite deceit and lying on the part of elderly subjects. Levine discusses the kinds of Conceptual Humanist experiences that led to her discovery of these problems. She offers approaches for correcting those practices through which social scientist have incorrectly stereotyped the elderly.

Part I demonstrates the complexity of the contexts in which some ethical issues arise in behavioral research. It also demonstrates the need to combine the methodological rigor and ingenuity of the experimentalist with the kinds of knowing that grow out of the more involved, intuitive, and perceptive relationships of the humanist and the divergent thinker. We see that no simple code of ethics can provide the sensitivity, understanding, or decision making approaches that are described in the following chapters.

References

Argyris, C. *Intervention theory and method*. Reading: Addison-Wesley, 1973.

Katz, J. *Experimentation with human beings*. New York: Russell Sage Foundation, 1972.

Jones, J. H. *Bad blood*. New York: Free Press, 1981.

Milgram, S. *Obedience to authority*. New York: Harper & Row, 1974.

Mitroff, I. I., & Kilmann, R. H. *Methodological approaches to social science*. San Francisco: Jossey-Bass, 1978.

Chapter 2

Alternatives to Deception: Why, What, and How?

Daniel M. Geller

The purpose of this chapter is to explore methods in social science research that do not rely on deception. Implicit in this inquiry into scientifically valid methods that minimize the risk of harm to research participants is the assumption that methods involving deception raise serious ethical and practical questions. Here, the term *research participants* refers not only to subjects but also to the experimenter and persons working for the experimenter. One of the aims of this chapter is to identify the methodological strengths and weaknesses of the alternative methods proposed in order to encourage both their use and further research into their advantages and limitations.

Most of the examples of deception that are addressed in this chapter, as well as the suggested applications of alternative methods, are taken from social psychology. This reflects the prevalence of deception methods in social psychology, my familiarity with them, and the generally recognized need for methodologically sound alternatives to deception. Since the social sciences share methods and problems, it should not be difficult for the reader to apply these examples to related disciplines.

The need for deception-free methods arises partly from the ethical issues concerning the rights of the subject or participant. These rights include obtaining the informed consent of participants and assuring that the participant leaves the study in no worse physical or psychological condition than when he or she entered it. Both of these rights of the participant may be compromised if deception is employed.

Is it possible, for example, to obtain *informed* consent from a prospective participant who is *not informed*? What if he or she is told that some of the details cannot be explained? What about the prospective participant who is forewarned or told of imminent deception but not told how or when it will occur? How do people feel about themselves and social psychologists after they learn that they have been duped by the researcher? When is it morally justified to conduct research in which informed consent is partially circumvented? The guidelines for human research of the American Psychological Association (1973) and the Department of Health, Education, and Welfare (1977) permit deception when there is no other way to effectively carry out the research. Although there are sound utilitarian arguments for some deception research, neither APA nor DHEW guidelines provide an incentive for the exploration or use of deception-free alternatives.

Before alternatives to deception are discussed it is necessary to identify the kinds of deception used in social science research and the reasons for their prevalence.

A Taxonomy of Deception

A research participant is deceived when any misinformation is given, misrepresentation made, or any incomplete information is implied to be complete. A taxonomy of deception developed by Sieber (1978) identified three types of deception. In *implicit deception* the real situation differs so greatly from what the participants expect that they act under incorrect assumptions. Usually this refers to situations in which participants are not aware that they are taking part in any experiment. For example, students in a classroom may be led to believe they are rating a visiting lecturer when they are actually participating in a study on first impression. Similarly, participants in a study on attributions made in a Watergate-type burglary were not aware that they were in an experiment until after it was over (West, Gunn, & Chernickey, 1975). *Technical deception* involves the misrepresentation of equipment and procedures. In Milgram's studies on obedience (1963, 1974) an impressive looking apparatus was identified as a shock generator. *Role deception* refers to the misrepresentation of other persons in a study, as when a confederate is presented as another subject or an experimenter poses as a customer in a store.

Why deception? Although logical arguments have not always been advanced to support the reliance on deception methods, they are nonetheless assumed by most persons familiar with social psychology or other social sciences that use deception. As an example, consider my own initiation into the relatively unquestioning use of deception methods.

In early 1971, before the concern over ethics in research became institutionalized in psychology with the publication of *Ethical Standards for the Conduct of Research with Human Participants* (American Psychological Association, 1973), but after Milgram's studies on obedience (1963, 1965) had provoked debate on ethical issues in research, three other graduate students and I decided to investigate how people respond to being ignored (Geller, Goodstein, Silver, & Sternberg, 1974). After learning that there was no prior research on this topic, we began investigating the phenomenon through informal role-playing simulations in which we pretended to ignore people who knew they were being ignored, but were asked to act as if they did not. Although we learned much about being ignored through these simulations, we decided to observe people's naive reactions to deliberate ignoring. After a few uncomfortable minutes, we divulged our true purposes and asked these unwitting victims how they felt. Before long we had developed a systematic laboratory procedure in which two confederates ignored a person who expected attention (it is actually more difficult than one would imagine). Never once did we, members of the faculty, or fellow graduate students question the use of deception. It was *assumed* that deception was the only appropriate means of observing spontaneous behavior, despite our preliminary success with simulation.

After the experiment had begun and we saw how effective the deception was we were almost faced with a revolt by the confederates. The confederates felt uncomfortable about deceiving the subjects after noticing the prevalence of emotional stress, loss of self-esteem, and self-blame that was common among the subjects even after a lengthy and sensitive debriefing session. As a consequence the confederates wished to discontinue the experiment; they were, however, persuaded to continue. Later, an analysis of the data revealed that the confederates were less effective in ignoring the participants after they raised these moral questions than they had been before.

This example illustrates some of the implicit reasons for the use of deception and some of its potential consequences, ethically and methodologically. Ethically, it points to the possibly lasting consequences of a deception that mimics a fairly common experience and that was not easily overcome by debriefing. Methodologically, one wonders how many other studies using deception may have been similarly affected by the arousal of conscience in confederates or experimenters.

This experience stimulated my own interest in alternatives to deception. It also suggests some possible reasons for the unquestioning acceptance of deception as a standard laboratory procedure in social psychology.

1. There is an untested but persistent notion that creating a false belief promotes spontaneous behavior by the participants, especially in a laboratory setting.
2. Implicit epistemological superiority is accorded to deception methods.
3. Social psychologists have been habituated to the use of deception and perceive a lack of alternatives.
4. The design of a clever deception procedure is rewarding to many researchers and highly respected by colleagues.
5. Deception methods predominate in the graduate training of social psychologists.
6. Deception methods maintain the power of the experimenter over the participant, who is typically and revealingly called the subject.

Although only anecdotal evidence is available to support most of the reasons for the prevalence of deception methods, arguments concerning the first two reasons, which relate to the scientific validity of deception methods, can be made. One might think that the faith placed in deception methods is based on solid evidence of its superiority; however, it is not. To my knowledge, there have been no specific attempts to assess the comparability of human behavior under the focused conditions of laboratory deception with behavior in the natural environment (often dubbed the "real world" by persons who presumably spend most of their lives in laboratories). It is, to be sure, a difficult task, one that is not fully met by explaining why the findings of the deception laboratory study may not necessarily be generalizable to other settings. Orne's (1962, 1969) work on some of the problems of deception methods comes closest, perhaps, but does so from a very biased approach and suffers from many of its own methodological flaws. Orne contends that participants are actively engaged in hypothesis testing of their own and, suspicious of the experimenter's stated motives, try to determine what is really going on and what is really expected of them. In so doing, participants may be responding to unintended features of the experiment, or demand characteristics, that provide clues to their expected behavior but are not being controlled. Although these notions have been conceptually valuable to researchers, Orne's demonstrations of the pervasiveness of demand characteristics have been unconvincing.

The acceptance of deception methods reflects the epistemological position social psychologists and other social scientists have granted it. For example, some researchers (Aronson & Carlsmith, 1968; Freedman, 1969) believe that any method can be evaluated on two critical dimensions: experimental realism, i.e., the extent to which the subject believes the situation to be realistic and takes it seriously, and mundane realism, i.e., the extent to which the events surrounding the participant in the experiment are similar to those encountered in the natural environment.

Deception methods are often said to be high in experimental realism if successfully implemented. Mundane realism usually varies as a function of the setting, being highest in field studies in which participants are not aware their behavior is being investigated and lowest in laboratory studies that do not succeed in overcoming the artificiality of the laboratory. Some proponents of deception methods seem to have ignored many of the problems implicit in the use of deception and have leveled their fervored criticism only at alternative methods (cf. Freedman, 1969). Only recently has it been suggested that both deception methods and alternative methods are simulations of behavior in the natural environment and that both must be subjected to the kind of epistemological scrutiny usually reserved for alternatives (Hamilton, 1976).

The Need for Alternative Methods

The methodological problems of deception methods have been given much attention in recent years and there is already some evidence of the consequences. The suspicion and distrust of actual participants and those likely to participate in the future, especially among college students, is well documented (Argyris, 1968; Cook, Bean, Calder, Frey, Krovitz, & Riesman, 1970; Fillenbaum & Frey, 1970; Kelman, 1972; Masling, 1966; Mixon, 1977; Seeman, 1969; Shulman & Berman, 1975; Stricker, Messick, & Jackson, 1969) and endangers the supply of the so-called "naive subject," without whom deception cannot succeed. Unless deception methods become the exception rather than the rule, they may further threaten the ability of social scientists to obtain the trust of any prospective participant whether deception is used or not. For example, a senior in one of my classes interviewed freshmen about territoriality and privacy among roommates. She found that many freshmen were reluctant to be interviewed. It seems that students were satisfied with the interviewer's assurance of anonymity and confidentiality, but, upon learning that she was in the psychology department, they became suspicious of her motives. It is noteworthy that this occurred at a university where there is no subject pool and where no deception research had been conducted under the aegis of the psychology department in recent years.

Another example involved my experience with adults recruited from advertisements in weekly New York City newspapers. Many of the volunteers for a role-playing simulation were inherently suspicious of our motives at first. Some feared (or, perhaps, hoped) they would be secretly "psychoanalyzed." Other participants reacted to our assurances of no deception with skepticism.

Many social scientists contend that it may be necessary to deceive in order to study some phenomena. If the ethical gains from conducting deception research outweigh the losses from either abandoning the study or deceiving the participant, then the deception might be justifiable on utilitarian grounds. In particular, there might be moral justifications in favor of deception for field experiments that do not expose participants to bizarre situations and are unlikely to affect the reactions of passersby to subsequent natural situations.

But what of laboratory studies where deception is deemed necessary? In such situations it seems essential, if informed consent is to be obtained, to forewarn prospective participants that some information will be withheld or that certain elements of the study may be manipulated, but that all will be revealed afterward. Forewarning, however, presents serious methodological problems as the participants may try to determine the nature of the deception and either make a good impression by acting appropriately (Riecken, 1962) or react against the pressure to do the expected (Masling, 1966). In such a study the burden is shifted to the debriefing session, which includes dehoaxing (Holmes, 1976a) and desensitizing the participant to reduce any distress experienced (Holmes, 1976b). Even with the most stringent debriefing (Mills, 1976) it may be difficult to assure that the participant feels no worse after the study than he or she did before.

Requirements of Alternative Methods

Clearly, the need for alternatives is evident for both ethical and methodological reasons. The requirements for ethical alternative methods are as follows.

1. There must be no use of warnings of imminent deception or deception itself.
2. The participant's agreement to take part in the study must be based on voluntary informed consent.
3. The honesty and integrity of the researcher must be maintained.
4. No physical harm to the participant should be permitted. Physical pain, such as electric shock, should not be used.
5. No psychological harm to the participant should be permitted. Any emotional stress imposed of absolute necessity should be minimal, temporary, and reversible enough that the participant feels no worse after the study than before.
6. The method chosen must be an appropriate means of understanding and assessing behavior in its natural setting. That is, high experimental and mundane realism should be sought.

Alternative Methods

The need for alternatives to deception was first recognized long before deception in research became the mode (Vinacke, 1954). This early moral plea was largely ignored until more than a decade ago when Kelman (1967) reexamined the issues surrounding deception. The final impetus in the search for ethical alternatives appears to have been a function of imminent and actual regulations on the protection of human participants in the early 1970s. The alternative methods to be discussed here are by no means exhaustive. The focus is on alternatives to laboratory deception methods. Three types of alternatives to deception are discussed: naturalistic observation or experimentation, deception-free laboratory experimentation, and simulation, of which there are several kinds. The advantages and limitations of each alternative, both ethically and methodologically, will be delineated. Alternatives to the deception used in participant observation studies (e.g., Festinger, Riecken, & Schachter, 1956; Humphreys, 1970) and survey research using unobtrusive measures (Webb, Campbell, Schwartz, & Sechrest, 1966) are not considered here.

Naturalistic Observation or Experimentation

Researchers often fail to take full advantage of opportunities to investigate behavior in its natural setting despite the high mundane realism and the potential generalizability of findings. The reason for this lies in the difficulty of establishing rigorous controls over variables. Without such control the internal validity of the study may be threatened and the usual advantage of field studies in terms of external validity or generalizability may be diminished.

The characteristic solution to the apparent conflict between control over the variables and threats to validity has been to design a field experiment in which some manipulation of the setting or persons is introduced. This is, of course, deception. Typical of this approach is the study of helping behavior in the subway by Piliavin and Piliavin (1972). In that study, a confederate posing as a passenger collapsed on the floor of a Philadelphia subway car while stage blood dribbled from his mouth; observers recorded the reactions of bystanders. Studies such as this, however, raise a number of ethical and legal questions (Silverman, 1975). Among these are questions about the use of deception (implicit, role, and technical deception in this study), misrepresentation of facts, entrapment, invasion of privacy, harrassment, and creating a public disturbance.

Solutions to the problems of designing a valid field study that does not involve deception or manipulation of behavior are possible; they only seem difficult because of our lack of familiarity with them. Observational techniques, combined with interviews, were used to study the norms which develop among people waiting in lines (Mann, 1969), thus avoiding the need to employ confederates to wait in line or break into the queue. The use of existing records or archival techniques has been documented by Webb et al. (1966). Similarly, many studies have used multiple correlation techniques to study the relationship between crowding or density and social pathology, using existing records and data obtained from interviews or questionnaires (cf. Altman, 1975). When the use of controlled experimental techniques is not possible and other methods seem inappropriate, quasi-experimental designs can be used (Campbell & Cook, 1976; Campbell & Stanley, 1966). For example, if a control group is not available for comparison or cannot be constructed, time-series methods can be used, in which the same persons or groups are sampled repeatedly. Quasi-experimental methods are not without methodological flaws, but neither are finely controlled deception studies in the laboratory with their concerns of demand characteristics, suspicion, and experimenter bias. Quasi-experimental methods may also require different statistical analyses than experimental studies, but these analyses can reduce the losses of control (Boruch, 1976; Boruch & Cecil, Chapter 10).

Deception-Free Laboratory Experiments

It is possible to assess behavior in a controlled laboratory setting without resorting to deception. One way to find out what participants are thinking or why they are behaving in a particular manner is to ask them. Although social scientists cannot rely on self-report, it is true that catching participants unaware is not the only means of understanding a participant's motivations. Social psychology has often relied on the assumption that the similar behavior of different persons in an experiment is attributable to the same cause (Taylor, 1976). Unfortunately, this cannot be known unless participants are asked, preferably in a way that minimizes response bias.

The emerging area of cognitive social psychology addresses these problems directly. Taylor (1976) points to the gap between theory and method in social psychology, a field that uses S-R (stimulus-response) methodology to assess S-O-R (stimulus-organism-response) theory. Carroll and Payne (1976) advocate the use of process-tracing techniques developed by cognitive psychologists, such as the verbal protocol, response time, and eye movement recording, as a means of assessing how participants make decisions. It is not difficult to realize the potential of such deception-free information-processing techniques in measuring attitudes or understanding attributions.

In a research project on reactions to visual stimuli in the urban environment, some of my students have already begun to use process-tracing techniques. These students are using fixation time, the amount of time a particular stimulus is looked at, as an indicator of evaluative response. Fixation time on urban scenes, which is expected to correlate with other measures, is hypothesized to be a function of features of the stimulus (e.g., complexity) and adaptation to the urban environment.

Although the use of process-tracing techniques is not new, they have not been widely used in social psychology. For example, in an effort to circumvent the problem of false reports of attitudes, Jones and Sigal (1971) convinced participants that their responses were being monitored by a machine that was so advanced that it would do them no good to try to cover up their real attitudes. This "bogus pipeline," as it was dubbed, allowed confidence in the accuracy of self-reports, to the degree of the participant's knowledge. However, the same confidence could conceivably be gained by using process-tracing techniques, without the need to resort to technical deception. If latency of response were used to indicate strength of attitude, firmly held attitudes might be more likely to elicit quick responses on agree/ disagree scales than weakly held attitudes. There are, of course, a number of problems associated with latency of response as a measure of attitude, but similar criticisms can be leveled at more traditional measures of assessing attitude. Additional research on such deception-free alternatives must be encouraged so that their advantages and limitations can be understood. Nevertheless, these alternatives are worth pursuing for their potential ethical advantage: they involve no deception.

In other experiments deception-free methods can be used without reliance on as yet untested alternatives. Consider a standard paradigm in social psychology in which self-esteem is manipulated in order to gauge its effect on a dependent variable, such as attributions of causality. Self-esteem is usually manipulated by providing the participant with false feedback on a personality inventory or his or her performance on a simple task. Possible but infrequently considered alternatives that do not involve deception are the use of actual self-esteem by providing true feedback on an important series of facts (e.g., grade point average for college students, with ability controlled). The relationship between self-esteem and attributions of causality could then be assessed using multiple regression analysis instead of analysis of variance. The results may have greater external validity because they do not rely on a single situational manipulation and are not likely to be influenced by suspicion or by the participant's attempts to interpret the demands of the situation.

Methodologically, deception-free laboratory experiments may have all of the advantages of control of any laboratory study while avoiding the handicaps of suspicion and reduced experimental realism. The moral issues raised by the use of deception and the concomitant erosion of trust between the participant and the experimenter are eliminated, thus permitting a cooperative relationship. This, in turn, is likely to minimize any fears that the participant might harbor that anonymity might not be preserved.

Simulations

The use of simulation as a means of understanding social behavior is not new in social science. In general, simulation refers to the establishment of a mock situation, or one that is not real, and asking participants to pretend or act as if it were real. Like all other methods it is not intrinsically deception free. One of the most effective and widely discussed simulations was the Stanford prison study (Zimbardo, Haney, Banks, & Jaffe, 1973), which used some implicit deception. Student volunteers who had agreed to role play, although they did not know whether they would play guards or prisoners, were unexpectedly picked up by real Palo Alto police cars and booked at the police station for unknown reasons before they were told it was all part of the study they had volunteered for weeks earlier.

Even when they do not include deception, simulations cannot be assumed to be intrinsically ethical. The Stanford prison study, and other simulations that will be discussed later, all caused intense emotional involvement in participants. Some of the moral issues involved in inducing such emotional distress have been argued and refuted elsewhere (Baumrind, 1964; Crawford, 1972; Milgram, 1964). Given the potential for intense involvement in simulations, researchers must consider whether any additional insights into human behavior can be gained that might justify the risks to participants. For example, the conclusions of the Stanford prison study were not entirely unpredictable in view of the findings of Milgram's study on obedience (1974) and the many real accounts of atrocities in prison and concentration camps.

Simulations can be categorized into three basic types: game simulations, field simulations, and role-playing simulations. Of these simulations role playing has the most developed potential as an alternative to deception because it can be readily adapted to many laboratory settings. Role playing has been used in an increasing number of studies in the last decade; its uses will be investigated in detail later in this chapter.

Game simulations are those in which participants, sometimes in teams, take roles in particular staged situations and maintain them until a desired outcome is reached or a given length of time has passed. They are, so to speak, serious Monopoly games in the arenas of war, business, international relations, education, community planning, and so on (Guetzkow, 1962; Guetzkow, Alger, Brody, Noel, & Snyder, 1963). The players play the game as if it were real, learning about themselves and the ways in which they can and do apply approaches and tactics after the game is over. Game simulations have also been successfully used as teaching methods (Gamson, 1978).

Boruch (1976) discusses the use of a game simulation called a "surrogate treatment program." For example, he notes that mock trials have been convened using real jury candidates, real judges, and real cases. Especially if convened simultaneously with an actual case, such simulations have the advantage of extremely high realism without raising any of the ethical and legal issues of the secret recordings of the Witchita Jury Case (Katz, Capron, & Glass, 1976).

Field simulations differ from game simulations in setting. They rely on the use of a highly realistic staged setting that encourages participants to believe they are participating in a natural event rather than a simulation. These simulations may be extremely involving for the participants and may last a long time.

The Stanford prison study lasted six days before it was terminated. One of the "inmates" appeared to have had an intense emotional breakdown, and was let out of the experiment. Even the experimenter (Zimbardo), in his role as prison superintendent, began to act as if it were real, concocting an elaborate scheme to put down a prisoner rebellion.

The Grindstone Experiment involved the defense of an island under simulated attack. The participants in the study, sponsored by the Canadian Friends Service Committee, were committed to nonviolent methods. Nevertheless, during its 31 hour duration many of the behavioral norms of nonviolence broke down (Olson & Christiansen, 1966).

One of the advantages of field simulations, like game simulations, is that no deception is involved, permitting the trust between the researcher and participant to be maintained. Methodologically, field simulations allow fairly extensive generalizations and offer extremely high levels of experimental and mundane realism.

These advantages, however, are accompanied by a disadvantage: the realism of the simulation can be so great that it has the potential to create intense emotional involvement among the participants. As demonstrated by the Stanford prison study, exposing participants to such a great potential for stress when they did not volunteer for the experiment with that expectation raises many moral issues. Can the experimenter fully inform the participant of the likely range of stress he or she might encounter? Is a verbal presentation sufficient to provide the participant with this information or would an audiovisual presentation be more appropriate? Investigators should be aware that research volunteers may have a tendency to believe that they can handle intense emotional stress; it seems to be unacceptable among many in our society to admit that one does not have an iron psyche.[1]

An example of a deception study that could have been conducted as a game or field simulation is one in which participants were induced to take part in a Watergate-type illegal burglary in order to assess actor-observer differences in causal attribution (West et al., 1975). Prospective participants were approached by a private investigator; if they agreed to meet him at a later date to discuss an unspecified project they might be interested in, they became participants. At the subsequent meeting the project was disclosed as the burglary of an advertising firm. Sponsorship was either by the Internal Revenue Service or a competing firm; reward was either immunity from prosecution, $2000, or nothing. A control group was also used. Participants expressed their willingness or refusal to continue with the burglary; only then were they told that they had been in an experiment and debriefed. The authors admit that participants may have suffered from a temporary loss of self-esteem but justify their procedures in a risk/benefit analysis. Major ethical issues of this study are discussed in a comment by Cook (1975).

How might the simulation techniques discussed above be used as alternatives in the "Watergate" study? (For sake of argument I will operate under the assumption, however tenuous, that the study made a sufficient contribution to be worth conducting.) A game simulation could be used to assess compliance and the attributions made. Even if participants were aware of the game, there is every reason to believe that they would take it seriously and respond spontaneously, as the involvement of such simulations tends to be high. A field simulation might be more ideally suited to this type of study. It could proceed exactly as did the deception study with one crucial difference: before the study began participants would be told that this was a simulation.

In *role-playing simulations*, like the other simulations discussed, participants are asked to pretend that a situation is real when it is not. Role playing is, however, unique in its flexibility of setting and players; it permits greater use of imagination than the other methods, making it ideal for laboratory use. The setting in a role-

---

[1] Although there is no specific evidence of this, college students have reported that they do not mind being deceived (Berscheid, Baron, Dermer, & Libman, 1973). Furthermore, over 83% of the participants in Milgram's (1974) studies of obedience to authority claim that they were glad to have participated in the research. Obedient participants did not differ from the defiant on this measure, contrary to what might be expected.

playing simulation can be complete with props or freely imagined. The roles of the players can range from the totally improvised to the highly scripted. It is even possible for one person to play more than one role.

Role playing is well suited to many experiments that usually rely on deception methods. Unlike the deceived subject, who must be kept unaware if the experiment is to succeed, the role player must be fully informed. The role player knows of any technical illusions and the existence of any actors (confederates or stooges in a deception study). But the role player's knowledge does not interfere; he or she is asked to suspend reality and act spontaneously, as if the situation were real. Especially when operating without a script, the role players are active participants in the research, creating their own roles with full awareness that they are the focus of the study. The role-playing participant's experience can be as real as that of a method actor or a child playing cops-and-robbers; it does not depend on being duped or deceived.

Role playing, although not labeled as such, was first proposed as an alternative to the "subterfuge and dishonesty" of deception by Vinacke (1954). Later, Brown (1962) theorized that the behavior of a role-playing subject would more closely approximate a life situation than that of a hoodwinked subject. It was not until 1967 that the results of the first attempt to design a role-playing study as an alternative to deception were published (Greenberg, 1967). In that same year, Kelman (1967) called for the use of role playing as an alternative to deception.

There is some confusion among researchers and critics over what constitutes role playing. Coutu (1951) distinguished role playing, the enactment of one's own appropriate role in a given situation, from role taking, imagining what another person would do in a particular situation. Coutu's distinction was largely unheeded; Greenberg's (1967) role-playing study actually involved role taking.

Unfortunately, this confusion has contributed to negative predispositions about role playing among social psychologists. Freedman (1969), an early and widely quoted critic of role playing, called it a return to the prescientific days of intuition and "psychology-by-consensus." In fact, his criticisms apply only to role taking, as exemplified by Milgram's (1963) finding that neither psychiatrists nor Yale undergraduates could predict the outcome of the obedience studies. Similarly, Aronson and Carlsmith (1968) placed role playing at the low end of the experimental realism continuum. Again, they seem to be referring to role taking, not role playing.

Several studies comparing various kinds of role playing with deception have met with some success in research on conformity (Horowitz & Rothschild, 1970; Wahl, 1972; Willis & Willis, 1970). Furthermore, role-playing simulations of Milgram's (1963, 1965, 1974) studies of obedience have met with success in terms of replications of results (Albrecht, 1973; Mixon, 1971, 1972; O'Leary, Willis, & Tomich, 1970). Mixon's studies contributed much to the understanding of role playing by differentiating nonactive role playing (similar to role taking) from active role playing and suggesting that differences in outcome among various role-playing studies might be a function of subtle variations in the instructions given.

In spite of the apparent success of these studies, role playing as an alternative method remained subject to much criticism as long as the criterion for success was simply similarity of outcome to studies conducted with deception methods. Miller

(1972) concluded that the prospects for role playing as an alternative to deception were doubtful, and cautioned that identical results between role-playing studies and deception studies do not necessarily imply identical causes. One key to assessing the effectiveness of role playing was alluded to by Greenberg (1967) and Wahl (1972), who suggested that the participant's involvement in the role-playing situation must be considered in interpreting results.

Role Playing as an Effective Alternative

In order for role playing to be considered an effective alternative to deception it was necessary to demonstrate that role-playing participants could experience as much emotional involvement in a situation as could successfully deceived participants, who were themselves presumed to get as involved as persons in a natural situation. Ideally, of course, role-playing simulations would not need to be compared to deception studies, but to assure the acceptance of role playing by skeptical social psychologists this approach was an essential first step.

Because of my interests in the issues of obedience to authority and and the consequences of deception on research participants (as demonstrated in my earlier discussions concerning deception in a study on being ignored conducted by Geller et al., 1974), I decided to conduct a role-playing simulation of obedience (Geller, 1978). Role playing was chosen as a method because of its previously exhibited potential in studies of obedience and its adaptability to a controlled laboratory setting.

In designing a role-playing simulation of obedience it was important to assess the success of role playing using two criteria: replication of results obtained by deception methods (outcome) and the experience of the participants, in obeying or disobeying the authority, as phenomenologically real (process). Process was measured by participant self-report, paper-and-pencil scales of role-playing ability, and, most importantly, ratings of emotional involvement. After extensive training on videotapes of participants in a pilot study, two independent judges viewed videotapes of the role-playing sessions and rated them on several nonverbal dimensions in order to assess involvement. The judges arrived at highly reliable ($r = .93$) ratings of involvement on a six point scale. The judged ratings were independent of the obedience or disobedience of the role players.

Participants role played one of three conditions of Milgram's (1963, 1965, 1974) studies on obedience to authority. In Milgram's baseline condition subject's were ordered to shock a confederate at an increasing level each time he gave a wrong answer on a learning task; in the experimenter absent condition the experimenter left the laboratory and gave orders to continue by telephone only if the subject called him for advice; in the victim's limited contract condition the confederate made a verbal agreement with the experimenter to be let out if he felt great pain, otherwise it was the same as the baseline condition. Using deception, Milgram (1974) found that obedience in these conditions was 65%, 22.5%, and 40%, respectively. Unlike deceived subjects, role playing participants knew that their behavior was the focus of the study, that the confederate was an actor, and that the shocks were not real. Role players did not know the results of Milgram's study , but were aware that they were participating in a replication of it to see how effective role playing would be. Elaborate precautions were taken to assure that participants understood what role playing was, why it was being studied, and when they were to begin role playing.

The predictions for this study were based on the belief that participants could respond to one of two sets of cues. The first cues, called the obedience set, were exactly the same as those in Milgram's study, and refer to the participant's response to the victim's protests and the experimenter's orders to continue. The obedience set results in either obedience or defiance and varies by condition, as Milgram has shown. The second set of cues, the role-playing set, refers to the participant's involvement in the role playing. If the participant is highly involved, he will be acting as if the situation is real, and therefore will respond according to the obedience cues, which would predominate. If the participant is not involved and is not taking the situation seriously, he will be responding according to his view of reality: that the shocks are not real. Therefore, when ordered to continue, the uninvolved participant will take the easy way out and administer what is obviously a fake shock, regardless of the pressure to obey or disobey. In the baseline condition, no difference between the most and least involved role players was predicted, since it is believed that participants responding to either set of cues would show high obedience (either as a function of Milgram's findings or as a function of the pretend situation). Since Milgram found that the results of the contract condition did not significantly differ from those of the baseline condition, no difference in the behavior of role players at different levels of involvement was expected in the contract condition. The crucial test of the effect of involvement lies in the experimenter absent condition. The obedience cues are diminished because of the reduced salience of the experimenter, so predicted obedience should drop among the most involved, who are responding to the obedience cues. The least involved, of course, are still responding to the fact that the shocks are not real, and should not be influenced by the experimenter's absence.

The results of this role-playing simulation confirmed my hypotheses. A multiple regression analysis revealed that only in the experimenter absent condition was the level of involvement (as measured by judged ratings only) a significant predictor of obedience. Breaking the results down by condition it was found that obedience among the most involved was 50% in the baseline condition, 22.2% in the experimenter absent condition, and 40% in the contract condition. These results are extremely similar to those found by Milgram. For the least involved there were no significant changes in obedience by condition, with respective levels of obedience being 70%, 55.6%, and 70% (for further details see Geller, 1978).

This role-playing simulation of obedience demonstrates the effectiveness of role playing as an alternative to deception. Role playing can replicate the outcome of studies done using deception and can also be experientially real for the participants. Like other simulations, role playing has the potential for high levels of experimental and mundane realism. The greatest impediment to the more widespread use of role playing as an alternative to deception (without comparing it to deception) is the problem of encouraging involvement in a higher proportion of the participants. The failure to assess role-playing ability using paper-and-pencil measures suggests that the ability to role play may simply be a function of experience and training, rather than any measurable predisposition. Further research to train volunteers in role playing before their participation in a study is needed.

Unfortunately, however, the very potential for emotional involvement in role playing that recommends it as an alternative method raises the same ethical issues that were discussed earlier concerning other simulations. As in any ethical decision, the weighing of risks and benefits, or the application of any moral standard, is ultimately subjective. Under many circumstances, especially those eliciting less intense stress than observed among many of the participants of this role-playing simulation of obedience, role playing would meet the criteria for alternative methods specified earlier. Role playing is probably best suited to the study of behaviors that are emotionally involving; if the emotional involvement is no more intense than that often encountered in life (as would be the case in studies on interpersonal attraction, loneliness and affiliation, and expectations for attention, such as embarrassment and being ignored), ethical problems could be virtually eliminated.

Conclusion

The search for effective alternatives to deception, for the methodological and ethical reasons discussed throughout this chapter, must continue. No one alternative can or should be expected to be appropriate for all or even most studies. Each method has certain methodological and ethical problems associated with it. In deception methods these problems are familiar; the investigator using deception knows about the problems of demand characteristics and believes that a careful and sensitive debriefing can reduce emotional stress. In any relatively new method the problems are not familiar, and it is more difficult to cope with them. Both the difficulties of alternative methods and the solutions to them will become apparent with use. In the meantime, there is no a priori reason for withholding epistemological parity from any one method (Hendrick, 1977). If the goal of experimentation in social science is to understand behavior in the natural setting, then the method must be carefully chosen to best reflect that behavior while meeting guidelines of ethical conduct in research.

References

Albrecht, M. *Conformity and dissent in the absence of consensus.* Unpublished master's thesis, University of Saint Louis, 1973.

Altman, I. *The environment and social behavior.* Monterey, Calif.: Brooks/Cole, 1975.

American Psychological Association. *Ethical standards for the conduct of research with human participants.* Washington, D.C., 1973.

Argyris, C. Some unintended consequences of rigorous research. *Psychological Bulletin*, 1968, *70*, 185-197.

Aronson, E., & Carlsmith, J. M. Experimentation in social psychology. In G. Lindzey & E. Aronson (Eds.), *The handbook of social psychology* (Vol. 1). Reading, Mass.: Addison-Wesley, 1968.

Baumrind, D. Some thoughts on ethics of research: After reading Milgram's "Behavioral Study of Obedience." *American Psychologist*, 1964, *19*, 421-423.

Berscheid, E., Baron, R., Dermer, M., & Libman, M. Anticipating informed consent: An empirical approach. *American Psychologist*, 1973, *28*, 913-925.

Boruch, R.F. Methodological techniques for assuring personal integrity in social research. Unpublished manuscript (NIE-C63), Northwestern University, 1976.

Brown, R. Models of attitude change. In R. Brown, E. Galanter, E. Hess, & G. Mandler (Eds.), *New directions in psychology: I*. New York: Holt, Rinehart & Winston, 1962.

Campbell, D., & Cook, T. D. The design and conduct of quasi-experiments and true experiments in field settings. In M. D. Dunnette (Ed.), *Handbook in industrial and organizational psychology*, Chicago: Rand McNally, 1976.

Campbell, D., & Stanley, J. *Experimental and quasi-experimental designs for research*. Chicago: Rand McNally, 1966.

Carroll, J. S., & Payne, J. W. The psychology of the parole decision process: A joint application of attribution theory and information-processing psychology. In J. S. Carroll & J. W. Payne (Eds.), *Cognition and social behavior*. Hillsdale, N.J.: Erlbaum, 1976.

Cook, S. W. A comment on the ethical issues involved in West, Gunn, and Chernickey's "Ubiquitous Watergate: An Attributional Analysis." *Journal of Personality and Social Psychology*, 1975, *32*, 66-68.

Cook, T. D., Bean, F. R., Calder, B. J., Frey, R., Drovetz, M., & Reisman, S. R. Demand characteristics and three conceptions of the frequently deceived subject. *Journal of Personality and Social Psychology*, 1970, *14*, 185-194.

Coutu, W. Role-playing vs. role-taking: An appeal for clarification. *American Sociological Review*, 1951, *16*, 180-187.

Crawford, T. J. In defense of obedience research: An extension of the Kelman ethic. In A. G. Miller (Ed.), *The social psychology of psychological research*. New York: Free Press, 1972.

Department of Health, Education and Welfare. Protection of human subjects. (Code of Federal Regulations, 45 CFR 46). Washington, D.C., 1977.

Festinger, L., Riecken, H., & Schachter, S. When prophecy fails. Minneapolis: University of Minnesota Press, 1956.

Fillenbaum, S., & Frey, R. More on the "faithful" behavior of suspicious subjects. *Journal of Personality*, 1970, *38*, 43-51.

Freedman, J. Role-playing: Psychology by consensus. *Journal of Personality and Social Psychology*, 1969, *13*, 107-114.

Gamson, W. A. *Simsoc: Simulated Society* (3rd ed.). New York: Free Press, 1978.

Geller, D. M. Involvement in role-playing simulations: A demonstration with studies on obedience. *Journal of Personality and Social Psychology*, 1978, *36*, 219-235.

Geller, D. M., Goodstein, L., Silver, M., & Sternberg, W. C. On being ignored: The effects of the violation of implicit rules of social interaction. *Sociometry*, 1974, *37*, 541-556.

Greenberg, M. Role playing: An alternative to deception? *Journal of Personality and Social Psychology*, 1967, *7*, 152-157.

Guetzkow, H. (Ed.). *Simulation in the social sciences*. Englewood Cliffs, N.J.: Prentice-Hall, 1962.

Guetzkow, H., Alger, C., Brody, R., Noel, R., & Snyder, R. *Simulation in international relations: Developments for research and teaching*. Englewood Cliffs, N.J.: Prentice-Hall, 1963.

Hamilton, V. L. Role Play and deception: A re-examination of the controversy. *Journal for the Theory of Social Behaviour*, 1976, *6*, 233-250.

Hendrick, C. Role-taking, role-playing, and the laboratory experience. *Personality and the Social Psychology Bulletin*, 1977, *3*, 467-478.

Holmes, D. S. Debriefing after psychological experiments: I. Effectiveness of post-deception dehoaxing. *American Psychologist*, 1976, *31*, 858-867. (a)

Holmes, D. S. Debriefing after psychological experiments: II. Effectiveness of post-experimental desensitizing. *American Psychologist*, 1976, *31*, 868-875. (b)

Horowitz, I., & Rothschild, B. Conformity as a function of deception and role playing. *Journal of Personality and Social Psychology*, 1970, *14*, 224-226.

Humphreys, L. *Tearoom trade: Impersonal sex in public places*. Chicago: Aldine, 1970.

Jones, E. E., & Sigal, H. The bogus pipeline: A new paradigm for measuring affect and attitude. *Psychological Bulletin*, 1971, *76*, 349-364.

Katz, J., Capron, A. M., & Glass, E. S. *Experimentation with human beings*. New York: Russell Sage, 1976.

Kelman, H. Human use of human subjects: The problem of deception in social psychological experiments. *Psychological Bulletin*, 1967, *67*, 1-11.

Kelman, H. The rights of the subject in social research: An analysis in terms of relative power and legitimacy. *American Psychologist*, 1972, *27*, 989-1016.

Mann, L. Queue culture: The waiting line as a social system. *American Journal of Sociology*, 1969, *75*, 340-354.

Masling, J. Role-related behavior of the subject and psychologist and its effects upon psychological data. *Nebraska Symposium on Motivation*, 1966, *14*, 67-103.

Milgram, S. Behavioral study of obedience. *Journal of Abnormal and Social Psychology*, 1963, *67*, 371-378.

Milgram, S. Issues in the study of obedience: A reply to Baumrind. *American Psychologist*, 1964, *19*, 848-852.

Milgram, S. Some conditions of obedience and disobedience to authority. *Human Relations*, 1965, *18*, 57-76.

Milgram, S. *Obedience to authority*. New York: Harper & Row, 1974.

Miller, A. G. Role playing: An alternative to deception; a review of the evidence. *American Psychologist*, 1972, *27*, 623-636.

Mills, J. A procedure for explaining experiments involving deception. *Personality and Social Psychology Bulletin*, 1976, *2*, 3-13.

Mixon, D. Behavior analysis treating subjects as actors rather than organisms. *Journal for the Theory of Social Behaviour*, 1971, *1*, 19-31.

Mixon, D. Why pretend to deceive? *Personality and Social Psychology Bulletin*, 1977, *3*, 647-653.

O'Leary, C., Willis, F., & Tomich, E. Conformity under deceptive and non-deceptive techniques. *Sociological Quarterly*, 1970, *11*, 87-93.

Olson, T., & Christiansen, G. *The Grindstone Experiment: Thirty-one Hours*. Toronto: Canadian Friends Service Committee, 1966.

Orne, M. On the social psychology of the psychological experiment: With particular reference to demand characteristics and their implications. *American Psychologist*, 1962, *17*, 776-783.

Orne, M. Demand characteristics and the concept of quasi-controls. In R. Rosenthal & R. Rosnow (Eds.), *Artifacts in behavioral research*. New York: Academic Press, 1969.

Piliavin, J. A., & Piliavin, I. M. Effect of blood on reactions to a victim. *Journal of Personality and Social Psychology*, 1972, *23*, 353-361.

Riecken, H. A program for research on experiments in social psychology. In N. Washburne (Ed.), *Decisions, values, and groups* (Vol. 2). New York: Pergamon Press, 1962.

Seeman, J. Deception in psychological research. *American Psychologist*, 1969, *24*, 1025-1028.

Shulman, A. D., & Berman, A. J. Expectations about subjects and experimenters in psychological research. *Journal of Personality and Social Psychology*, 1975, *32*, 368-380.

Sieber, J. E. Personal communication. 1978.

Silverman, I. Nonreactive methods and the law. *American Psychologist*, 1975, *30*, 764-769.

Stricker, L., Messick, S., & Jackson, D. Evaluating deception in psychological research. *Psychological Bulletin*, 1969, *71*, 343-351.

Taylor, S. Developing a cognitive social psychology. In J. S. Carroll & J. W. Payne (Eds.), *Cognition and social behavior*. Hillsdale, N.J.: Erlbaum, 1976.

Vinacke, W. Deceiving experimental subjects. *American Psychologist*, 1954, *9*, 155.

Wahl, J. M. Role playing vs. deception: Differences in experimental realism as measured by subject's level of involvement and level of suspicion (Doctoral dissertation, University of Oregon, 1972). *Dissertation Abstracts International*, 1973, *33*, No. 98, p. 44. (University Microfilms No. 73-7974.)

Webb, E. J., Campbell, D. T., Schwartz, R. D., and Sechrest, L. *Unobtrusive Measures: Nonreactive research in the social sciences*. Chicago: Rand McNally, 1966.

West, S. G., Gunn, S. P., & Chernickey, P. Uniquitous Watergate: An attributional analysis. *Journal of Personality and Social Psychology*, 1975, *32*, 55-65.

Willis, R., & Willis, Y. Role playing versus deception: An experimental comparison. *Journal of Personality and Social Psychology*, 1970, *16*, 472-477.

Zimbardo, P., Haney, C., Banks, W., & Jaffe, D. The mind is a formidable jailer: A Pirandellian prison. *New York Times Magazine*, April 8, 1973, pp. 38-60.

Chapter 3

Random Assignment of Clients in Social Experimentation

Ross F. Conner

Social reformers regularly propose new solutions for the many social problems confronting our society. Some of these potential solutions are developed into innovative social projects; thus "new, improved" programs come to be implemented in health, education, welfare, and other social service areas. Alas, the potential solutions to problems in these areas far exceed actual, genuine solutions. One recent study of the effectiveness of a large sample of new programs in the areas of surgery and anesthesia revealed that these particular new programs were effective only about half the time (Gilbert, McPeek, & Mosteller, 1977, p. 685). It is doubtful that the demonstrated effectiveness of other types of novel social reform programs in areas such as education and welfare would exceed this rate. Indeed, the percentage of successful programs in these latter areas probably would be lower since all of the health programs studied by Gilbert, McPeek, and Mosteller initially had been thought to be very effective, based on preliminary testing.

We must, therefore, evaluate the effectiveness of social programs, both new and old. The field of evaluation research addresses this issue, since it involves the study of all aspects of program evaluation. One important part of evaluation research is outcome or impact assessment of the effects of social programs. Many evaluation researchers advocate one particular method for outcome assessment because of its singular ability to link program activities with client outcomes: social experimentation using a true experimental evaluation design. Tukey (1977), for example, strongly recommends this method in a discussion of health interventions:

> Many of us are convinced, by what seems to me to be very strong evidence, that the only source of reliable evidence about the usefulness of almost any sort of therapy or surgical intervention is that obtained from well-planned and carefully conducted randomized, and where possible, double-blind clinical trials. (p. 679)

This sentiment is shared by other researchers for evaluations of health programs as well as for evaluation of educational programs, welfare programs and the like (Cook & Campbell, 1979; Riecken & Boruch, 1974; Rossi, Freeman, & Wright, 1979). The most important aspect of a true experimental design is the assignment on a random basis of potential clients either to a treatment group ("experimental") which receives the new program or to a no-treatment group ("control") which does not receive the program.

"What is this you are recommending?" a critic might ask. "You want to assign people—real human beings—randomly and not on the basis of need? And, you are going to deny clients a potentially beneficial service? Why, this is patently unethical!" On first hearing, the objections that this critic raises seem valid, indeed, almost self-evidently valid. After later reflection, however, one is likely to conclude that the ethical situation is not as clear as this critic assumes.

The Coronary Drug Research Project (Canner, Berge, & Klint, 1973; Coronary Drug Project Research Group, 1975) illustrates the complexity of the ethical dilemmas associated with social experimentation. This 5-year, nationwide study assessed the relative effectiveness of different drugs which were then commonly used to treat heart attack victims. The clients were men, aged 30 to 67 years, who had experienced a heart attack. Men eligible for the study were told the purposes of the social experiment, including the fact that each participant would be assigned randomly to receive one of several types of drugs or, in the control condition, no drug at all. If he chose to participate, a client signed a consent form agreeing to be in any of the six study conditions (five involving drugs; one control). All clients received identical opaque gelatin capsules, the contents of which were unknown to clients and clinic personnel alike. Over the 5-year course of the study, clients were given follow-up examinations every 4 months.

How, some readers may ask, can we possibly justify denying potentially beneficial drugs to the heart attack victims in the control group? Even if the clients give their informed consent, is it ethical to subject them to such a procedure in the name of science? As these questions make clear, there are serious ethical issues that need to be addressed. These issues, however, are not as simple as these questions would make them appear, and the answers are likewise complex. One outcome from the Coronary Drug Research Project highlights this fact. Because of the "denial" of any drug to those in the control condition, the social experimenters discovered that two of the drugs were significantly worse than no drug at all (measured in terms of group mortality). When this finding was uncovered midway through the study, the researchers immediately terminated these two drug conditions and quickly disseminated the results to the medical community, many of whom had been prescribing these two drugs routinely to heart attack patients. The ethical issues now become more complex. Was it ethical for doctors to prescribe these two drugs, or any drugs, before they were sure of their effectiveness? Is it ethical to allow clients to assume that heart attack drugs are beneficial when this belief is based more on faith than on fact?

The purpose of this chapter is to explore in depth these ethical issues and others concerning the use of random assignment in forming experimental and control groups in social experimentation. Following a description of randomization and several examples of its use, both in traditional laboratory settings and in social reform program settings, the value premises that underlie decisions to use social experimentation will be discussed. Then, three primary ethical issues will be analyzed from the different perspectives of those most centrally involved in the social experimentation process: the client, the program director (or service provider), and the researcher (or evaluator). Finally, a general principle will be presented which can help guide those involved in social experimentation in resolving ethical issues. This paper, then, analyzes one particular social research approach and explores the ethical issues involved in this approach.

Random Assignment

A central tenet of quantitative social science research methodology is the importance of assigning subjects at random to experimental conditions. Through randomization, a researcher is able to distribute *subject*-related outcome variations evenly across experimental conditions and, thus, observe the unique effects of *experiment*-related outcome variations. In this way, causes (i.e., different experimental conditions) can be linked to effects (i.e., different outcome measurements). The importance of randomization is stated quite strongly in one well-known social research text:

> randomization . . . is one of the greatest intellectual achievements of our time. It is not possible to overrate the importance of the idea and the practical measures that come from it to improve experimentation and inference from obtained results. (Kerlinger, 1973, p. 123)

As long as quantitative research was conducted in the laboratory, random assignment presented no significant ethical problems. If the laboratory researcher thinks about the ethical implications of random assignment at all, he or she probably views this method of selecting subjects for particular conditions as a fair method for allocating the more demanding, more difficult, or more boring conditions. In a laboratory study, for instance, of the effect of information-source expertise on attitude change, some subjects have to serve as controls to provide a baseline measure against which to assess the effects of high- and low-expertise sources. These control subjects receive some information but it is intentionally boring and unrelated to the presumably exciting and subject-involving attitude topic. In their assessment of risks to subjects in laboratory studies of this type, the human subject institutional review boards with which this author is familiar do not question the ethics of random assignment.

When the social researcher moves outside the laboratory into the field, random assignment still can be used and, depending on the focus of the research, still may present no ethical problems. Field experiments typically are identical to laboratory experiments in that the focus of the research (i.e., the independent variable) is under the control of the experimenter. The main difference is that the setting is more realistic (see Bickman & Henchey, 1972, pp. 1-6). In these cases, random assignment may present implementation problems but rarely ethical problems. This is illustrated in a study by Abelson and Miller (1967) of the effect of personal insult on negative attitude change. The procedure was for a "roving reporter" (actually the experimenter) to stage two-person debates between strangers (one of whom was, in fact, a confederate of the experimenter) sitting near each other in a park in New York City. The basic design involved eight combinations of the three conditions (insulting vs. neutral remarks by "opponent"; opponent leaves vs. opponent stays; and, crowd present vs. no crowd). (In addition to these eight conditions, there were two other "no persuasive intent" conditions included as control conditions.) Except for the crowd present or crowd absent conditions (which were run on particular randomly selected days), the other conditions were determined instantly by the confederate who, once a subject agreed to participate, felt in his pocket for the next number on a perforated paper role with a randomly determined sequence of numbers. The confederate then began to act appropriately for the condition. Although there are important ethical issues in this field experiment (e.g., should people peacefully sitting on a park bench and minding their own business be drawn into a study without their explicit knowledge and consent?), random assignment of subjects is not one of them. Randomly selected no-treatment control subjects in field experiments could be considered the lucky ones whose behavior is simply observed (or manipulated to a lesser degree than that of experimental subjects) to provide baseline data.

The ethical situation changes dramatically when we move to the area of social experimentation. Unlike laboratory and field research, social experimentation involves innovative or ongoing social reform programs aimed either at ameliorating problems of those in need or at improving programs for those already being served. An example of the former would be a special recreation-plus-meals program for senior citizens; an innovative computer-based reading program for elementary school children would be an example of the latter type of social reform program. Social experimentation, in its purest form, is a particular approach to planning and researching (or evaluating) these reform efforts (Riecken & Boruch, 1974). This approach entails, first, random selection of a sample of potential clients from among the population of eligible clients, and, second, random assignment of part of the sample to an experimental (or treatment) group and of the other part of the sample to a control (or no-treatment) group. In this way, the effectiveness of the reform program can be determined scientifically.

The use of the true experimental (or control group) research design, of which random assignment is an integral part, has been advocated by a number of researchers in the evaluation research field (e.g., Campbell, 1969; Campbell & Stanley, 1966; Cook & Campbell, 1976; Riecken & Boruch, 1974; Rossi, 1977; Rossi, Freeman, & Wright, 1979; Suchman, 1967). This advocacy has been based on the unique ability of this particular design to link program or organizational changes with outcomes and, thus, to permit scientific conclusions about causes and effects. There is not, however, universal agreement that a true experimental design should be employed in these settings. Some researchers (e.g., Franklin & Thrasher, 1976; Guttentag, 1973; Stufflebeam, 1969) have challenged its use, in whole or in part because of the ethical dilemmas it entails. Other researchers have challenged or defended the use of experimentation for other reasons (see Mitroff & Bonoma, 1978, or Patten, 1978, for challenges and Boruch, 1976, or Cook & Campbell, 1979, for defenses).

Those with whom the social scientist necessarily shares control in social experimentation (program clients, administrators, directors, and staff) also have their own perspectives on the ethics of social experimentation. The social experimenter's desire to assign social service clients randomly to experimental or control conditions may generate resistance from program staff and clients because the proposed intervention, which they believe is beneficial, would be denied to the clients in the control group. Should a group of social service clients be denied, even temporarily, a presumably beneficial service to demonstrate scientifically that the service is, in fact, beneficial?

The answer to this ethical question and others in any particular case is complicated because the final decision is not the researcher's alone. This fact is reflected in the use of the label "clients" in social experimentation rather than "subjects." The relationship between social researchers and the objects and conditions of their study differs in laboratory and field experimentation as compared with social experimentation. In laboratory studies in particular and in field experimentation, the researcher has almost total control of the situation. In social experimentation, the researcher never has total control and, instead, shares control with the other participants. The evaluation researcher initially must negotiate the conditions of the research with supervisors, managers, directors, clients, and other parties associated with the social experiment; as the study proceeds, renegotiation frequently is required due to disruptive, unforeseen circumstances or new, unexpected developments. Because power and control are shared, decisions about the research, such as one to assign clients randomly, cannot be made unilaterally by the researcher. In the discussions between researchers and program directors which precede the initial approval or disapproval of the use of a control group, a central topic of discussion is certain to be the ethical issue of denying a presumably beneficial service to people in a control group in the interest of scientific experimentation.

Random Assignment in Evaluation Research

The control group research design (or the true experimental design) used in evaluation research is based on the traditional laboratory design for experimental work. In this classical design, the researcher selects an independent variable (or several independent variables) that he or she can adjust to different levels, and a dependent variable that is used to measure changes due to the independent variable. For example, a laboratory researcher may be interested in the effects of different doses of a drug (independent variable) on sick patients' temperature (dependent variable). From a group of 75 patients, the researcher randomly assigns 25 to receive injections of a low dosage level of the drug; 25 other patients are randomly assigned to receive a high dosage level. The remaining 25 patients are not given the drug but do receive an injection of saline water. Then, the researcher measures patients' temperatures to assess the effects of different dosage levels or of the saline placebo (i.e., an inert treatment given for its psychological effect). In the laboratory setting, the researcher typically has total control of the assignment of the subjects, the administration of the treatments, and the measurement of the effects.

This laboratory model required some adjustments for social experimentation (Campbell & Stanley, 1966; Campbell, 1969; Reicken & Boruch, 1974; Suchman, 1967; Weiss, 1972). In contrast to the laboratory researcher, the social experimenter has less control over the research process because of the more complex nature of the setting and the treatment. For this reason, certain extra precautions are necessary. For example, the dependent variable measurement on both experimental and control groups occurs twice: prior to the implementation of the treatment with the experimental group (pretest) and again following the conclusion of the treatment (posttest). Unlike the laboratory researcher, the social experimenter often does not have the luxury of replicating his or her study several times to assure that chance variations have not occurred and that randomization has equated the groups. Consequently, although a pretest technically is not required (since randomization should equate the two groups on the dependent measure), it usually is given to be sure that the two groups are, in fact, equal. If the groups are not equal, clients names can be put back into the pool and random assignment can be done a second time prior to the start of the treatment.

Three examples of actual evaluation research projects that have used a control group design will help to clarify some major differences between the laboratory and the nonlaboratory implementation of random assignment. These particular examples were selected because they represent different types of projects and because reference material on each project is published and available to the interested reader. Other examples can be found in Boruch, McSweeny and Soderstrom (1978) which lists 300 evaluation projects involving a true experimental design.

The New Jersey Negative Income Tax Study and subsequent similar studies in Seattle and Denver have used random assignment of clients to control and multiple experimental groups (Haveman & Watts, 1976; Pechman & Timpane, 1975; Rossi & Lyall, 1976). The general goal of all of the studies was to determine the effects of guaranteeing poor families a certain minimum income. If the family's income rose above the level of the payments (i.e., the negative taxes), these were reduced by a graduated percentage of the base level. By graduating reductions in base income, the program's planners hoped to avoid the disincentive to work resulting from the 100% reduction that characterized the typical welfare program at the time. In the New Jersey study, about 1300 families were randomly assigned to eight different conditions, involving different income guarantee levels as well as different tax rates on earned income. One of these conditions was the control condition where families were not guaranteed a certain income and no special restrictions were placed on earned income. In this control condition, families were free to use the regular welfare services available to all poor families. The control families received $10 per month to compensate them for the time spent completing monthly data questionnaires. This payment, although not intended as such, was an important, welcome supplement to the incomes of some of the control families. In these cases, the control condition became a very low-payment treatment condition, decreasing to a limited extent the researchers' ability to compare the various guarantee-tax rate treatments to a true no-treatment group. The findings from the New Jersey study demonstrated that families did not stop working when they received a guaranteed minimum income.

The studies of the effectiveness of the television show "Sesame Street" (Ball & Bogatz, 1970; Bogatz & Ball, 1971) provide a second example from the evaluation research field of a true experimental design using random assignment. The study of Sesame Street's first year (Ball & Bogatz, 1970) was intended to be a true experimental study which compared viewers and nonviewers. At the outset, children were assigned randomly either to viewing or nonviewing conditions. Due, however, to the researchers' lack of control over which children actually viewed or did not view the show, many nonviewers became viewers at their own instigation. Consequently, the researchers had to change the first year design to a quasi-experimental comparison group design. The researchers learned from their first-year experiences, and the second year study (Bogatz & Ball, 1971) was implemented as planned, primarily through the selection of sites where the show was available only with a UHF adaptor (Los Angeles, Calif.) or via cable (Winston-Salem, N.C.). Children in both cities were randomly assigned to viewing or nonviewing groups for the 6-month study, and viewers were given either a UHF adaptor or a cable. Children in both groups were tested individually on a variety of cognitive skills at the outset of the study and again 6 months later. At the end of the study, homes with children who had been in the control group were given a complimentary cable or UHF adaptor. The results showed that the television show was generally effective but more so in some areas of learning than in others (see also Cook, Appleton, Conner, Shaffer, Tamkin, & Weber, 1975; Cook & Conner, 1976).

The final example of a social experimentation study comes from the medical field. Conducted in England in areas around London, this study assessed the effectiveness of home care following a serious heart attack compared with hospital care after such an attack (Mather et al., 1971; see also Caro, 1977). Men under 70 years of age who had suffered an acute myocardial infarction within the previous 48 hours were the potential study clients. These 1,203 men were placed first into one of three general groups based on their preferences for home or hospital care and on the decisions of the 458 participating family physicians of these men: elective home, elective hospital, or randomization group. The 343 men placed into the randomization group were those for whom either home or hospital care was acceptable. These men were assigned randomly to either home or hospital care by their physician who opened a sealed, numbered assignment envelope from a set of such envelopes. A comparison between the random-home group and the random-hospital group (in this case, the control group) in terms of total deaths within 28 days of the heart attack showed a 4.4% lower mortality rate for the random-home group (mortality rates: random-hospital = 14.2%; random-home = 9.8%). The authors conclude that the general practice of admitting heart attack patients automatically to the hospital should be reconsidered in light of these results.

These three studies demonstrate how control groups and random assignment are used in social experimentation. Three aspects of the control condition are noteworthy. First, the control group members were not misled about the real purposes and conditions of the experiment, as frequently occurs in laboratory studies. Instead, as potential clients, they were given a full explanation of the study, then asked to give their informed consent to participate in any of the study groups. Second, unlike laboratory control groups that usually receive no treatment whatever, the social experimentation control group clients did receive a type of treatment: the usual, ordinary services available to everyone. In the Sesame Street case, for example, the control group children were free to participate in any educational activities ordinarily available to them. Now, in part because of its proved effectiveness, Sesame Street would be part of the "ordinary treatment" available to all children. When the show began in 1969, however, this was not true; Sesame Street was a special, new program of potential benefit to young children. Finally, there were definite benefits from participation for the control group members beyond the "for-the-good-of-science" rationale usually used to justify the absence of any tangible benefits to laboratory control subjects. These benefits reward control group participants and reduce inequities among the study participants. Although social experimentation control group members did not experience the new treatment, they did receive some extra benefits during the study (i.e., the money paid to controls in the New Jersey study or the regular medical attention in the medical study) or following the study (i.e., the free television cables or UHF adaptors given to controls in the Sesame Street study). These aspects of control group use are related to the value premises that underlie social experimentation.

Value Premises of the True Experimental Design

There are four value premises that underlie arguments favoring the use of control groups in social experimentation. These premises differ from those applicable to laboratory work and are fundamental to the analysis of ethical issues to be presented in the next section; consequently, it is important to identify these premises before exploring individual ethical issues.

Status Quo Activities

The first premise is that all research clients have a right to status quo activities. That is, any social service or organization activity that currently exists as part of the usual array of services or activities should be available to all potential clients. This means that individuals who are placed in the control group usually *do* receive services or maintain their regular activities (hence the label "status quo"). In the evaluation of a new school reading program, for example, children in the control group participate in the usual reading program while children in the experimental group receive the new program.

This is a very different situation from the laboratory model of the true experimental design, where the control group members receive no treatment or service. To return to the hypothetical example discussed earlier, sick patients in the placebo control group received no treatment and were prevented, in effect, from seeking other treatments (e.g., visiting another doctor for an injection). This procedure is followed in the laboratory to assure that there is a true no-treatment group to use in comparing the treated group or groups.

In the nonlaboratory adaptation of the true experimental design, a placebo control group typically is not used because the researcher's main interest is to compare the new program with the usual, status quo program, not to compare the new program with no program. Consequently, in evaluation research projects, control group members usually are not prevented from seeking other available services; indeed, in some cases they are encouraged to use these other services and even are referred to them.

Informed Participants

The second value premise that underlies the use of control groups is that all individuals involved in the study are informed about the purposes of the study and about the existence of a control group. In laboratory studies, participants in both experimental and control groups are sometimes unaware of the real purpose of a study or of the existence of different groups. Members of a placebo group necessarily are deceived to some extent about the efficacy of their "treatment." In the extreme case, they are completely unaware that a placebo is being used. In the least extreme case, they are informed prior to the study that certain people will receive a placebo but that the identity of these people will not be known during the study.

In a social reform program, however, the main purposes of the program are known to all, at least in general outline. A new reading program, for example, is intended to help children read better; a new rehabilitation program for juvenile delinquents is aimed at reducing subsequent delinquency. In addition, the evaluation plan for the program is usually known to all, particularly if the plan involves a control group. At the outset, the existence and necessity for the control group are explained to potential clients. Typically, clients provide oral or written consent that they understand and accept the purposes of the program and its evaluation. Then, clients are assigned randomly to the experimental or control group. There is no deception involved in the process at any stage.

Equal Right to Scarce Resources

A third value premise that underlies control group use is that individuals should have an equal right to the benefits of a new and presumably better service if one is available. New social programs, which are assumed to be more beneficial than current programs, are rarely, if ever, available to everyone who is eligible. Consequently, an equitable method is necessary for selecting those individuals who will participate in the program. Random selection of participants assures that each individual has an equal chance of being selected and precludes intended or unintended discrimination against potential clients. Through this selection procedure, a control group of eligible participants is formed naturally.

This premise can be viewed in another way. If a harmful service is to be inflicted on a group of individuals, each individual should have an equal chance of avoiding the service. An example of this would be the draft lottery which was used in the United States for several years. Young men were selected essentially at random (i.e., by birthdate) to join the military or to stay at home (Feinberg, 1971).

Scientific Utility

The last value premise that underlies advocacy of control groups is the most familiar: control groups have great scientific utility. As stated earlier, the use of control groups is the only method available to determine whether changes in participants can be attributed causally to service program activities. Although other methods have been developed (e.g., quasi-experimental comparison groups), these other methods do not permit definitive answers about cause and effect because of initial differences between the experimental and comparison groups. The use of randomly constituted control and experimental groups precludes these initial differences on all dimensions, both those dimensions known and relevant to the program and those unknown and seemingly irrelevant (see Conner, 1977, for further details).

These four premises constitute the general rationale for the use of random assignment and control groups in evaluation research. Social scientists who advocate social experimentation base their general arguments, explicitly or implicitly, on these premises. The third premise discussed above is the one most frequently cited: equal right to scarce resources. In the abstract, these value premises are sensible and compelling. In any particular case, however, all of the premises may not apply. Consequently, the justification for the use of control groups and of the associated random assignment procedure is never absolute. If, for example, there is no scarcity of resources and all potential clients can be served, ethical questions about the use of control groups cannot easily be resolved with an appeal to the general premises. In most instances, the four premises are valid but to greater or lesser degrees depending on the circumstances of the program. Because of these program-by-program variations, no simple formula can be devised to answer the ethical questions that arise in the course of planning and implementing a control group study. Instead, researchers must assess the relevance of the premises to particular situations to make informed ethical judgments. Careful consideration of the applicability of these four value premises in a particular case typically will aid a researcher in selecting procedures which optimize social as well as scientific interests. These two interests are not necessarily antithetical: the satisfaction of social interests (e.g., fair allocation of scarce resources) also can benefit scientific interests (e.g., formation of experimental and control groups), and the satisfaction of scientific interests (e.g., random selection) can facilitate social interests (e.g., equity and justice). This complementarity will be discussed in more detail in the following section.

Primary Ethical Issues

There are three ethical issues that frequently are of central concern when social experimentation is considered for particular cases. These issues are (1) the potential for denial of a valuable service to eligible clients, (2) the equitable allocation of scarce resources to a large group of eligible recipients, and (3) the provision of evidence of program effects. These issues are complex and multifaceted. The definnition of each issue, indeed, even the recognition of an issue, depends on the perspective of the participant in the situation. Consequently, in the discussion to follow, careful attention will be given to each of the main perspectives in the situation: the client, the service provider, and the researcher. (The terms "actors" and "roles" are used below in a conceptual sense in describing these perspectives in a research project; the theatrical connotation, which would imply some artificiality, is not intended.) To analyze these three ethical issues fully, we first must identify the assumptions that underlie them, then assess the validity of the assumptions from each of the perspectives or roles. In some cases, one individual will have dual roles: service provider and researcher. In this case, it becomes particularly important to understand and delineate the different perspectives in order to make ethical research decisions that optimize social and scientific interests.

Denial of Service

The most frequent issue raised about the use of a control group in social experimentation is whether eligible clients are being denied a potentially beneficial service. There are two main assumptions behind this statement. The first assumption is that a service or program (i.e., some logic organization of activities) is occurring. Second, there is an assumption that the service is beneficial to and, hence, desired by clients.

Assumption of occurrence of service. There is usually little, if any, question in the minds of staff that a service is occurring. The service provider has planned the components of the program, has organized them in some more or less systematic fashion, has implemented the planned service, and devotes the entire day to service provision or related activities. From the clients' or researchers' perspectives, however, the occurrence of services is not self-evident. Clients and researchers typically are not involved in the planning of services and so are not as personally invested in the service as are the providers. Clients experience the service as it is implemented, with little or no knowledge of the background or intent. Consequently, clients are in the best position to judge the services actually delivered. Researchers assess the service through providers and clients. When researchers are employed by the providers, and "experience" the service first through the providers, the researchers' view of the services actually delivered may be somewhat more biased toward the providers' view than the clients' view. Nonetheless, the researcher is in a better position than the provider to judge which services, in fact, occur.

From both the clients' and researchers' perspectives, then, there may be no actual services provided or the services experienced by the clients may be very different from the services intended for them. As an example, consider the Sesame Street case. In spite of careful planning and implementation (i.e., airing) of the show and special attention to the selection of homes to receive the show via cable, the target children may not see the show because bigger brothers and sisters who control the television set prefer to watch other shows. Indeed a variation of this scenario occurred for the first few years of Sesame Street: the more economically disadvantaged children for whom the show was intended watched less often than did their more advantaged counterparts (see Cook et al., 1975).

The Sesame Street case also could provide a hypothetical example of how actual services can be very different from intended services. Imagine that the creators of Sesame Street intended the show only to be an educational experience. Upon learning that television viewing surveys showed that many households watched the show regularly, the creators assumed that children were learning as intended because homes continued to tune in the show. Careful analysis of the situation, however, indicates that children are not learning anything but are being entertained very effectively. Parents are glad to have the inexpensive babysitting service, and continue to have their children watch the show. In this case, the service delivered, though not the intended one, is a benign one; in other cases, the "service" actually delivered could be a harmful one.

In sum, unless the occurrence of a service can be demonstrated, there is no basis for an ethical dilemma over the denial of a nonexistent service to clients. To be sure, another ethical issue is raised, namely, one of truth in advertising (i.e., the promotion of one service but the provision of no service or of quite a different service). To assess service occurrence, it is necessary to document the services actually provided. Because the absence of service or the occurrence of a very different service is not uncommon in social programs (see Freeman, 1977), the practice of process monitoring has been advanced as an essential component of a complete program evaluation. Once a service can be demonstrated to be occurring, the quality of the service should then be examined.

Assumption of beneficial service. The occurrence of a service that is beneficial is the second assumption on which an ethical dilemma over denial of service is based. This assumption, though closely related to the first, is conceptually separate and becomes particularly relevant if the service is, in fact, harmful to clients. For service providers, this assumption is basic to all their activities, so basic that it is often taken for granted by them. The *raison d'être* for a program is to help clients; consequently, the idea that it might be making the situation worse is not even considered (e.g., Gaylin, Glasser, Marcus, & Rothman, 1978).

Researchers are less likely to assume that the program is beneficial since their primary role is to be skeptical about the benefits of a program. Nonetheless, researchers are prone, because of their close association with service providers, to view a program as more beneficial than it may in fact be. Clients generally are least likely to accept this assumption automatically, particularly if they have participated in other programs. Clients, like researchers, realize that social programs have rarely, if ever, achieved all of their goals and usually fall far short of goal attainment. Consequently, clients and researchers are more skeptical of the benefits claimed for a new social program than are the service providers.

This skeptical attitude on the part of the clients is particularly likely to occur when clients have been the recipients of other social programs (e.g., economically disadvantaged families) and when programs have been created for clients rather than sought out by them (e.g., the New Jersey Negative Income Tax Study). In these cases, it has been the author's experience, based on studies of and work with social reform programs using or attempting to use a control group research design, that clients are usually skeptical that there will be any benefits from the program and instead are concerned that the new program will simply be added trouble for them in terms of paperwork, strangers, and the like (e.g., Conner, 1977). When questioned about their concern that they might be denied a beneficial service, some of these clients smile cynically. As one parent said, concerning an educational program, "I *prefer* to have my kid in the control school; at least I know what will happen there." This woman and other clients like her admit that the status quo may not be a good one but that it is at least a known quantity. If the new program can be demonstrated to be an improvement, their clients will be concerned about missing a beneficial service. If clients are concerned with *demonstrable* benefits, then clients can understand the need for good research on program effectiveness. Indeed, when they realize that there can be good research done on program effects, clients can become research supporters; this point will be discussed in more detail under the third primary ethical issue, evidence of program effects.

Because of differing perceptions of the likelihood of benefit among service providers, researchers, and clients, the extent to which denial of benefits presents an ethical problem varies among these actors. Because they do not automatically see benefits, clients and researchers do not automatically see ethical problems. Service providers are more likely to see this as a critical ethical issue. This is particularly true of the subgroup of service providers composed of administrators and others who are directly involved with the program and with clients on a day-to-day basis. This occurs because the primary sources of knowledge about the program for these people are official program documents, special reports by the project director, and the like—sources that tend to be especially positive in their view of the program. For this reason, this subgroup is prone to overestimate the degree to which clients both view the program as beneficial and desire to be part of it. This subgroup understandably reasons that, with such a clearly beneficial service available, clients denied the service will surely complain loudly. Consequently, this subgroup will tend to argue against a control group design, using this unproved rationale. Researchers should take special care to education program administrators about the study and to emphasize that clients do not automatically want the services that have been developed for them.

In these cases, then, clients do not necessarily want the new service and are glad not to be involved in it. In other cases, clients clearly desire services and are eager to participate, either because they know or have been led to believe that the program will be beneficial to them. If the clients' knowledge of the program benefits is based on good evidence (i.e., on good prior research), it clearly would be unethical for an evaluator to recommend that the service be denied to a control group of clients. Indeed, if a program's benefits had already been proven, there would be no need to run a control group study. The more likely case is that clients have been led to believe that the services will be beneficial, without sufficient proof of effectiveness. The ethical burden in this instance, then, is on the service provider who has raised expectations on the basis of faith not fact. It is likely that these expectations develop from the program itself (via promotional brochures or word-of-mouth). These expectations can be controlled by careful explanation of the program's goals coupled with an explanation of the need to study the effectiveness of the program. The evidence that is available (Conner, Rosenthal, McNeil, & Rohlf, 1979; Wortman, Hendricks, & Hillis, 1976) indicates that clients can understand and accept the need for research on program effectiveness.

When the roles of service provider and researcher are taken by the same person, it is particularly difficult for him or her to consider objectively the validity of the assumption of beneficial service. This is completely understandable, since the service provider probably has worked long and hard to plan, fund and, finally, institute the innovation. In the course of performing these activities, the service provider is likely to change his or her view of the benefits of the service from anticipated, expected goals to self-evident *faits accomplis*. Consequently, it is difficult for the service provider to shift to the researcher perspective and to see the need to question objectively whether the service is beneficial. The author himself was in this dual role in one instance, and the service provider perspective preempted the researcher perspective (much to his chagrin!). Because the likely supremacy of the service provider perspective in a person with this dual role, it is wise to add an objective third party to the project to serve in the researcher role, even if only for several days as a consultant. This third party should be given enough independence to articulate the researcher perspective, whatever its implications may be for the project. Only in this way can a valid resolution be reached between the needs of service provision and of research.

Equitable Allocation of Scarce Resources

The second primary ethical issue surrounding the use of random assignment and control groups in social research concerns the method of allocating scarce program resources. Social or organizational programs typically cannot be given to all who need them, unless designed for a very small population and funded by a very generous source. Most planners and implementers are forced to make compromises between what they want and what is possible because resources are limited.

It is at the point of selecting program clients that the reality of scarce resources relates to the use of control groups. If places in the program are limited, service providers are confronted with the need to allocate these places in an equitable manner. Some allocation methods pose an ethical problem because potential clients vary in the likelihood of being selected. This ethical problem can become a public relations problem, and a legal problem as well, if potential clients later learn that they were not given a chance to be in the program and decide to complain or sue for redress.

One of these inequitable client selection methods is by self-selected referral. For example, the director of a new health program may contact several fellow directors of other social programs for names of clients. In this case the director has not picked clients personally, which obviously would be inequitable, but, due to self-selection of referral sources, he or she indirectly has favored some potential clients. Possible clients who are not known to these other program directors or clients whom these other directors choose not to mention (for whatever reason) are not considered.

Another inequitable selection method which is more common is the first-come, first-served procedure. Many program staff mistakenly believe that this method is fair because the staff have no part in the process, directly or indirectly. Although this may be true, this selection procedure is very susceptible to client manipulation in ways that are unknown to program staff. The news that a program is soliciting clients may circulate from person to person in only one or a few social networks. Consequently, all the clients who appear at the program office on the first day of registration may be friends or may come from one particular neighborhood or one office; in either case, the group of enrollees will not be a representative sampling of eligible clients.

For service providers as well as for clients, the equitable allocation of limited places in a social program is an important problem. This is one problem that the researcher, using random selection, can solve for the program. Following an active and extensive recruiting campaign, the researcher randomly selects clients for the program from a list of all eligible clients, in the process forming experiment and control groups.. The control group members, then, were just as likely to have been chosen as the treatment group members. A new ethical problem can arise at this point if the researcher and service provider have not dealt honestly with those on the eligibility list. Clients must be informed prior to randomization than only a limited number of places are available and that selection for the places will be by a random draw so that everyone's chances are equal to everyone else's. Otherwise, clients who are not selected will feel misled and perhaps cheated, thinking that some "under the table" method was used to choose clients.

In resolving the ethical problem of equitable allocation of scarce resources, the researcher creates a control group as a by-product. While the treatment group members are being assigned randomly, the control group members are also being assigned at no extra cost in time or effort. On occasion, selection into the control group provides some benefits to the control group members which, though far short of the "potential" benefits to the treatment group, are welcomed. In some medical programs for example, physical examinations may be a pretest for both experimental and control groups. In the course of the examination, a serious physical problem may be discovered for a control group member which can then be treated. Likewise, parents of children in the control group of an educational program evaluation sometimes find the testing which typically occurs to be informative. The New Jersey Negative Income Tax Study provides a good example of this type of positive consequence of control group selection: the control group families were quite pleased to receive an extra $10 per month, given to them as compensation for their time in completing forms.

Evidence of Program Effects

The last ethical issue of primary concern to us is the degree of responsibility that service providers and researchers have to provide evidence of program effects. This issue has different aspects when viewed from the perspective of the service provider or that of the researcher.

The service provider. In establishing a new service program or in perpetuating an old one, a service provider is sanctioning the activities of the program. In new programs, this sanction is usually very explicit: the program staff members are strong believers in the benefits of the program. In older programs, the sanction is more implicit and conveyed more by staff's continued participation in the program than by explicit statements and endorsements. In either case, a message is conveyed to potential clients and to the public at large that this program is good and is worthy of attention, participation, and support, both moral and financial.

It is the responsibility of the service provider to recognize that this implicit sanctioning is occurring and to be aware of the actions that may follow from it. Clients, for example, may be able to choose between two social programs which offer a similar service: Program A and program B. Imagine, however that program A is slightly more expensive or requires more time or is located a little further away than program B. Imagine, too, that program A is more effective than program B. Since both programs appear to the client to be functioning adequately, the client chooses program B on the basis of tangible factors like time or location.

Clients have a right to information about program effectiveness. Service providers need to determine the extent of this right for their program. The best information which links program treatments to effects on clients comes from a research study using random assignment. With information from a study of this type, program staff can be most confident that clients have the information they need to make informed, considered decisions. Service providers also have the responsibility of explaining to potential clients the limitations or qualifications of the data on program effectiveness. It is not sufficient to hand the client a long, technically complex report and expect him or her to digest the report's implications.

The researcher. If a social program has a program researcher working on the staff, this is a clear message to clients, policy makers, and funders that this program is assessing effectiveness. Service providers can assume that they no longer need to devote their time and energy to documenting service effectiveness since this is the task of the program researcher. Clients may assume that the researcher's presence will assure a worthwhile service. The researcher needs to be aware of these expectations of others involved with the program. Moreover, he or she has a responsibility to be sure that these other people understand what the researcher can and cannot do and what the research plan he or she has developed will and will not provide.

There are different approaches to social research which will provide useful program information but will not document program effectiveness. For example, input analysis can reveal the number of clients, the number of hours of treatment, the number of program staff, and the like. Likewise, process monitoring can provide information about the events that occur between clients and staff, about the pattern of client behaviors, and so forth. None of these data, however, addresses the question of program effectiveness. The researcher will know this at the outset of his or her study and so has a responsibility to inform the program staff of this fact.

If a researcher has committed him or herself to an outcome assessment, then the researcher has an obligation to undertake certain steps. Program goals must be determined and ways must be established to measure them. In addition, the researchers must plan a comparison, using a control group or a quasi-experimental comparison group, of those who receive the program and those who do not. Fulfilling these obligatory steps are necessary but not sufficient conditions for a productive outcome assessment. As the Sesame Street first-year study showed, even the best laid plans can break down due to unforeseen circumstances. Without these steps, however, an outcome assessment cannot occur.

To avoid any misunderstandings, it is advisable for a researcher to prepare a written description of the research plan which describes the goals to be measured, the criteria to be used to assess achievement of each goal, and the plan to be used to assess program effects. By doing this early, the researcher is reducing the likelihood that unrealistic expectations will develop on the part of program staff. As the research progresses and changes become necessary, the researcher should keep the staff apprised of changes in the plan and any corresponding changes in the products. By doing these things, the researcher will be fulfilling his or her responsibilities to plan and implement the most rigorous design to obtain the best information possible about program effects. Rutstein (cited in Gilbert, McPeek, & Mosteller, 1977, p. 337) takes a very strong stand on the obligation of researchers to design rigorous studies:

> It may be accepted as a maxim that a poorly or improperly designed study involving human subjects . . . is by definition unethical. Moreover, when a study is in itself scientifically invalid, all other ethical considerations become irrelevant (e.g., obtaining informed consent).

We have not discussed the clients' perspective because clients are frequently unaware that program effectiveness can be assessed. When they learn this, however, clients usually become research supporters since they are the primary beneficiaries of changes, made on the basis of program research findings, intended to make the services better.

Conclusion

In the previous sections, different ethical issues have been explored. The resolution of each issue in any particular case is rarely easy and occasionally only leads to new issues. The value premises described earlier do not apply to all social programs and, when they are valid, vary in their degree of importance. For these reasons, it is difficult to order the ethical considerations or to weigh them in degree of importance in a general way. Each research project is unique and, consequently, so are the surrounding ethical issues.

Two considerations, however, concerning ethical decision making in the use of random assignment and control groups are similar from project to project. First, no social researcher should employ social experimentation automatically in evaluating a social program. The researcher who does not carefully consider the total program context before selecting a research design may find that he or she not only has a useless study but also has distorted or even destroyed a program by trying to force it into an inappropriate mold. Social experimentation often requires adjustments in program processes (e.g., overrecruitment of potential clients) which sometimes may change the entire character of the original program. If this is going to be the case, social experimentation ethically cannot be used. Prior to implementation of any research plan, then, the social researcher must plan his or her study carefully and assess the likely intrusiveness of the requirements of social experimentation.

A second consideration that applies to all research settings is that the clients' viewpoints should be considered carefully in developing a research plan. The one common aspect of all social reform programs is that they exist to help clients. These programs have as their overriding goal the amelioration or termination of particular client needs or the improvement of the clients' situation. Since clients are the reason for the existence of these programs, clients should play a central role in the planning, implementation, and evaluation of the programs. In the past, service providers had the central role in social programs; they planned and implemented programs on the basis of their assessment of client needs, as well as of program effectiveness. Recently, researchers have entered the scene to help service planners and providers with these tasks. Now, client needs are determined by researchers who ask representative groups of clients about their needs. Likewise, program effectiveness is determined by measuring changes in client attitudes and behaviors rather than by accepting only service provider assessments of client changes.

The next step, which has occurred in only a minority of programs, is to bring clients or their representatives into the planning, implementation, and evaluation process and give them a central role. In regard to some social program evaluations, clients can play a major role in all phases of the process. When evaluation planning begins (which ideally is just as program service planning begins), representative clients can be a part of the planning team. In this case, the evaluation researcher asks clients and service providers to discuss and agree on program goals and objectives. At the same time, the evaluator assesses the extent to which the four value premises presented earlier apply in the situation. The evaluation researcher then devises a preliminary research plan and dependent measures to assess program success, both of which are discussed with clients and service providers and revised based on their input.

In implementing a research plan, particularly a control group study, researchers can benefit from close contact with clients. The randomization process need not be mystified: it can be explained and demonstrated in ways that permit genuine understanding by clients. This understanding can lead to truly informed, considered judgments by clients about their willingness to participate in an experimental or control group. This was demonstrated in an experimental study, using college students who were clients for a special extracurricular activities program (Wortman et al., 1976). The study showed that experimental and control group clients who had been informed thoroughly about the evaluation procedures and had volunteered to participate did not differ in their subsequent attitudes toward the program or their willingness to continue their participation. Although this study did not involve major social services, other studies on more typical social reform programs also suggest that clients will accept randomization if it is explained to them (Conner, 1977; Conner et al., 1979).

At the end of a research project, client participation is also critical. Once the study results are completed, client input is essential in explaining some findings and in formulating recommendations for program changes. Since clients will be the main beneficiaries of these suggested changes, they have a strong interest in pressing service providers for the changes. Greater client involvement in the interpretation and dissemination of results should help to increase research utilization.

In sum, clients should be given a central role in social experimentation. Their involvement not only will improve the quality of studies and the meaningfulness of results, but it will also aid in the resolution of many ethical problems. Rather than speculating on whether clients will feel that they have been denied a service due them, service providers and researchers should ask clients. Likewise, rather than hoping for an equitable selection of eligible clients, service providers and researchers need to enlist the help of clients to guarantee a fair selection. Finally, to assess program effectiveness, researchers should make clients their advisors to be sure that important questions are addressed and that meaningful answers are produced, disseminated, and utilized. Ethical problems arise primarily when social researchers are trying to make decisions for other people (e.g., potential clients) without informing and consulting them. By bringing all relevant parties together in an open and equal exchange throughout the course of a study, a social researcher will be able to answer many ethical questions as they arise.

Acknowledgments. The author is grateful to Newton Margulies and Joan Sieber for their suggestions on earlier drafts of this chapter. Some of the content of this chapter is based on Conner (1980).

References

Abelson, R. P., & Miller, J. C. Negative persuasion via personal insult. *Journal of Experimental Social Psychology*, 1967, *3*, 321-333.

Ball, S., & Bogatz, G. A. *The first year of Sesame Street: An evaluation.* Princeton, N.J.: Educational Testing Service, 1970.

Bickman, L., & Henchey, T. *Beyond the laboratory: Field research in social psychology.* New York: McGraw-Hill, 1972.

Bogatz, G. A., & Ball, S. *The second year of Sesame Street: A continuing evaluation* (Vols. 1 and 2). Princeton, N.J.: Educational Testing Service, 1971.

Boruch, R. F. On common contentions about randomized experiments for evaluating social programs. In G. Glass (Ed.), *Evaluation studies review annual* (Vol. 1). Beverly Hills, Calif.: Sage, 1976.

Boruch, R. F., McSweeney, A. J., & Soderstrom, E. J. Randomized field experiments for program planning, development, and evaluation: An illustrative bibliography. *Evaluation Quarterly*, 1978, *2*, 655-695.

Campbell, D. T. Reforms as experiments. *American Psychologist*, 1969, *24*, 409-429.

Campbell, D. T., & Stanley, J. C. *Experimental and quasi-experimental designs for research.* Chicago: Rand-McNally, 1966.

Canner, P. L., Berge, K. G., & Klint, C. R. The coronary drug project. New York: American Heart Association, Monograph 38, 1973.

Caro, F. G. *Readings in evaluation research* (2nd ed.). New York: Russell Sage Foundation, 1977.

Conner, R. F. Selecting a control group: An analysis of the randomization process in twelve social reform programs. *Evaluation Quarterly*, 1977, *1*, 195-244.

Conner, R. F. Ethical issues in the use of control groups. In R. Perloff & E. Perloff (Eds.), *Values, ethics and standards in program evaluation*. San Francisco: Jossey-Bass, 1980.

Conner, R. F., Rosenthal, S., McNeil, J., & Rohlf, D. Participants' reactions to randomization. Paper presented at the Evaluation Research Society Annual Meeting, Minneapolis, Minnesota: 1979.

Cook, T. D., Appleton, H., Conner, R. F., Shaffer, A., Tamkin, G., & Weber, S. W. *Sesame Street revisited*. New York: Russell Sage Foundation, 1975.

Cook, T. D., & Campbell, D. T. The design and conduct of quasi-experiments and true experiments in field settings. In M. Dunnette (Ed.), *Handbook of industrial and organizational psychology*. Skokie, Ill.: Rand-McNally, 1976.

Cook, T. D., & Campbell, D. T. *Quasi-experimentation: Design and analysis issues for field settings*. Chicago: Rand-McNally, 1979.

Cook, T. D., & Conner, R. F. Sesame Street around the world: The educational impact. *Journal of Communications*, 1976, *26*, 155-164.

Coronary Drug Project Research Group. Clofibrate and niacin in coronary heart disease. *Journal of the American Medical Association*, 1975, *231*, 360-381.

Feinberg, S. Randomization and social affairs: The 1970 draft lottery. *Science*, 1971, *171*, 255-261.

Franklin, J. L., & Thrasher, J. H. *An introduction to program evaluation*. New York: Wiley, 1976.

Freeman, H. E. The present status of evaluation research. In M. Guttentag (Ed.), *Evaluation studies review annual* (Vol. 2). Beverly Hills, Calif.: Sage, 1977.

Gaylin, W., Glasser, I., Marcus, S., & Rothman, D. *Doing good: The limits of benevolence*. New York: Pantheon, 1978.

Gilbert, J. P., McPeek, B., & Mosteller, F. Statistics and ethics in surgery and anesthesia. *Science*, 1977, *198*, 684-689.

Guttentag, M. Evaluation of social intervention programs. *New York Academy of Sciences*, 1973, *218*, 3-15.

Haveman, R. H., & Watts, H. W. Social experimentation as policy research: A review of negative income tax experiments. In G. Glass (Ed.), *Evaluation studies review annual* (Vol. 1). Beverly Hills, Calif.: Sage, 1976.

Kerlinger, F. N. *Foundations of behavioral research* (2nd ed.). New York: Holt, 1973.

Mather, H. G., Pearson, N. G., Read, R. L. Q., Shaw, D. B., Steed, G. R., Thorne, M. G., Jones, S., Guerrier, C. J., Eraut, C. D., McHugh, P. M., Chowdhury, N. R., Jafary, M. H., & Wallace, T. J. Acute myocardial infarction: Home and hospital treatment. *British Medical Journal*, 1971, *3*, 334-338.

Mitroff, I., & Bonoma, T. V. Psychological assumptions, experimentation, and real world problems: A critique and an alternate approach to evaluation. *Evaluation Quarterly*, 1978, *2*, 235-260.

Patton, M. Q. *Utilization-Focused Evaluation*. Beverly Hills, Calif.: Sage, 1978.

Pechman, J. A., & Timpane, P. M. (Eds.). *Work incentives and income guarantees: The New Jersey Income Tax experiment*. Washington, D.C.: The Brookings Institution, 1975.

Riecken, H. W., & Boruch, R. F. *Social experimentation: A method for planning and evaluating social intervention*. New York: Academic Press, 1974.

Rossi, P. H. Testing for success and failure in social action. In P. H. Rossi & W. Williams (Eds.), *Evaluating social programs*. New York: Seminar Press, 1977.

Rossi, P. H., Freeman, H. E., & Wright, S. R. *Evaluation: A systematic approach*. Beverly Hills, Calif.: Sage, 1979.

Rossi, P. H., & Lyall, K. C. *Reforming public welfare: A critique of the negative income tax experiment*. New York: Russell Sage Foundation, 1976.

Stufflebeam, D. L. Evaluation as enlightenment for decision makers. In *Improving educational assessment*. Washington, D.C.: National Education Association, 1969.

Suchman, E. *Evaluation research*. New York: Russell Sage Foundation, 1967.

Tukey, J. W. Some thoughts on clinical trials, especially problems of multiplicity. *Science*, 1977, *198*, 679-684.

Weiss, C. H. *Evaluation research: Methods of assessing program effectiveness*. Englewood Cliffs, N.J.: Prentice-Hall, 1972.

Wortman, C. B., Hendricks, M., & Hillis, J. W. Factors affecting participant reactions to random assignment in ameliorative social programs. *Journal of Personality and Social Psychology*, 1976, *33*, 256-266.

Chapter 4

Creating Ethical Relationships in Organizational Research

Philip H. Mirvis and Stanley E. Seashore

When social and behavioral scientists leave their laboratory, clinical practice, or survey center to conduct research in organizations, they are not fully prepared for the challenge of being ethical. The ethical problems encountered in real-life settings take on unique and disconcerting features arising from the fact of social organization. In these cases, researchers are dealing with a social system composed of people who have positions in a hierarchy and who, in the collective identity as an organization, also have relationships with supporters, consumers, government, unions, and other public institutions. As a result, researchers cannot approach participants in the study as independent individuals because they behave within an interdependent framework of rights and responsibilities. Nor can they invoke existing distinctive guidelines for dealing with employees, managers, clients, or sponsors because all have overlapping interests that are sometimes in conflict. Finally, they cannot single-handedly manage the ethical dilemmas that arise because they are a weak force in a field of powerful forces, with only limited means for ensuring moral action or for redressing moral lapses. Questions are raised for researchers of their responsibilities, not only to individuals but also to the social system that encompasses them, for according to law and to custom, to harm a living system is analogous to harming a person. Consider some of the questions in a field experiment recently conducted in branches of a large metropolitan bank:

Research in Organizations: Some Ethical Questions

In this study, there was developed an information system that would gather financial, behavioral, and attitudinal data (from records and directly from employees) and return it periodically to work groups for problem solving and decision making. In presenting this idea, the social scientists asserted for themselves a role of "action researchers," where *action* meant working with a task force of bank employees to operationalize and implement the program, and *research* entailed evaluating its effect on employees' participation and work performance.

Is it ethical in a case such as this to implement a change program that promotes one set of values, processes, and goals at the expense of others? One manager welcomed the information system as it enabled him "to involve everyone in the management of the branch"; another resented it because "it took management . . . out of [my] hands." In proposing the system, the researchers chose an action role that was contrary to the detached and dispassionate posture recommended by many in their profession. In fulfilling its requirements they counseled some managers on the effective use of the information and confronted others over its ineffective use. One manager felt this helped him "get off my fanny"; another felt it was "shoved down [my] throat."

What is the meaning of voluntary consent, confidentiality, and privacy in the case of persons whose employment contract stipulates the participation in studies, revelation of personal data, and inspection of behavior, all as simply "part of the job?" In this instance, several managers wanted to participate in the study, while others asked not to be involved. In the research design, branches were matched as to size, location, and other factors in such a way that some eager managers were assigned an inactive part and reluctant others were "persuaded" to join in. Steps were taken to protect the privacy of managers and the confidentiality of data collected for the information system. One manager reported, however, that he was not certain his data wouldn't be seen by "the boys downtown (top management)." When it was discovered that an official had "asked" a manager to see the reports for his branch, neither were the researchers so assured.

Under what conditions are the benefits greater than the risks of providing (or withholding) experimental treatments, descriptive data, or evaluative interpretations that could be used to improve an organization, hire or fire its members, or influence their welfare on the job? One manager used the information to guide weekly problem solving meetings, improve customer service, and promote employee development. The supervisor in the branch said it gave them a "common tool to concentrate on as a group." Another manager used the information to identify "uncooperative" employees and force their resignation or transfer; for those who remained, he used it to explain "why we have to do certain things." The supervisor said the system gave the manager a tool to "rake people over the coals." She found it hard to cope with the stress and "not carry it home in the evening."

There are few moral principles that can be applied to these situations: those principles that address the values, processes, and goals of research programs merely acknowledge the power implicit in hierarchy, in the researcher's sponsorship, and in vested interests in organizations; those that provide for voluntary consent, confidentiality, and privacy ignore that organizations necessarily are, in part, systems of compliance, coercion, and public accountability; those that ensure a favorable balance of benefits and risks assume the researcher is able, with confidence, to specify and control the demands and consequences of a study and is immune from co-optation over its course. Furthermore, in organizational research, the usual protective strategies of debriefing or care of participants cannot be effectively invoked. Yet, in comparison to other research, its impact, whether for good or evil, may be magnified in intensity and scope.

To address the ethical problems in organizational research, therefore, we propose that the researcher needs to consider his or her relationships not only with the participants in the study, but also with their *roles* as employees, managers, members of an organization, and members of society. This chapter relies on role theory and its related concepts to describe ethical dilemmas that arise in organizational research and to propose means to moderate them. Role concepts bridge personal and institutional behavior by representing both the requirements that social systems have for their members and the personal identity that members invest in the social system. Viewed as *role systems* (Katz & Kahn, 1978), organizations can be seen as sets of relations among people which are maintained, in part, by the role expectations they have for one another. When communicated, these expectations delimit the behavior of members of the organization and their rights and responsibilities with respect to others in their role system.

A researcher studying an organization also assumes a role and forms role relations with others in the organization. He or she communicates role expectations to them and is the recipient of their communications. In this chapter we take the view that *most of the ethical concerns in organizational research arise from the conjuncture of these roles*. In the first sections, we develop this perspective by describing the roles and by examining the sources of role ambiguity and conflict in a research effort. This affords the reader concepts for analyzing ethical dilemmas in organization research. It provides practicing researchers with guidelines for clarifying their roles, anticipating role conflicts, and responding to them through policy and planning decisions.

Ethical decision making, however, is embedded in action; its essence in organizational research is the considered choice among alternative courses of action where the interests of all parties have been clarified and the risks and gains have been openly, mutually evaluated. Thus, the responsibility of the ethical decision maker is not to impose clear and compatible roles on the research participants; rather it is *to create roles* that are mutually clarified and compatible and, in creating them, *to affirm general ethical norms governing human research*. In later sections of this chapter we explicate this view by describing ethical norms in research and by presenting a case example of multiple research relationships where the participants invoked them to jointly address the role pressures they encountered in an ethical and productive way.

Throughout this chapter, it is our contention that most ethical dilemmas in organizational research arise not from personal immorality, but from the researcher becoming entangled in a network of multiple roles and in the conflicting expectations derived from them. Thus, the challenge of being ethical lies not simply in the application of moral prescriptions, but rather in the process of creating and maintaining research relationships in which to address and moderate ethical dilemmas that are not, and cannot be, covered by prescription. We conclude by proposing that research training and a code of ethics be developed that are compatible with this perspective. In offering these proposals, we look ahead to a future in organizational research in which the risks of ethical conflict increase, but the institutional, professional, and personal benefits of acting ethically increase as well.

Roles and Organizational Research

When entering a larger organization, social scientists encounter a complex, established role system regulating relationships among individuals and groups. Moreover, they bring to the setting their own existing role relations with colleagues, the profession, the home institution, and the sponsors and users of his research. Their relationship with the host organization can be represented as an intersection of these two role systems. Behavior in this new, combined system is influenced in some respects by the previous history, norms, and role relations in each subsystem, and in some respects by the new dynamics of the research effort. Figure 1 depicts this intersection. It shows the relationship between the researcher and the participants, each nested within their immediate role systems which are, in turn, nested within a larger social system, the society, and its attendant ethical norms.

New roles and role relations are created at the region of intersection through the exchange of role communications. This process can be either aided or impeded by the initial role expectations of the parties. All cultures, whether societies or formal organizations, provide standard role models that can be tentatively invoked, and tested for their applicability to new situations. Yet, in the case of organizational research, sponsors may hold one set of expectations for the researcher, the home institution may hold another, and, since few organizations have established role models for researchers, factions in the organization may hold still other expectations. On first encounter, the itinerant researcher is likely to be confronted with a wildly disparate array of role messages, all derived from different sets of culturally established role models. Only rarely will they all be compatible. Thus, the researcher's task is not simply *role taking*, but also *role making* (Graen, 1976).

Pictured in this way, role definition can be seen as a personal, interpersonal, and organizational process in which individuals' responses to themselves, to one another, and to one another's roles can bring about the formation of clear and compatible, or, alternatively, unclear and incompatible role definitions. In this light, the prob-

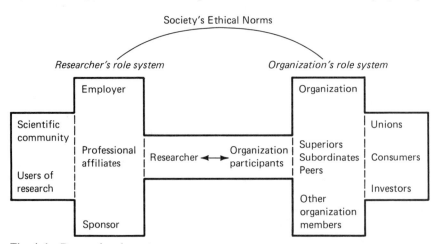

Fig. 4-1. Research role system.

lems encountered by the researchers in the bank study described earlier can be reconsidered.

In that study, one set of role expectations came from reference groups and role models in the researcher's own "back home" role system. As members of a profession, the researchers accepted responsibilities to solicit the informed and voluntary consent of the participants and, as action researchers, assumed such added responsibilities as involving employees in the joint design of the project and consulting with managers in its use to solve problems participatively. They explained to the organization the necessity and implications of such a role.

Nevertheless, from the beginning, both managers and employees tried to fit them into established role models already familiar to the firm. Top management, for example, viewed the researchers as "off beat" (academic) but inexpensive consultants (the study was externally funded) whose job was to demonstrate a way in which branch morale and performance could be improved. Hence, they felt justified in "persuading" managers to participate and in "asking" to review the confidential reports in one branch where such a gesture from the "boys downtown" might stimulate further improvement. Following the formation of the task force and the empowerment of lower-level personnel, by contrast, many employees began to see the researchers as partisans providing them a means with which to communicate their ideas and frustrations directly to management. In one branch they were emboldened to resist a branch manager's decision, taking control, in the manager's words, "out of my hands." Some managers responded by sharing their control, but another powerful bloc portrayed the researchers as "outsiders" attempting to wrest their power away from them. One manager therefore used the data to reassert his power, isolate "uncooperative" employees and remove them, and "rattle the [teller] cages" of those who remained. The personnel manager, a key stakeholder, made wary by the research team's funding from the Department of Labor, feared they might be in a position to spur employee initiatives toward unionism; by the end of the study he credited the researchers for harnessing employees' energies, thus, not coincidentally, for diverting them from union drives.

Even in such a relatively simple situation, the social scientists' roles were defined, redefined, confused, and ultimately brought into conflict with other roles. As events unfolded, there were powerful pressures and incentives for the researchers to adopt the roles preferred by one or another of the participant or stakeholder groups. In this study, as in others, the competing role expectations produced an ethical dilemma: the researchers' responsibility to increase employee participation (required by the research design and approved by all levels of management) was in direct conflict with their responsibility to not diminish the standing of those managers who were unable or unwilling to work participatively with their staffs. As it happened, those branches in which the managers used the new information system participatively showed improvements in morale and teller performance, training, and turnover. In contrast, in branches where managers did not use the data participatively, employees felt disillusioned and behaved accordingly: morale declined and turnover increased, in many cases well above preexperimental levels (Nadler, Mirvis, & Cammann, 1976).

This consequence, and many others that arise in organizational research, can be traced to the process of role definition, clarification, and resolution of conflict. It is our thesis that when social scientists, as members of one role system, and organization members, as members of another, begin a research effort, the ethical problems must be anticipated, diagnosed, and treated in light of this intersection of role systems, and resolved through collaborative effort and appeal to common, transcendent goals.

This view of ethical conduct in organization research runs counter to the common predilection toward viewing behavior largely in terms of personal values and intentions. There is a long history, for example, in organizational psychology of attributing ineffective role performance to the regrettable deficiencies of organization members who are unmotivated, unwilling, or unable. Hence, the emphasis in the field on motivation, selection, and training. This line of thinking is also endemic in other fields of social science, for example, in community settings where social psychologists have often "blamed the victim" of social and political circumstances. Turned inward in this same spirit, social scientists have blamed unethical conduct on the immorality or ill intentions of researchers.

To be sure, there are some who knowingly, willfully, or carelessly misrepresent themselves and their role in a research relationship and expose the participants to unjustified risk. There are those, too, who intentionally violate accepted norms of ethical conduct. The immorality of their actions derives from their motivations, however, so these researchers can be "blamed" for their unethical conduct. But to restate our views, we believe that most ethical dilemmas in organization research arise not from such personal immorality, but from researchers becoming entangled in a network of ambiguous or conflicting roles and role expectations.

Role Ambiguity in Organization Research

One notable characteristic of established organizations is the pervasive and detailed understanding the members have of one another's roles. This understanding is, for the most part, sustained, reinforced, or modified through acts or interactions that indirectly convey role-defining and role-maintaining meanings. There is not much explicit talk about roles; thus, there is little facility for the purposeful design of novel roles, such as those of organizational researchers. It is not surprising, then, to find the first stages of a research project, like those in any process of new role definition, to be marked by misunderstanding and uncertainty.

The first source of role ambiguity in an organizational study is the *uncertainty over which persons and groups should be considered a part of the research effort.* During the first weeks of a project, the researcher's contact is often limited to a few people in key functional areas, and to those in general management or administration. At the same time, there are others in the organization who have legitimate concerns about the study. The task of the researcher is to identify these parties and initiate role communications with them. Included among them are people and groups participating in the study and, when its scope warrants, other stakeholders such as union officials and those in other work areas who will be affected by the results. In most instances those parties at interest are readily identifiable as legitimate senders and receivers of role messages. Less well identified are those who do not or cannot effectively communicate their expectations, and those who are unknowingly excluded.

Ambiguity in Disjunctive Role Systems

One of the authors, Seashore, was engaged by the top officials of a large firm to design and conduct an extensive action research project involving several thousand employees, several years of time, and a large amount of expense. Preliminary discussions over a period of several months led to meetings with the Board of Directors and to contractual agreements that included extensive and complex understandings about the identification of significant parties, role definitions, and the procedures for engaging participants and soliciting their cooperation. It became known to the research team that within the firm there was an established social scientist (X) whose interest might be pertinent to the study. Meetings were arranged for acquaintance, but did not proceed smoothly as X perceived the research team as intruders on the local scene, competitors for scarce research resources, a threat to the model of applied social science that X had been patiently building within the firm, and purveyors of methods and theories that seemed to X of suspect validity. These views were expressed candidly, thoughtfully, and repeatedly, with the suggestion (privately expressed) that the actions of the research team were unethical.

The research team representatives were in a quandary. X had been explicitly excluded (by others) from the planning of the study, with the implication that X should continue to be excluded. Although no clear reasons were given, several possible explanations came to mind including some that could not be addressed directly with X without violating the ethical norms of confidentiality already established with others. Adding to the quandary was the realization that X had competencies of important potential value to the conduct of the study.

In the ensuing weeks it became clear that the exclusion of X was not thoughtfully intended, nor seriously desired, by anyone. However, efforts to restructure the fractured role system proved unavailing. Invitations to include X in the research team were perceived as threats of co-optation and exploitation. Steps by X to modify the research plan in ways more compatible with X's own organization role and research preferences were unacceptable to the research team (judged highly valuable for a later stage of the research process, even though irrelevant or harmful for early stages). X refrained from sabotaging the project, although the temptation must have been great.

In the end, the project was abandoned, for several different and compelling reasons, with the ready consent of all interested parties. The social scientists were caught at the disjunctive borders of different role systems, at first, without full cognizance of one another's role commitments, and, then, with means foreclosed for creating compatible role relations. The research team withdrew to their home base; X left the firm; both felt ethically virtuous and respectful of one another, but distressed at the mutual damage (Klein, 1976).

There are many reasons why individuals and groups with significant interests at stake may remain excluded from an organizational research project. Characteristics of the researcher, such as age, sex, race, or background, may disincline some parties from coming forward to present their interests. In these cases, the formation of a research team or of an in-house liaison group that attempts to match its own composition with that of major organizational groups can increase the likelihood that the researchers will be able to identify and respond to the interests of these parties (Berg, 1977). Conflict between hierarchical or functional groups may also lead one group to exclude themselves or be excluded from a study. In such instances, it is incumbent on the researchers to be alert to, and openly examine, the potential harm associated with such exclusions and, at a minimum, establish contact with the excluded groups to clarify the aims and intentions of the study. The failure to do so invites coercion or co-optation of or by the excluded and poses unanticipatable risks to the researcher and the participants.

Merely identifying the parties to a research effort does not clarify the part they are to play in the study. A second source of role ambiguity is the *uncertainty the researcher and the participants have about one another's roles and role responsibilities*. In order to seek clarification of the researcher's role, for example, organization members may focus selectively on different role messages. They may respond to the researcher's employer, sponsor, and other cues from the researcher's role set. In addition, they may generalize from past experiences or from the folklore that surrounds them. Recently a team of researchers from the Institute for Social Research (ISR) conducted a survey of employees in a division of a large service organization. Ten years previously a similar survey had been conducted by other members of the Institute, but with inadequate provision for feedback of the data by the management throughout the division. As a belated consequence, some employees initially refused to cooperate with a new group of "rip-off artists." Even after a decade, the role definition derived from this earlier study, remembered by some and transmitted to others, rose to haunt the researchers in their efforts to define a new role.

The researcher's observed behavior may in time provide the ultimate source of role information to the participants. Until then, imputed role stereotypes still have to be overcome. It is commonplace, for example, for a researcher who enters an organization through management to be seen initially as their agent. In the same way, those following in the steps of engineers may be assigned to the role of "time and motion experts," while those working through the personnel department are sometimes assumed to be "corporate shrinks." Seldom does the researcher's behavior conform to the negative aspects of such stereotypes. Nevertheless, assigning the researcher a stereotyped role can lead to a self-fulfilling prophecy. Thus, it is incumbent on researchers to communicate clearly, explicitly, and, by behavioral example, their intended role definitions. As a corollary, they must also clarify their roles to themselves.

There are many roles that social scientists can assume in organizational research and each implies the use of particular means toward intended ends. They may, for example, be entering an organization to study it unobtrusively, to intervene in it experimentally, to help it, or some combination of these. Through these means they may be there to study problems, diagnose them, or ameliorate them. *Clarifi-*

cation of the choice of role helps researchers to distinguish their own role responsibilities and the anticipatable *risks* and *benefits* that follow from the choice of means and ends. An *open* role clarification, moreover, provides a basis from which to consider what *unintended consequences* might follow from the choice of one as opposed to another role (Michael & Mirvis, 1977).

In addition, an open role clarification helps to *distinguish the coordinate role responsibilities of the participants*. They, too, need to determine whether they are to be passive subjects, active participants in a change program, uninvolved observers in the role system, or clients who should expect to receive specific benefits. Organizational field studies, like those in the laboratory, have their demand characteristics. Participants often have to "guess" at the researchers' intentions and define their own roles accordingly as subservients, colleagues, accomplices, or saboteurs. It is incumbent on researchers to limit the guesswork by working closely with the participants to define their respective roles and to arrive at mutually understood (if not always initial or preferred) role definitions. The failure to do so may leave unclear the full range of risks and benefits in a study and leave unidentified the interests and existing role requirements of some of the participants. One way of clarifying roles is through the negotiation of a research "contract" that identifies the interests of the researcher and participants, and explicates, as best possible, the rights and responsibilities of their respective roles.

The final source of role ambiguity in a research project is the *uncertainty over the role of other stakeholders* in both the researcher's and organization's role system. It is quite common, for example, for organization members to question an academic's motivations in helping them or to suspect collusion between them and their sponsors. Indeed, it seems quite incredible to many people in organizations that anyone would laboriously gather information for its own intrinsic interest, without intent to employ it in trade or in self-serving action. Yet, if organization members often err in imputing such malevolence to the researcher, researchers err in seeing organization members as participants without outside interest. More often than might be suspected from research reports, organization members co-opt researchers and exploit their activity or results for personal or organizational gain. Thus, in clarifying roles, it is also important to clarify role relations to other stakeholders in the role system. Through stakeholders' ties to the researcher or the participants, such parties may gain access to confidential data or subvert the intended aims of the project to further their own. Moreover, they are likely to succeed unless their role in the project is foreseen and clarified. For researchers, the ethical consequences that follow from being duped are equal to those from willful deception.

Role Conflicts in Organization Research

Ethical dilemmas often arise *not because roles are unclear but because they are clearly in conflict*. Whether individual, as in the case of foremen in their role as supervisors of hourly employees and as subordinates of first line management, or institutional, as in the case of union and management or manufacturing and inspection functions, role conflict is a prevalent fact of organization life. Academic researchers are well aware of role conflict, too, as the role demands of teaching are often incompatible with those of research.

In a field research project, social scientists occupy a boundary position and receive role defining messages not only from persons in their own role system but also from the participants and stakeholders in the organization. This greatly enlarges the sources of legitimate role communications. It also increases the likelihood of *role conflict between the researcher and the participants and the researcher and various stakeholders*. Consider such conflict in a research project in which Seashore collected confidential data from and about managers in an organization regarding their leadership style, effectiveness, personal health, and family. Late in the study, the president of the firm, faced with a crucial decision, asked the researcher for a private opinion about the promotional qualifications of one of these managers. The researcher felt ethically committed to his assurance of confidentiality, and to opinions based on confidential data, and declined to comment even though believing that the information would benefit an individual he admired and judged to be of very high managerial potential. The president considered it unethical of the researcher to withhold information about a very "public" person in a position normally exposed to scrutiny.

Whose sense of ethical behavior should prevail? The researcher's professional role gave priority to privacy and confidentiality, the president's to the use of all information of benefit to the firm. Shortly thereafter, the person in question saw fit "voluntarily" to resign, a loser in some subterranean combat in which there was no chance for compromise between roles respectful of private and organizational interests.

Role conflict may also exist *between participants, between participants and stakeholders, and between stakeholders* themselves as regards a research project. This latter kind of conflict faced Mirvis and a colleague when they requested research collaboration from a business firm and one member of the Board of Directors objected because he did not want the firm to be a "guinea pig" for a study funded by a government agency. Upon discussing his concerns, it was discovered that he feared the study, a social audit, would result in the unintended consequence of legislation by the agency mandating social reporting. The researchers assured him this was not their intent or that of the funding agency and included this assurance in their funding request. Imagine the shock when, in meeting with representatives from the agency, they discovered that some officials hoped to implement such audits nationally. In objecting to this, they told the representatives quite explicitly that this was not their own intent and that, moreover, they had offered their assurances to the host organization on the matter. Whether that objection or the attitude from which it arose contributed to the funding decision is indeterminate. In any case, the agency withdrew its support.

Role conflict can also arise from *within a researcher, a participant, or a stakeholder*. An example is seen in the case of one participant, a top manager, in an organization in which there was general assent to an arrangement under which all feedback of research information would be to a designated committee that would "own" the data and have full control over its internal distribution and use. The manager appreciated the merit of this arrangement as it clarified responsibilities and powers on an unaccustomed matter, and was intended to forestall potential role conflicts and ethical quandaries among several parties, including himself and the research team. Soon thereafter, the same manager, for plausible reason, firmly demanded that some of the research material be provided directly to himself before it became accessible to the committee. In his view, the inherent responsibilities and rights of a plant manager superseded the specifically designed protective role system he had helped to create. What can, should, or must the research team do in such a circumstance?

There is simply no way to escape such role conflicts in organizational research. The more conflict, and the more parties that hold conflicting expectations, the more stressful the situation becomes. At some point, researchers (like their subjects) are "damned if they do and damned if they don't" and suffer the role strains associated with this situation.

These strains become painfully personal when researchers experience role conflict within themselves. Such a personal role conflict relatively new to social scientists has come forward in recent years now that they are seen as professionals offering valuable services. Physicians, lawyers, and clinical psychologists, for example, assert the ethical principle that they are obliged to serve, if they can, any and all clients in need who so request. Social scientists, formerly protected by the public presumption of their incompetence or irrelevance (not to mention the high principle of academic freedom), have been spared such an ethical demand. This may be changing. Seashore, for example, was scolded sharply for ethical malfeasance when he declined to be engaged in research for a certain organization, for the reason that he did not personally value the organization's purposes. Others may be inclined to adopt a role in which they seek to change the organization and its mission.

Lest the conflict between the researcher's personal values and his or her role in giving service to a client seem only an emerging issue, a current one concerns the researcher's personal values and research methodology.

A Professional Role Becomes Painfully Personal

One of the authors, Mirvis, undertook a participant-observer study of Alcoholics Anonymous groups. He attended meetings regularly and, under the norms of AA, was accepted into membership simply by the act of attending. While not himself in need of AA's services, his motives were wholly supportive of the purposes of the organization. At one meeting, a co-worker from the researcher's base organization showed up and abruptly Mirvis' professional and personal roles became sharply incompatible. Fortunately, the dilemma could be resolved by establishing his professional purposes with the colleague, who then helped arrange and legitimate an "open" role for further observation.

This illustrates, again, a need for the social scientist studying organizations to expect ethical dilemmas when his or her professional role impinges on personal standards and values.

To cope with the role pressures emanating from several parties, from a single individual, or from within himself, the researcher must anticipate them. Research role conflicts are predictable, for example, when working with groups already in conflict. Thus, it is important for the researcher to clarify his or her role with respect to labor and management, supervisors and subordinates, competing departments, and public versus private interests. Similarly, it is important to clarify the nature of research roles with anxious employees and with "trapped administrators," who themselves may hold conflicting expectations. Finally, it is important that the researcher clarify his or her stance with respect to research and action for much of that conflict is internal to the researcher who must favor one or else compromise both (Seashore, 1976).

Besides clarifying roles, it is incumbent on the researcher *to build role relations with the participants and stakeholders and between them*. In this way he or she can provide for the joint and collaborative examination of the intended means and ends of the research and the unintended consequences, can establish procedures for the acknowledgment and resolution of role conflicts, and can negotiate his or her role such that it is mutually compatible with the roles and role relations in the organization. This raises an important distinction between the ethical implications of role ambiguity and of role conflict. Ambiguity, in all instances, is potentially accessible to moderation by the researcher and the parties involved, limited mainly by the time and energy available and by the occasional agreement that some ambiguity is preferable to premature clarity. Role conflict, by contrast, is sometimes unmanageable except by incorporating such conflict into the research relationships themselves. Thus, creating a role that is mutually compatible with the role system of the host organization does not necessarily imply equal concern for all competing interests. One form of compatibility is openly to take sides and, then, with the full cognizance of the "other" side, behave accordingly. This carries with it the implication that the researcher may be denied access to complete and valid data from some of the participants or be unable to counter efforts to discredit or sabotage the research. It must be recognized that ideals of impartiality and scientific validity themselves have ethical implications. These values can be realized only in the study of organizations where all parties honor them above others, or else in the conduct of trivial research. Thus, having clarified roles and built role relations, it is incumbent on the researcher *to clarify the ethical basis of the research and to openly examine value conflicts in the research relationships*.

Ethical Norms in Organization Research

The prior pages have detailed, in the language of role theory, some of the inevitable sources of ambiguity and conflict that can, and often do, create ethical dilemmas for the organizational researcher. Fortunately, there exist superordinate ethical and social norms that serve to dampen their adverse consequences and facilitate the achievement of research objectives with a tolerable balance of risk and gain. However ill defined these may seem to be, social systems place limits on the actions that may be taken by individuals acting in their roles, and advance standards to be upheld that protect their members and ensure the system's own survival. Regardless of role pressures and the benefits to be gained from acting otherwise, social behavior is governed by some widely shared norms regarding freedom, self-determination, democracy, due process, equity, and so on.

Thus, much as roles differentiate the parties in a research effort and carry distinctive expectations, norms embody general expectations and bind the parties together. When studying an organization, researchers encounter the norms of their role system, the host organization, and the larger society, some of which have legal standing. These norms form the ethical basis for the research, not just because they are lawful or even based on accepted moral principles, but also because they apply to the demands of concrete situations.

The norms of the parties in an organizational study are in some respects more protective and constraining than in, say, a laboratory experiment. It is usually the case in organizations, for example, that when members accede to the organization the power to make policies and institute procedures, they expect honest and equitable treatment in return. This provides an ethical basis for the organization's decision to sponsor a research study, whether the intention is to benefit its members directly or contribute to the society's storehouse of knowledge from which its members derive indirect benefits. It implies that the organization will inform its members of the aims and intent of the study and solicit their voluntary consent when they are to participate directly in it. Should the organization abuse that power, however, the researcher, asserting a norm of self-determination, may be justified in openly seeking to empower employees or in terminating the study (Laue & Cormick, 1978). Similarly, should the researcher prove incapable or incompetent, the organization, asserting a norm of due process, may be justified in terminating the research effort (Bermant & Warwick, 1978).

There are in place, too, some institutional structures to enforce these norms. Institutional Review Boards are increasingly involving social scientists and knowledgeable outsiders who are familiar with the exacerbated questions posed by organizational research in evaluating proposed projects. Organizations themselves are formulating research policies and expecting researchers to be well versed in the risks and benefits associated with their work. Researchers themselves are undertaking peer reviews. In one study, two researchers from the ISR devised a plan for the longitudinal analysis of data that required the designation of organizational units for comparison on grounds that were, in part, a matter of subjective judgment. The analytic outcome was deemed implausible by some individuals qualified to have an opinion. The norms of the research community then required an independent inquiry to review data sources, analytic decisions, and possible sources of error. As it happened, no errors were detected, but norms of the community regarding respect for data were properly asserted as a matter of ethical responsibility.

There are occasions, however, when the norms governing research relations are unclear and must be clarified in the context of those relations. For example, organizations collect a myriad of data about employees, some of which is reported to government, shareholders, and managers, and some of which is held in private. In seeking access to this data for research purposes, Mirvis has informed employees, but not solicited their specific consent when examining data that are public or broadly accessible, but has done so when the data are confidential, as in the case of personnel files, or private, as in the case of employees' opinions as measured through a survey or interview. As common as this practice may be, it has also been common practice for this researcher to affirm this norm with the organization and establish its common interpretation.

There are occasions, too, when the applicable norms are in conflict. In an evaluation effort recently completed, the researchers discovered that the special personal relationship of the (unaffiliated) change agent with an employee contributed significantly to the failure of the intervention. Asserting a norm of scientific candor and completeness the researchers felt an obligation to report this feature of the findings to the scientific community. At the same time, publication would have embarrassed the change agent and potentially threatened a fellow professional's future. In addition, the reputation of the organization member involved might also have suffered. Thus, the researchers faced a dilemma where their normative responsibilities to the scientific community were at odds with the protective norms that governed their research relationship with participants. They resolved the matter by discussing it with the change agent and then camouflaging the nature of the relationship in public reports, deleting documentation, and falsifying information that might have led to the parties' identification. In their judgment (and consistent with their values) the risk to individual welfare outweighed the benefits of an accurate account of events.

In cases where one set of ethical norms is in conflict with another, the researcher has the responsibility to invoke the additional norm that the conflict be confronted openly, fully, and honestly. This is not to say that all parties' values will be (or should be) honored in its resolution. It does imply that they will be represented and asserts that the conflict be settled by reason and reciprocity, rather than by the preemptive use of power or the selfish reversion to personal whim.

The norm of reciprocity can govern any research relationships that are extended in time and that bring roles and norms into conflict. To establish it, the task of the ethical researcher is not only to create a research role and establish its attendant norms, it is also to *build open working relationships with the parties at interest such that the ethical dilemmas that do arise can be examined with reciprocal interest for each other's interests and values*.

Defining and Clarifying Roles and Resolving Role Conflicts: A Case Example

We have proposed that forms of organization research pose ethical problems that lie beyond the scope of the current canons of ethical treatment of clients and research subjects and cannot be confronted effectively or ethically by a researcher guided only by their prescriptions. The reasons for this can be traced to the complexity of role systems in which the participants and the researchers are immersed. Such problems, however, can be anticipated from awareness of these impinging role systems, and this anticipation can also guide forward planning and action to the end of avoiding, moderating, or productively resolving them when they do arise.

Although this view may be widely acceptable in the abstract, its application is another matter. There has not yet emerged a sufficient body of shared experience, tested procedure, or institutionalized practice to make application easy. There are in progress, however, events that hold promise for clarification and instructive example. Increasingly, social scientists are reporting not only their research theories, methods, and results, but also their treatment of ethical matters. Examples include analyses of researcher and client relations in organizations (Argyris, 1970), the recent collection of candid reports of failures by organizational change agents and project directors (Mirvis & Berg, 1977), and research cases analyzed in terms of role relations (Klein, 1976). With the accumulation of such cases and analyses, social scientists will have available a more experiential and less speculative codification of ethical issues and appropriate response strategies.

The authors, along with colleagues, have been engaged for several years in a research program in which an explicit effort is being made to anticipate ethical issues that arise from role relationships and to create social structures, shared norms, and decision processes capable of coping with them. Since the work is still in progress, it is premature to attempt a detailed description and evaluation of these efforts to act ethically, but mention of some of the strategies employed is pertinent here. The points mentioned are not offered as tested prescriptions, to be emulated by others, but only as an interim report on efforts to find workable approaches to the choice of ethical actions.

The research program is concerned with the conduct of demonstration projects aimed at improving effectiveness and the quality of working life in both private and public sector organizations (Drexler & Lawler, 1977). Certain features of the set of field studies need to be mentioned. First, the typical case involves a longitudinal assessment of the progress and outcomes of organizational change programs undertaken by a joint labor-management committee, composed of representatives from management and from employees or their union(s), and aided by an external consultant(s). The committee's charge is to review problems and change opportunities, and help initiate actions and solutions. The duration of their efforts, lasting a period of at least 3 years, makes inevitable changes in circumstances, personnel, and roles that can neither be planned nor anticipated by the assessment team. Second, the typical case presents an impressive, if not appalling, array of intersecting role systems, each with legitimate interests to be accommodated; these involve the firm's management, the union(s), the external consultant(s), research funding agencies, a third-party agency to coordinate activities at the site, and a team of ISR staff members. Finally, the ISR team is authorized to observe events over the period, obtain such data and measurements as they see fit, and make a public report describing and appraising the outcomes; while such a provision for independent evaluation and public reporting is not unprecedented, it is rare in organization life.

The general strategy employed to address the potential ethical issues has involved (1) initial efforts to define roles; (2) early attempts to clarify roles and to reach agreements, in writing, defining the interests of the several parties along with their role responsibilities; (3) anticipating possible sources of role conflict and responding to them through policies and decision making procedures; and (4) providing for the resolution of remaining conflicts through collaborative effort, review of research relationships, and continuous legitimation of the ethical basis of the research. A few examples will illustrate concretely the steps taken to clarify roles and build role relations and the agreements negotiated to affirm ethical norms in a novel set of role relations.

Defining Roles in a Quality of Work Life Project

1. The joint committee will be composed of equal numbers of representatives chosen by the management and by the union.
2. The external consultant(s) will be selected by the committee, will work under the direction of the committee, and will agree to an independent evaluation.
3. ISR representatives will serve as the independent evaluators and will be permitted to attend, take notes, and review documents pertinent to committee meetings.

At the start of this project, top management and labor officials discussed their interests separately with the Third Party Agency and then met jointly as members of a steering committee to negotiate the ground rules for their participation. These negotiations culminated after about one year in a letter of agreement, signed by the presidents of the organization and of the union. Thereafter, a pilot site was selected and a local site committee was formed, composed of representatives elected or appointed by the local management and union. This committee oversaw site activities.

The consultants in the project were selected by the site committee. Their specific role was negotiated with the committee itself. Some, for example, defined themselves as educators, other as facilitators, and still others as change consultants. Although this reflected their preferences as to title and billing, in part, it also reflected the consultants' own role definitions and their expectations of the host organization. As an additional condition of employment, the consultants agreed to an independent evaluation.

Members of the ISR assumed this independent evaluation role. In this position, they defined themselves as neutral observers and through policy and practice sought to maintain impartiality. On occasion, this proved problematic. At one site, for example, local management objected to the purposefully casual attire of the evaluator claiming that no one should "represent management dressed like a slob." After the repercussions of this matter reached the corporate and union brass and returned, with a reaffirmation of the original understanding, the evaluator's independence had been symbolically, if somewhat comically, affirmed. He thereafter appeared more clearly as a representative of ISR, not the management, often *sans cravat*.

Clarifying Roles and Role Relations

1. All participation by members of the organization in committee meetings will be voluntary.
2. The management and the union assure that no member of the organization will suffer loss of or reduction in pay, loss of or reduction in benefits, or be suspended or terminated, as a result of activities stemming from the project.
3. Either management or the union may terminate the project and agreements associated with it, for any reasons, upon 24 hours notice.

4. The management will provide to ISR personnel such operating and fiscal information from its records as are needed for the evaluation of the project; ISR will hold confidential all such information except as release is authorized by the management.
5. The personal provision of information to ISR from organization members shall be voluntary and under assurance that the privacy and anonymity of informants will be maintained.

As the project got under way, the signed letter of agreement, its dissemination throughout the organization and union, and the broad communication associated with it ensured the informed consent of the participants, which was formally obtained from their proxy representatives on the steering and site committees. In addition, it ensured that the participation was voluntary; it gave both management and the union the unilateral right to terminate the project "within twenty four hours of notice." The agreement stipulated that no committee members would "lose pay or benefits for attendance at such meetings." The same stipulation applied to management and nonmanagement employees who participated in experimental projects authorized by the committee. In addition, they were assured that they would not "suffer loss of or reduction in pay, loss of or reduction in benefits, or ... be suspended or terminated as a result of activities stemming from the project."

The agreement also established the financial contribution of management and the union to the project and the control over disbursement of the funds. In addition, it stipulated that no experimental programs would "affect any previous collective bargaining agreements" without prior approval of the parties. Finally, the agreement formalized union and management roles as "joint clients" of the consultants and the evaluation researchers, through their representation on the site committee.

This formal contract covered key issues regarding informed consent, voluntary participation, funding for the program, protection of participants, and formalization of role relationships. To cover their week-to-week role relations with the consultants and committee members, the evaluators also negotiated more informal *role contracts* with them that detailed their respective rights, duties, and responsibilities in the study and established the basis of exchange in their role relations. As part of their responsibility to these "clients," for example, the evaluators agreed to review their instruments and evaluation plans with the site committee in return for having access to organizational records and to the employees themselves. The intent was to further ensure the informed consent of the participants, through their representatives, and to familiarize them with the aims of the research. When practiced, however, it also enhanced the quality of the research, as the committee members suggested new and relevant sources of information and better ways of phrasing questions or gathering data from respondents. In addition, it improved the quality of the research relations as committee members were consulted about and contributed to the evaluation effort. Finally, it enriched the quality of the findings as it established a climate of mutual trust and reciprocity in which the participants were encouraged by their peers to cooperate with the researchers and honestly to express their feelings about their work.

Responding to Potential Role Conflict

1. The joint committee will be empowered to direct the project and will decide for itself its internal rules for decision making (all have chosen to decide by consensus).
2. The committee shall not take any action which violates, abrogates, or extends the union-management contract unless authorized through the normal negotiation process.
3. ISR will review their instruments and evaluation plans with the joint committee and be responsive to their suggestions and criticisms.
4. All visits to the project site be representatives of the external sponsors, the coordinating agency, or the ISR team will be subject to the consent and conditions provided by the joint committee.
5. ISR will provide factual information from its records to the committee, and only to the committee, upon request, but will not provide opinions, interpretations, or recommendations based on those data; the control over the dissemination and use of the data will rest with the committee.
6. The external consultant(s) will have no privileged access to ISR's research data.
7. During the course of the project, ISR will not make public any information concerning the project without the consent of the joint committee, except for information previously made public by others.
8. Following completion of the project, any public reports by ISR will be subject to the review and consent by the management, by the union(s), and by the consultant(s) as to factual matters and as to the release of previously confidential information, but not as to opinions and interpretations made by ISR staff.

There were ongoing and competing tensions between the researchers' role as independent evaluators and their role as interdependent members of a role system. Oftentimes their role responsibilities were unclear. In reviewing items for their evaluation surveys, for example, researchers were often asked to include diagnostic questions relevant primarily to the interests of committee members or the consultants. Similarly, when observing committee members or change activities, the evaluators were sometimes asked for their opinions. In other instances, their roles appeared to conflict with those of the other parties. For example, in administering their evaluation surveys they aroused employee's expectations for change and in feeding the data back, they indirectly contributed to the intervention itself.

In order to anticipate these role conflicts and respond to the ethical dilemmas they could have produced, the researchers formulated policies to clarify their roles and role responsibilities and codify norms. An example of this was the issuance, with the aid and consent of the site committee and consultant, of a "statement of intent regarding the return of research information to the experimental site." This statement varied somewhat from site to site, but specified at a minimum that data provided during the study would be factual, *but without ISR interpretation or opinion*, and would be made available equally to management and to union representatives on the site committee who would control its further dissemination and use. In addition, the statement provided that *only data sought by the committee or the consultant* would be returned, and then only when it did not violate ISR assurances of confidentiality or exceed budgetary provisions. Such a statement was intended to balance the role pressures facing the researchers by affirming their rights as independent observers while also acknowledging their responsibilities as contributing members to the complete role system.

The researcher's role responsibilities, of course, extended to the other parties in the role system. Guidelines were established for the early external distribution of data to other social scientists that provided for the protection of the anonymity and confidentiality of data from site participants and the privacy and professional interests of the consultants, the researchers, and the site organization. Similarly, a statement of intent regarding the public release of information was developed which allowed for the prior review of the material by all parties and attested to their rights to challenge "the correctness of factual information" and the "release of previously confidential information," but not "interpretations, opinions, or evaluations by ISR staff." At one site, this statement even provided for a "written rebuttal" by the consultant or any committee member should they have disagreed with those interpretations, opinions, or evaluations.

Such agreements seem excessively legalistic and rigid when abstracted from their context. Each of the provisions negotiated in agreements at the start and throughout the projects affirm ethical norms binding on clients and researchers: norms such as those pertaining to protection of participants' welfare, preservation of scientific interests, avoidance of coercion, minimization of risk, and the like. It is significant that under such terms, the achievement of ethical solutions to operational problems is plainly a matter of concern to all the parties, and not only a matter of the researcher's judgment. In all instances, the provisions were elaborated through discussions or through the precedent of earlier, specific actions. In many cases, the original specifications were altered by informal agreement to meet the necessities of unanticipated conditions. Such role contracts have been applied not as inflexible credos, but as a reminder of original intentions to conduct research ethically.

The reader should not assume that all this attention and effort has resulted in unqualified success in the management of ethical dilemmas. The approach has been successful, so far, in the sense that the research requirements have been met and the researchers' role has been tolerated in all places, even honored in some, despite the stresses that accompany organizational change programs. Nevertheless, if mention were made of all ethical dilemmas encountered and painfully resolved or tolerated in some fashion, it would form a long list in which co-optation of the researchers undermined scientific interests and mutual distrust brought about the participants' interests into conflict with the evaluation role. In sites where these pressures were managed more effectively, the strategies of the researchers, broadly speaking, were to work with the other parties to maintain the integrity of the evaluation role and to fulfill their mutual responsibilities to ensure that the research was conducted ethically.

Table 4-1 provides a summary of these and the more general strategies for clarifying ambiguous roles and resolving role conflicts in organization research. Implementing these strategies is indeed a challenging undertaking. Yet if the ethical

Table 4-1. Strategies for Addressing Ethical Dilemmas in Organizational Research

Source	Strategy	Ethical norm
Role ambiguity		
Regarding which persons or groups are part of the research	Creating an in-house research group composed of all parties implicated directly or indirectly in the study.	Anticipating coercion or cooperation of or by uninvolved parties, researcher, participants, and stakeholders; examining risks and benefits; identifying personal, professional, scientific, organizational, job holder, and stakeholder interests.
Regarding the researcher's role	Communicating clearly, explicitly, and by example the intended role; clarifying the intended means and ends; examining potential unintended consequences; providing for an informed participation.	
Regarding the participant's roles.	Clarifying role responsibilities and rights; providing for informed consent and voluntary participation; establishing procedures to ensure anonymity, confidentiality, job security, and entitlements; providing for redress of grievances and unilateral termination of the research.	
Regarding the stakeholder's roles.	Clarifying role responsibilities and rights; establishing procedures to ensure participant's anonymity, confidentiality, job security, and entitlements.	
Role conflict		
Between researcher and participants; between researcher and stakeholders; within researcher.	Creating and building role relations; providing for joint examination of intended means and potential unintended consequences; establishing procedures for resolution of conflict through joint effort within established ethical norms.	Avoiding coercion of or by uninvolved parties, researcher, participants, and stakeholders; acting with knowledge of risks and benefits; protecting personal

		professional, scientific organizational, job holder, and stakeholder interests through collaborative effort and commitment to ethical basis of the research.
Between participants; between stakeholders; between participants and stake-holders; within participant or stakeholder.	Organizing full role system; providing for collaborative examination of intended means and ends and potential unanticipated consequences; establishing procedures for resolution of conflict through collaborative effort within established ethical norms.	
Ambiguous or conflicting norms		
Within or between researcher participants, and stake-holders.	Clarifying ethical norms for research; providing for collaborative examination of unclear or incompatible norms; establishing procedures for resolution of value conflicts through collaborative effort.	Establishing ethical basis of research.

norms on which they are based are unduly slighted, then research in organizations could not be done ethically, effectively, or at all.

Looking Ahead

The social science research profession, like other professions, faces a near future of turmoil: ethical norms are in flux; we are becoming less encapsulated in environments of our own making; and, we will more often work on issues of concern beyond our disciplinary interests. Yet, *to look closely at the role and normative conflicts in future research efforts not only ensures the discovery of ethical dilemmas, but also makes them more salient and vexing.*

This can, of course, lead to paralysis as the increasing attention to analyzing risks and benefits, obtaining consent, and managing role relations takes precious time and energy away from research. *Becoming fixated on ethics itself has ethical consequences.* As Benne (1959, p. 66) notes, "Making valid distinctions between neurotic anxieties and ethical concerns is a 'learned' rather than a 'natural' ability." Thus, it is not simply a matter for researchers to "behave ethically," for as we have sought to show, ethical action does not follow from good intentions alone. Instead it is incumbent on researchers and organizational participants to learn how to conduct research ethically. The social science community recognizes this need. When Seashore began his research career, there was great naiveté about ethical consequences in organizational research. Today, as Mirvis began his, naiveté itself is unethical.

One place to begin to address ethics in organization research is in the pre- and in-service training of social scientists. Already a body of knowledge is being developed to help identify the roles and role responsibilities of organizational consultants (Benne, 1959), organization development practitioners (Walton & Warwick, 1973), group trainers (Glidewell, 1978), and evaluation researchers (Sieber & Sanders, 1978). The normative values that govern research relations have become the subject of study (Warwick & Kelman, 1973). In the same vein, social scientists are addressing their role in the larger society (Gouldner, 1962) and the social and political consequences of their research activities (Guskin & Chesler, 1967). All of this heightens awareness of the ethical conflicts in research and also creates a climate in which to learn to conduct research ethically.

To further this purpose, we would suggest that social scientists more often apply their knowledge of social organization to their own research activities. Their knowledge of roles and role relations, for example, could be used to define their roles as researchers and to diagnose the ethical problems that are faced in a research effort. Similarly, their methods of policy analysis and contingency planning could be applied to address the foreseeable conflicts and to respond to the second- and third-order consequences of the research. Finally, their knowledge of the intra- and interpersonal skills of organizing could be used to help build role relations in order to cope with uncertainty about risks and benefits and to manage the ethical dilemmas that arise.

Among the several social and behavioral science disciplines, the psychologists have the most richly developed and documented ethical guidelines as well as institutionalized agencies for surveillance of practice and resolution of public complaints. The current documents of the American Psychological Association (1963, 1967, 1973, 1975), however, have evolved largely from clinical and counseling practice, from research with unorganized subjects, and from a preoccupation with collegial relationships; they do not adequately address the issues that arise in the context of organizational settings. The other social science disciplinary groups have even more rudimentary ethical provisos, and generally lack organizational mechanisms for the accumulation of experience, codification of issues, and exposure of cases to the healing properties of light, air, and public debate. None of these disciplinary groups, so far as we know, offers any effective guidance for the in-service training and supervision of organization researchers or practitioners (Alderfer & Berg, 1977). Most importantly, no explicit counsel is given to researchers regarding their responsibilities to work closely with members in the organization to anticipate, prepare for, and openly confront the role conflicts and normative differences that precipitate ethical dilemmas in organization research.

Up to this point, there have been no systematic efforts to formulate ethical guidelines specific to organization research. Stone (1978) has identified a "potpourri" of ethical questions researchers face in every study; others, notably Argyris (1970), have examined one or more ethical questions in depth. But now, as researchers' roles become increasingly differentiated, research relations increasingly tangled, and the consequences of "unethical" behavior increasingly dire, the need for common concepts for analyzing ethical dilemmas and common principles for resolving them becomes pressing. There should be arrangements for the public airing of ethical dilemmas, presentation of rationales for choosing a course of action, and derivation of general principles. Preparation of a casebook on ethical standards for organization researchers would be a good next step along the way.

Such a casebook would deal with familiar generic issues, but treat them in the context of organization research. Among the specific questions would be: (1) How can the anonymity of organizations and the privacy of individuals be appropriately respected when they occupy social roles that are inherently, or even legally, exposed to scrutiny and in which the distinction between personal and public interest is obscure? (2) What is the meaning of voluntary consent given that organizations are open systems and countless individuals may be indirectly implicated in research? (3) What is the meaning of informed consent when organizational processes are set in motion and take on their own dynamics without anyone knowing, with confidence, the outcomes? (4) How can principles of confidentiality be operationalized when it is not obvious who or what social entity "owns" the information? Examining these and related issues with attorneys, ethicists, union representatives, managers, and other interested citizens would add a diversity of viewpoints and provide the basis for a common ethical code.

As researchers reflect on and act within their roles, one ethical principle of the American Psychological Association surely must apply. That is the first principle, that the researcher is personally responsible for the ethics of the research effort. The Milgram (1965) studies showed vividly how people can behave unethically because of their role in a social setting. Surely as researchers we often behave like Milgram's subjects, letting social habits and coercions supersede our "personal" values. One aim in applying role theory to the conduct of research is to enable researchers to look critically at their own roles and role relations. We believe that by analyzing research relations in terms of roles and the norms that govern them, researchers shed light on their ethical dilemmas. Likewise, by contemplating these dilemmas, they also shed light on their choice of roles.

That phrase "choice of roles" sharpens the view we advocate, for it implies that there exists in any situation an array of alternative roles that potentially can satisfy ethical criteria. But, it does not imply that the ethical researcher need only choose a role and then hold it to its prescriptions. The thrust of our argument is directly contrary, for we believe that roles are not "taken"; they are conferred on people and affirmed or modified through assertion, negotiation, and consensus. In a relatively brief, simple, contrived, and power imbalanced relationship, as in the "medical model" of professional behavior in relation to a client, the professional may gain instant acceptance of his or her own "choice of roles"; but a social scientist studying an organization can do so only by choosing a roles so innocuous that no other roles are significantly implicated or by identifying with a powerful group of supporters capable of insulating him or her from the normal role-forming obligations.

At the beginning of this chapter, we proposed that ethical choice is embedded in ation and that its essence is the considered choice among alternative courses of action where the interests of all parties have been clarified and the risks and gains have been openly, mutually evaluated. Those who, from a distance, adjudge this or that role model to be unethical are strangers to the problems of field research in organizations. We have described our own research, our own moral choices, and have proposed role theory as a means for understanding ethical quandaries encountered in organization research. When conducting such a study, the researcher is immersed in action and can only fitfully guide it with abstract moral reflection. Role theory, to be relevant to ethical decision making, must be useful in action. We believe it can be applied to research in organizations, but come to the conclusion that while it cannot be prescriptive as to the "content" of the researcher's role, it can be prescriptive as to the "processes" that can lead to a tolerable (and temporary) consensus among all interested parties regarding a moral course of action. This view does not lessen the researcher's personal responsibility for his or her choice of role or role behavior. On the contrary, it requires that the social scientists choose and fulfill an acceptable public role or leave the scene.

Neither organizational nor research roles are biological, but they do seem to have a built-in survival mechanism. They perpetuate order in the research relationship and, within that order, perpetuate themselves. This can lead to the presumption that following current ethical role prescriptions, including those presented here, is an assurance of ethical conduct. But ethics are not inherent in role behavior. Just the reverse: Ethical conduct in research requires criticism of roles, norms, and the institutions that sustain them. To be ethical then, we must be critical of our roles in institutions, the norms that govern these roles, and the institutions themselves. This critique can inform ethical decision making. It can also free us to conduct research ethically.

Acknowledgment. Portions of this manuscript appeared in the *American Psychologist*, 1979, *34*, 766-780. Copyright 1979 by the American Psychological Association, reprinted/adapted by permission of the publisher and author.

References

Alderfer, C. P., & Berg, D. N. Organization development: The profession and the practitioner. In P. H. Mirvis & D. N. Berg (Eds.), *Failures in organization development and change*. New York: Wiley-Interscience, 1977.

American Psychological Association. *Ethical standards of psychologists*. Washington, D.C.: American Psychological Association, 1963.

American Psychological Association. *Casebook on ethical standards of psychologists*. Washington, D.C.: American Psychological Association, 1967.

American Psychological Association. *Ethical principles in the conduct of research with human participants*. Washington, D.C.: American Psychological Association, 1973.

American Psychological Association. *Standards for providers of psychological services*. Washington, D.C.: American Psychological Association, 1975.

Argyris, C. *Intervention theory and method*. Reading, Mass.: Addison-Wesley, 1970.

Benne, K. D. Some ethical problems in group and organizational consultation. *Journal of Social Issues*, 1959, *20*, 60-67.

Berg, D. N. Failure at entry. In P. H. Mirvis & D. N. Berg (Eds.), *Failures in organizational development and change*. New York: Wiley-Interscience, 1977.

Bermant, G., & Warwick, D. P. The ethics of social intervention: Power, freedom, and accountability. In G. Bermant, H. C. Kelman, & D. P. Warwick (Eds.), *The ethics of social intervention*. New York: Hemisphere, 1978.

Drexler, J. A., Jr., & Lawler, E. E. III. A union-management cooperative project to improve the quality of work life. *Journal of Applied Behavioral Science*, 1977, *3*, 373-386.

Gouldner, A. W. Anti-minotaur: The myth of a value-free sociology. *Social problems*, 1962, *3*, 199-213.

Glidewell, J. C. Ethical issues in and around encounter groups. In G. Bermant, H. C. Kelman, & D. P. Warwick (Eds.), *The ethics of social intervention*. New York: Hemisphere, 1978.

Graen, G. Role making processes in organizations. In M. D. Dunnette (Ed.), *Handbook of industrial and organizational psychology*. Chicago: Rand-McNally, 1976.

Guskin, A. E., & Chesler, M. A. Partisan diagnosis of social problems. In G. Zaltman (Ed.), *Processes and phenomena of social change*. New York: Oxford University Press, 1967.

Katz, D., & Kahn, R. L. *The social psychology of organizations* (2nd ed.). New York: Wiley, 1978.

Klein, L. *A social scientist in industry*. Essex, England: Gower Press, 1976.

Laue, J., & Cormick, G. The ethics of intervention in community disputes. In G. Bermant, H. C. Kelman, & D. P. Warwick (Eds.), *The ethics of social intervention*. New York: Hemisphere, 1978.

Michael, D. N., & Mirvis, P. H. Changing, erring, and learning. In P. H. Mirvis & D. N. Berg (Eds.), *Failures in organizational development and change*. New York: Wiley-Interscience, 1977.

Mirvis, P. H., & Berg, D. N. (Eds.). *Failures in organizational development and change*. New York: Wiley-Interscience, 1977.

Milgram, S. Some conditions of obedience and disobedience to authority. *Human Relations*, 1965, *18*, 57-76.

Nadler, D. A., Mirvis, P. H., & Cammann, C. The ongoing feedback system: Experimenting with a new managerial tool. *Organizational Dynamics*, 1976, *4*, 63-80.

Seashore, S. E. The design of action research. In A. W. Clark (Ed.), *Experimenting with organization life*. New York: Plenum, 1976.

Sieber, J. E., & Sanders, N. Ethical problems in program evaluation: Roles, not models. *Evaluation and Problem Planning*, 1978, *1*, 117-120.

Stone, E. *Research methods in organizational behavior*. Santa Monica, Calif.: Goodyear, 1978.

Walton, R. E., & Warwick, D. P. The ethics of organization development. *The Journal of Applied Behavioral Science*, 1973, *6*, 681-698.

Warwick, D. P., & Kelman, H. C. Ethical issues in social intervention. In G. Zaltman (Ed.), *Processes and phenomena of social change*. New York: Wiley-Interscience, 1973.

Chapter 5

Vulnerable Populations: Case Studies in Crowding Research

Chalsa M. Loo

This chapter deals with selected ethical issues that arise in research on the effects of crowding, with particular emphasis on broad issues pertaining to informed consent. These include the use of "participant advocates," and debriefing procedures tailored to the participants' needs, assessing the effectiveness of debriefing procedures in removing imposed discomfort, assessing the degree of imposed harm on participants, accommodating the circumstances and needs of the community by addressing problems involved in conducting research in the community and determining community attitudes toward the investigated variables, and minimizing feelings of powerlessness on the part of subjects.

The study of the effects of stressors such as crowding poses particular ethical problems for social scientists. A major problem arises from the conflict between the scientist's responsibility to society to produce scientifically valid, socially beneficial research, and the responsibility to protect human subjects from harm and to respect their autonomy. This problem arises in research on the effects of stressors such as crowding because scientific validity requires empirical evidence of any adverse effects, yet the scientist is obligated to avoid causing harm to human subjects. To minimize the possibility of causing harm to subjects, the scientist can conduct research on nonvulnerable[1] persons, or can study the effects of safe, high-density conditions that are mild and nonstressful. These alternatives, however, involve ethical problems as well.

The study of vulnerable populations in their natural settings may pose considerable threat to privacy and autonomy since these populations have little power to prevent the investigator from observing, possibly misinterpreting, and publishing information about their lives. However, since vulnerable populations are those most

---

[1] In this chapter, a *vulnerable population* is defined as a population of persons who, relative to the majority of society, have less power, opportunity, or freedom to determine outcomes in their lives or to make decisions that affect their situation because of their age, physical or mental condition, race, economic or political position, or a captive status.

likely to live in crowded conditions in the real world, the study of nonvulnerable populations has less social benefit or relevance. The study of vulnerable participants in a laboratory setting where issues of privacy are less salient increases risk of causing harm to the participants and failing to respect their autonomy since vulnerable participants have fewer options and thus fewer ways to cope with stress. However, the generalization of findings from nonvulnerable samples in a laboratory setting to vulnerable populations in the real world may be invalid, thereby causing social injury or societal injury.[2]

The study of safe high-density conditions in which no harm is caused to human subjects and consequently no negative effects of crowding are found raises a similar set of ethical problems. If the scientist generalizes from this setting to more crowded conditions and other settings, the likelihood of causing social or societal injury is great if, in fact, severe crowding is detrimental to certain segments of the population or to the population as a whole. Yet, testing only safe density conditions leaves untested the effects of extreme and continuous crowding.

Throughout this chapter, it is argued that errors in construct validation and in generalization of findings beyond the limits of the sample studied can result in serious social and societal harm; for each research setting, valid measures and appropriate procedures and interpretations are required. Attention is given to these ethical issues as they relate to two different settings in which crowding research is conducted: the laboratory setting and the natural setting. Case examples are used to illustrate these issues. Two studies are described: a laboratory study of autistic children, and a survey of Chinese-Americans in San Francisco's Chinatown. Procedures for the protection of human subjects, as they apply to laboratory settings and to survey research in ethnic minority communities, are discussed. Finally, these issues are generalized to the study of the effects of other stressors.

Recent Concern for Ethics of Research and the Usefulness of Case Examples

In recent years, academic psychologists have engaged in a critical examination of the ethics of psychological research on human participants. Review committees in research institutions have made data collection and funding contingent on the use of safeguards to protect human participants and in so doing have increased our awareness of values and procedures as they apply to participant welfare, scientific validity, and scientific significance. Increased awareness of ethical issues can also

---

[2] In this chapter, *social injury* refers to detrimental effects to particular segments of the population and *societal injury* refers to detrimental effects to the larger society, as a result of dissemination or application of invalid conclusions. For example, if social scientists and policy makers generalize from short-term crowding research conducted using normal children to long-term crowding of emotionally disturbed children, *social harm* is done to emotionally disturbed children who are subsequently and mistakenly allowed to remain in crowded classes as a matter of policy, and *societal harm* accrues to the society that enters into such a mistaken policy.

come about through a discussion of ethical dilemmas that have arisen in actual research. These case examples can serve a useful teaching function to researchers. As any one dilemma challenged the individual researcher with some tormenting decision, so it can challenge our thinking about what constitutes ethical research and what alternatives and approaches are available to the researcher.

Recent Concern for Research on Crowding and Its Effects on Human Behavior

In 1970, social scientists began to address problems of overpopulation, advancing urbanization, and environmental deterioration (Bartz, 1970; Craik, 1970; Fawcett, 1970; Wohlwill, 1970). It was largely this concern that stimulated the development of research on crowding and its effects on human behavior. Calhoun's (1962) striking findings of disastrous and pathological effects of crowding on rats prompted investigation into the effects of crowding on humans in order to determine whether analogies from "mice to men" were appropriate and whether people subjected to crowded cities and crowded living conditions would suffer a similar fate. Since that time we have gained some knowledge about the effects of crowding and about problems involved in studying such a phenomenon.

Laboratory Research on the Effects of Crowding

Most of the psychological research on the effects of crowding on human behavior has been laboratory research conducted in university settings. This is probably because most of the first crowding researchers were academic social psychologists; undergraduate students were very accessible participants and the university laboratory was a convenient setting as well as a setting in which variables could be more easily controlled. The study of stressors such as crowding poses particular ethical problems in laboratory research, and the nature of these problems depends on whether the population studied is vulnerable or not.

Generalizations Made from Research on Nonvulnerable Participants

When effects of crowding are investigated on nonvulnerable populations in a laboratory setting and no harmful effects of crowding are found, there is a risk that a misleading or incorrect conclusion might be drawn that crowding is not harmful to all humans under any condition. In actuality, the study may only demonstrate that under a particular type of density manipulation in a university laboratory setting, nonvulnerable participants who performed some particular task do not demonstrate significant effects of crowding.

None of the ethical principles in the conduct of research with human participants adopted by the American Psychological Association discusses validity as an ethical issue, yet invalid research generalizations that lead to "social injury" or "societal injury" do constitute an ethical issue.

How can conclusions that are drawn from laboratory research on crowding lead to "social or societal injury?" Critical policy decisions on prison conditions, housing projects, health, and educational standards can be based on the findings of crowding research. For example, a legal suit was brought against the State of New York by inmates of a state prison who argued that the crowded conditions in the prisons constituted an inhuman condition (*Ambrose et al. vs. Malcolm et al.*, U.S. District Court, Southern District of New York, 76 Civ. 190). Two social psychologists served as expert witnesses, one for the defense, one for the prosecution. Laboratory research in which no harmful effects of crowding were found was presented as evidence by the expert witness for the defense to justify the position that crowding has no harmful effects on humans. However, the differentiation between vulnerable and nonvulnerable research participants was not made; the psychologist drew largely from research findings on nonvulnerable participants and research conducted in a laboratory setting when the party in question (prison inmates) represented a vulnerable population as defined by their captive status and represented a population residing in a natural setting (a prison). There is recent evidence that the effects of crowding on vulnerable participants are detrimental and significantly more negative than the effects of crowding on nonvulnerable participants (Loo, 1978a; 1978b). Therefore there is danger in generalizing from results conducted on nonvulnerable populations. If generalizations from studies in which no harmful effects of crowding were found are invalid for some groups, harmful consequences may come to persons who exist in crowded conditions because policy makers may be unlikely to ameliorate crowded conditions on the basis of the conclusions drawn.

Harm to Research Participants

The social and public policy question of whether crowding is harmful to humans may be impossible to answer through laboratory research when ethical considerations prevent the investigator from causing harm to the participants. If the investigator's responsibility to prevent physical and psychological discomfort or harm to the participants means that a laboratory experiment is terminated before analyzable data can be collected, then it may be impossible to scientifically determine crowding effects in a controlled laboratory setting. Moreover, if, in order to protect the participants' welfare, a researcher studies a high-density condition that is not dense enough to constitute crowding, it may also be impossible to determine scientifically the effects of crowding.

Vulnerable Participants: A Case Study

The Need for Research on Vulnerable Participants

Paradoxically, while the majority of the research on crowding effects has been conducted on nonvulnerable participants, it is more important to study the effects of crowding on vulnerable participants such as the urban poor, the institutionalized, or those with few choices or alternatives in their work and living situations because these are the people who are most likely to live and work in crowded conditions in real life. Moreover, very little research has been conducted on individual differences in response to density conditions. A determination of possible differential effects of crowding on various groups of people needs to be made. The identification of "high risk" populations would alert us to the development of preventive or ameliorative measures for such populations. Differential treatment or planning approaches for community, neighborhood, housing, classroom, and treatment facilities can be developed for differing populations if knowledge of differential effects of crowding can be obtained.

The ethical dilemma of harm caused to research participants versus valid research is most likely to arise when vulnerable participants are studied because the level of stress experienced is likely to be greater for such persons and their control over the experimental situation is likely to be more limited than for nonvulnerable participants. This is clearly illustrated in a study we conducted on the effects of crowding on autistic children.[3]

Case Study Description and Results

In deciding to study the effects of crowding on autistic children, we had in mind the need for research on vulnerable participants and the need for differential research on crowding effects, as has already been mentioned. Autistic children are characterized by their avoidance of interpersonal contact of any kind; therefore, they represent a population hypothesized to be most negatively affected by close interpersonal contact that exists in crowded conditions.

A laboratory design was selected because we were striving to control as many variables as possible. The purpose of the study was to investigate the effects of spatial density (in which the size of the room varied) on autistic children using a repeated measures design. The children attended a special day center for autistic children. Their ages ranged from 5 to 9 years. They were scheduled to be observed in a university playroom (containing a variety of new toys) for two sessions, each session lasting 1 hour. The children's behaviors were observed by research assistants located behind one-way mirrors.

The teachers had requested permission to observe the sessions from behind the one-way mirrors and this request was granted. In order to keep the teachers' presence from distracting the research assistants, arrangements were made so that the teachers could observe and listen from a separate one-way mirrored room. In retrospect, we found that the teachers had served a role of "participant advocate" by assuring that no harm should come to the participants. These teachers were very sensitive to the psychological well-being of the children. They had worked for months on a behavior modification program aimed at eliminating the autistic behaviors of these children. The teachers were briefed on the importance of assessing the effects of environmental conditions and amount of space on children with problems.

---

[3] The study on autistic children was an undergraduate senior thesis conducted under my faculty sponsorship.

In planning our study, we had only one previous study to which we could refer in which a similar population had been studied. This study (Hutt & Vaizey, 1966) compared the behaviors of five autistic, five brain-damaged, and five normal children, ages 3 to 8, under three social density conditions (six or less children, 7-11 children, and 12 or more children). These participants were either in-patients or day-patients in a hospital setting. Two adults, usually nurses, were always present in the room. Autistic children were found to spend significantly more time on the boundary of the room as density increased, unlike the normal and brain-damaged children who showed no effect of density on time spent on the boundary of the room. No mention was made of any behavioral changes in the frequency of autistic behaviors as a function of density, but then these behaviors were not variables that were investigated. No mention was made of ethical dilemmas that arose for the investigators while conducting their research. Therefore, we were not prepared for the problems that arose in our study.

Before describing the problems, mention should be made of the ways in which our study differed from Hutt and Vaizey's, since the differences may provide some insight into the origins of events in our study. In terms of ethical issues our study differed from Hutt and Vaizey's study in two ways: our study had "participant advocates" and the participants in our study were in a noncaptive situation. These factors will be discussed more fully.

Kelman (1972) has suggested that the researcher take precautions to counteract the powerlessness of "disadvantaged" participants. One counteracting method is to assign research guardians for the participants. In Tanke and Tanke (Chapter 6, companion volume) the question of who will be an effective guardian of the interests of a special subject population is addressed. In Hutt and Vaizey's study the reason for the presence of the nurses or other adults, their role, and their relationship to the children were not specified. In our study, the teachers served as "participant advocates."

In Hutt and Vaizey's study, the participants were "captive" participants in an institutional setting and therefore the researchers had considerable control over their participants. In our study the presence of "participant advocates" in a situation in which the participants were not captive meant that our control over the participants was substantially less.

The resulting behaviors were these: during the first of two planned sessions, numerous autistic behaviors and distress were evidenced. One child twiddled his fingers in front of his eyes, another child rocked his body back and forth, one leaned forward in a hypnotic-like stance, one child cried helplessly, and another child continually screamed.

The research assistants and the teachers had different responses to the children's behavior. The teachers became very distressed at the behaviors evidenced by the children and deemed it unwise to allow the children to return for the second session. In their assessment, the long-range scientific benefit that such research might have for children was not worth the short-term loss of seeing the children in their center distressed and demonstrating autistic behaviors more accentuated than usual. Since ethical research practice requires the investigator to respect the individual's freedom to discontinue participation at any time (Principle 5 of the American Psychological

Association's, 1973, *Ethical Principles in the Conduct of Research with Human Participants*), and since the teachers served as spokespeople for the participants, the study was terminated.

On the other hand, the research assistants were somewhat, but not seriously, alarmed by the children's behaviors. They had been prepared for most of these behaviors by training sessions in which the characteristics of autistic children had been discussed and observed on film. The research assistants, therefore, did not expect the children to act like normal children. Had the decision regarding termination of the study been theirs, they probably would not have assessed the situation to warrant termination.

Issues Raised by the Case Study

Several issues and questions were raised by the events of this study. First, who should determine whether participants are harmed? Second, how does one determine whether participants are harmed and if they are, how does one determine the degree of harm? Third, how does one determine reversibility of harm and what procedures might remove undesirable consequences to participants? Fourth, can the effects of crowding on autistic children or other vulnerable participants be ethically conducted in the laboratory setting while maintaining scientific validity and social relevance?

Who should determine if participants are harmed? Tanke and Tanke (Chapter 6, companion volume) pose the possibility that a caretaker in an institution for the emotionally retarded may not be the most effective guardian for this very population in conducting research. In our study, were the teachers the best people to determine whether the study should be terminated? After all, there were differences of opinion; the teachers and research assistants reacted somewhat differently to the events that occurred. The teachers knew the behaviors that were usual for each of the children. The researchers did not have this information and therefore could not assess how deviant the children's behaviors were compared to their "normal" behavior. On this criteria, the teachers were better able to determine whether harm had been imposed on the participants and were therefore more appropriate to serve as "participant advocates." At the same time, they may not have been able to weigh the scientific and social merits along with their concern for the participants. This is because the teachers had an emotional and professional investment in the participants' behavior and a vested interest in seeing these children behave as normally as possible. The degree to which these children displayed normal behavior was a reflection of their therapeutic effectiveness. While the teachers had been briefed on the importance of assessing the effects of environmental conditions and amount of space on children with problems, their commitment to the pursuit of scientific knowledge, even in the ultimate interest of children with developmental disabilities or disorders, was far less than their concern for the present well-being of the children.

In retrospect, perhaps we had not adequately prepared the teachers for the experiment. We had not discussed with them the possibility that autistic behaviors would be exaggerated in the crowded condition. In addition, we had not fully discussed the scientific and social significance of the research we were conducting so that they might objectively weigh the benefits and costs of the effects.

How does one determine whether participants are harmed? Could a determination of whether harm had been imposed have been made in a more objective way? Preparatory to the experiment, research assistants in collaboration with the teachers might have determined what the children's base-line behaviors were in their day center setting, a setting familiar to the children. Without base-line data the extent of harm or distress experienced by deviant population groups is best judged relative to their usual behaviors rather than by what is usual for normal populations.

What procedures, if any, remove undesirable consequences? How does one determine the degree of reversibility of the harm and what procedures might remove undesirable consequences to the participants? Ethical considerations require the investigator to remove undesirable consequences for the participant that result from research procedures (Principle 9 of the American Psychological Association's, 1973, *Ethical Principles in the Conduct of Research with Human Participants*), and debriefing often serves to undo such distress or harm.

Our past experience of observing normal children in various density conditions taught us that even though there were instances of distress or aggression in the play session, most of the children reportedly liked the play sessions. Furthermore, the debriefing activities (which consisted of individually talking with each child and serving them as much juice and crackers as they wanted) eliminated any residual feelings of distress or unhappiness for those few who evidenced these feelings after the play session. However, we had not discussed with the teachers what procedures would constitute effective and appropriate debriefing for autistic children. Our regular debriefing procedure may not have been suitable to the particular needs and characteristics of autistic children, particularly when in contact with a stranger. Thus, we might have discussed with the teachers what would have constituted appropriate debriefing procedures for these children and we might have conducted some pilot testing to determine the effectiveness of such debriefing procedures.

Prior to the experiment an assessment of what degree of deviation from base-line behaviors could be effectively removed by debriefing procedures might have been collaboratively done by the research assistants and the teachers, thereby reducing differences in the evaluation of the degree of harm imposed by the experimental procedure on the participants.

Can laboratory research on vulnerable participants be ethically conducted? Lastly, the experience forced a consideration of whether the study of the effects of crowding on vulnerable participants should be conducted in laboratory settings at all. It is possible that the preparatory debriefing and base-line behavior assessment procedures may not have been possible or would not have worked out. In such a case there may be no ethical way to study the effects of crowding on autistic children in a laboratory setting. Perhaps research on vulnerable participants can only be conducted in a natural setting where crowded conditions already exist and where crowding need not be artificially imposed by the investigator. Perhaps ethical considerations for the welfare of the participants limit the researcher who conducts laboratory research to the study of only *nonvulnerable* participants. If this is so, and the study of vulnerable populations is of greater applied relevance than the study of nonvulnerable participants, then the appropriate setting for research on crowding effects needs to be seriously reconsidered. In fact, the proper setting for studying the effects of crowding on vulnerable participants might by necessity be a natural setting.

If there is no natural setting in which a particular type of vulnerable participant can be found, then there is probably no necessity for such research because there is no real-life situation to which the results can be applied. If, however, there are natural settings of crowding where vulnerable participants reside, the researcher may have to relinquish the advantage of strong causal inferences obtainable from tightly controlled laboratory studies in order to study the phenomenon in the field and thereby avoid the ethical problems involved in studying the effects of crowding in a laboratory setting.

The dilemmas of scientific significance and scientific validity versus participant welfare occur primarily in laboratory research and occur less often in field or survey research. The condition of high density is introduced by the experimenter in laboratory research and any harmful consequences attributable to crowding must also be attributable to the experimenter. In field or survey research, any harmful consequences of crowding that exist are not attributable to research procedures.

In summary, the case study just described demonstrated two conditions that would facilitate determination of harm imposed on vulnerable participants, namely, through the use of "participant advocates" and a condition of noncaptivity for the participants. The case study also demonstrated two conditions in which an assessment of the risk and benefits of the research might be made: first, through a determination of base-line data for participant behaviors, and second, through a determination of the effects of a debriefing procedure designed specifically for the participants. The last issue addressed concerned the selection of the appropriate research setting in accordance with consideration of the applied relevance of the research and the ethical issues that make data collection or scientific validity difficult to obtain.

Ethnic Minority Groups in a Natural Setting: Research in Chinatown: A Case Study

The study of crowding in a natural setting poses different problems and issues in terms of ethical research and decision making. The study of crowding in a natural community setting often involves conducting survey research on ethnic minority populations since it is usually ethnic minority groups who live in crowded conditions. Moreover, the study of crowding in a community setting often involves consideration of, and sensitivity to community issues, since the community constitutes one unit of analysis for the study of crowding in the real world.

In this section, ethically sensitive procedures for conducting research on ethnic minority populations in a community setting will be presented. I will be drawing on a case study of research presently being conducted, an interview survey research study in San Francisco's Chinatown. San Francisco's Chinatown was selected as a community in which the effects of crowding could be studied because it represents the most crowded community in California and the second most crowded community in the United States, and because serious and controversial housing and city planning issues presently exist for this community.

The purposes of the Chinatown housing and health study are multiple. The independent variables cover background variables, situational variables, psychological variables, objective density/housing variables, and stress-illness variables. The dependent variables include the perception of community crowding, the perception of dwelling crowding, and dissatisfaction with the community and dwelling unit. The study will investigate which of the independent variables best explains each of the dependent variables. In addition, the relationship among the following variables will be analyzed: population density, within-dwelling density, perceptions of crowding, and stress-illness variables. We plan to interview a large sample of Chinese-American residents, randomly selected by households in Chinatown. An equal number of households will be sampled from the three areas of Chinatown (Core Chinatown, Residential Chinatown, and Expanded Chinatown); these areas differ from one another in their population density or in their degree of racial homogeneity. Core Chinatown is composed of 89% Chinese-Americans and its population density is 228.1 people per acre. Residential Chinatown is composed of 67% Chinese-Americans and its population density is 121.9 people per acre (about half the density of Core Chinatown). Expanded Chinatown is composed of 35% Chinese-Americans and its population density is 119.9 people per acre (*Chinatown 1970 Census: Population and Housing Summary and Analysis*, 1972). Expanded Chinatown's population density is essentially identical to that of Residential Chinatown but the number of Chinese-Americans in this area is nearly half that of Residential Chinatown.

Culturally Invalid Interpretations

"Social injury." When survey research on the effects of crowding is conducted on ethnic minority groups, ethically sensitive procedures must be used to prevent culturally invalid interpretations from being made which in turn may cause "social injury" to the ethnic minority group being studied or to other ethnic minority groups to whom the interpretations may be generalized. This relates directly to the issue of "social injury" that can result when conclusions are generalized inappropriately from one type of setting and one type of participant to other settings and types of participants. Invalid conclusions can cause "social injury" to those segments of the population for whom the conclusion may be invalid. Social injury can prevent a group of people from elevating their quality of life or it can prevent federal, state, or city officials from elevating the quality of life of persons living in crowded conditions. Attempts to improve living conditions are not likely to be made if it is believed that residents are satisfied with their existing conditions or if it is believed

that crowding is not stressful and not correlated with adverse consequences. If in fact crowding has negative consequences for some persons, then inappropriate generalizations are particularly serious for those whose lives are most distressed economically, socially, or because of race and who live in crowded conditions. Social injury of this nature is, in my mind, as unethical as imposing physical and psychological harm to research participants; it differs only in that its effect is more indirect and thus less conspicuously attributable to the investigator. In effect, I am arguing that research interpretations that lead to the prevention of needed improvements are as harmful as imposing distress on volunteering participants. When harm comes to nonvulnerable participants as a result of research procedures, the participants enter the study in a state of "no discomfort, harm, or danger" and the procedures lead to a state of "temporary or lasting discomfort, harm, or danger." However, some members of low-income, ethnic minority groups who live in crowded conditions may be living daily in a state of "temporary or lasting discomfort, harm, or danger." Research conclusions that have public policy consequences can potentially lead to either a maintenance, an exacerbation, or an amelioration of this state. Thus, scientific and cultural validity is essential for the welfare of people, but especially for those who are more oppressed.

Alternative Interpretations for Chinese-Americans

Invalid conclusions may result from instruments, measures, or questionnaire items that are not culturally relevant. Invalid conclusions may also result when interview responses are not understood within their cultural context. For example, if no relationship between crowding and measures of stress are found for Chinese-Americans, an interpretation that crowding has no negative effects for Chinese-Americans may be incorrect if conceptual and linguistic equivalency have not been achieved, or if the respondents' answers are not understood within the Chinese-American cultural context. I raise the issue of culturally valid interpretations because the literature (*American Institute of Planners Newsletter*, 1967; Anderson, 1972; Schmitt, 1963) suggests that Chinese do not find crowding stressful and, in fact, like crowded conditions. Since Anderson, an anthropologist, and Schmitt, a statistician, say they found no evidence of behavioral pathology in Hong Kong, they argue that crowding is not necessarily harmful to Chinese. Anderson (1972) maintained that for Hong Kong Chinese much of the crowding is voluntary and not forced, that noise is desirable or at worst ignored, and that solitude is not valued except for religious or meditational purposes. Schmitt (1963) claims that the successful tolerance of high densities and overcrowding stems from long-established Chinese traditions of affinity for close quarters, natural gregariousness, and family cohesiveness. He suggests that Americans redirect their values along the Chinese lines in order to better accommodate themselves to high density. The *American Institute of Planners Newsletter* (1967) quotes a construction supervisor who, when asked about the effects of doubling the floor area of low-cost apartments in Hong Kong, said "With 60 square feet per person, the tenants would sublet." The implication of the supervisor's reply is that Chinese either do not need more space, do not value or want more space, or can cope without much space. Robert Sommer (1969) uses this quote to demonstrate cultural differences in interpersonal distancing.

I do not feel that the type of anthropological approach used by Anderson nor the type of correlational analysis used by Schmitt (using aggregate data on crime rates) represent the most appropriate method of measuring Chinese attitudes toward crowding nor the consequences of crowding for Chinese. What's possibly wrong with their approaches and interpretations? Take for example a situation in which Hong Kong Chinese are asked "Would you want more privacy?" If Hong Kong Chinese said "No," this may not mean that they do not value or want solitude or privacy. The word "privacy" may be interpreted to imply "selfishness," in which case their response would be an unselfish one, namely, "No." Alternatively, Hong Kong Chinese may respond with "No" because they may have never experienced living conditions other than the crowded ones in which they live and are therefore unable to see more privacy as a realistic alternative or unable to conceptualize of what is outside their realm of experience (Woo and Seto, personal communication, 1977). In response to Schmitt's suggestion, it seems that if Americans have experienced spacious living and city conditions while Hong Kong Chinese have not, it may be impossible for Americans to redirect their values along Chinese lines to better accommodate themselves to high density. It may not be cultural values that differ; rather it may be differences in past experiences and perceived available choices that account for response differences between Hong Kong Chinese and white Americans. Questions about past living experiences and perceived alternative choices need to be determined to fully understand the meaning of responses dealing with density and privacy.

Furthermore, the response that Chinese tenants would prefer to sublet if offered twice as much space is also subject to interpretative question. Chinese traits of working toward long-term goals and the ability to delay gratification (Young, 1972) may not have been considered by those who conclude that Chinese do not want more space. An appropriate probe to the question that was asked of the supervisor would have been to inquire about Chinese motives for their preferences of rent over space. It is possible that Chinese would prefer to sublet in order to save money to move to a larger flat in a less crowded area (Ja, personal communication, 1977). In addition to saving for a larger flat, survival needs, financial debts, or familial responsibilities might also be reasons for the preference to sublet than to use the space. Having food or needing to care for relatives may be a higher priority than having more living space. Thus, a preference to sublet does not necessarily mean that Chinese do not feel stressed by crowding or do not want more space. It may simply mean that the need for space is a lower priority than certain survival or familial needs.

Lastly, it should be noted that no researcher has directly surveyed Chinese respondents about their attitudes toward crowding, whether they find crowding desirable or undesirable, and their opinions regarding the effects of crowding. Conclusions and generalizations have been made from indirect measures and from observations by outsiders. In the case of perceptions and attitudes on crowding and the need for privacy, interpretations are most likely to be valid when observations are checked by asking about the issues in question and when conclusions are checked for accuracy with members of the studied population. I am open to the possibility that crowding may not have negative effects or may not be disliked, but I would like to know that such conclusions are derived from culturally valid measures and that the opinions of Chinese were obtained.

Procedures for Participant Welfare

The ethical principles of the American Psychological Association state that psychologists must carry out their investigations "with respect for the people who participate and with concern for their dignity and welfare" (American Psychological Association, 1973, p. 1). In this section of the chapter I will consider procedures for participant welfare. Where appropriate, examples will be taken from the survey of Chinese-American residents of Chinatown that is currently being developed. Three topics will be covered: first, accommodations to the character, circumstances, and needs of the community; second, approaches that provide benefits to the participant and the community; and third, approaches that minimize feelings of powerlessness or embarrassment for the participant.

Accommodations to the Nature, Circumstances, and Needs of the Community

Accommodations to the nature, circumstances, and needs of the community include two topics: first, addressing potential problems of conducting research in that community, and second, determining community attitudes towards the variables to be investigated.

Addressing problems involved in conducting research in the community. In developing survey research on crowding, housing, health, and stress in San Francisco's Chinatown there were many historical, cultural and situational factors that posed possible difficulties for data collection, respondent accessibility, or respondent cooperation. First, no large-scale survey research had ever been conducted in Chinatown other than the U.S. Census. Second, many Chinatown residents are thought to distrust white Americans and white-dominated institutions due to fears of anti-Chinese discrimination, inability or difficulty in conversing in English, or fear of deportation.[4] Third, due to low wages, many Chinatown residents work long and unconventional hours. Husbands and wives whose working hours do not coincide may only see each other a few hours in a day. If both parents work in the late afternoon and night, children may rarely see one or both of their parents upon returning home from school. Fourth, in September of 1977 a gang-style murder at the Golden

---

[4] To circumvent white racist immigration laws that singled out the Chinese for systematic exclusion (1882-1943), many Chinese laborers entered the country through illegal channels. Since the turn of the century, a constant fear of deportation has existed in American Chinatowns, borne of a history of unannounced raids and arrests without warrants by Immigration Service officials or local policy looking for illegal aliens and leftist leaders. (Ben Tong, personal communication.)

Dragon Restaurant, which killed five and wounded 11, caused tension among Chinatown residents and even among some of the interviewers. All four of these conditions posed potential problems for the interviewers and the researcher in terms of respondent accessibility, cooperation, and data validity.

In our plans to try to accommodate the study to these potential problems we made several decisions. First, we decided to try to cover as many hours as possible for interviewing times to accommodate respondents with unconventional working hours. Interviewers were also prepared to work cooperatively, transferring assigned respondents should their available time or the Chinese dialect of the respondent be better matched by another interviewer.

Second, we recognized that survey research in a community can be beset with setbacks and delays, and that the interviewing phase of the research must be appropriate to the events and circumstances of the community. In this case, interviewing immediately after the murders would not have been appropriate and may well have resulted in a high refusal rate. The timetable of the pretesting phase of the research was slowed down until the fear born of the murders dissipated. If a researcher is obsessed with meeting rigid deadlines to the extent that community circumstances are not taken into account, a disservice may be done to the research, the interviewers, and the community.

Third, we matched the race and culture of the interviewer to the respondent, for purposes of scientific and cultural validity. Ethnic minority members may be less likely to trust or be self-disclosing to an interviewer who is a non-Chinese-American and an outsider. The motives of the researcher may be suspect and there may be concern that the results, if not correctly interpreted, may be damaging to the community or to the image of the ethnic minority group.

Several research studies suggest that scientific validity is sacrificed when a white interviewer interviews a black respondent. Williams (1964) found differences between responses of blacks to threatening questions as a function of whether the interviewer was black or white. He states that some of the differences were large enough to indicate that serious errors in interpretation would be made by researchers using these data for substantive interpretations of black attitudes. Williams goes further to assume that greater response bias occurs in situations of greater social distance between respondent and interviewer. Katz, Robinson, Epps, and Waly (1964) found that hostile impulses aroused by test instructions were expressed to black testers by black respondents but repressed with white testers. Clark (1965) reports that traditional standardized questionnaires and interview responses resulted in superficial verbal responses or evasions from Harlem respondents who found the procedure pretentious. Thus, a black respondent is likely to respond in a cursory, unelaborated fashion, expressing neither active resistance nor friendly openness to a white interviewer, and the interviewer who does not interpret such behavior correctly may misinterpret the respondent's attitude, incorrectly assume response validity and be unaware that the respondent may either feel exploited or intimidated.

No research has been conducted on the effects of race of interviewer on Chinese-Americans. While we must be careful not to generalize from one ethnic group to another, it is likely that an interviewer who is a non-Asian-American is at a disadvantage compared to a Chinese-American when it comes to interviewing Chinatown residents, particularly immigrants. Chinatown residents may project characteristics of power onto a white interviewer, consequently the interviewer may be perceived as intimidating to some and exploitive to others. At the same time, however, a non-Chinese-American interviewer may provide the participant with a sense of anonymity. The first effect would be negative in terms of rapport and comfort, the second may be positive in the sense of confidentiality.

In our study, interviewers served as consultants as well as interviewers. Selecting interviewers whom Chinatown residents could trust meant that the interviewers could collect important feedback regarding questionnaire design and format, interview procedures, linguistic equivalency problems, and culturally relevant questions during the pretest phases of the research. Interviewers of the same race and culture of the respondents were selected through role-playing interviews. These interviewers were bicultural (most were born and raised in Hong Kong and had lived in the United States for around 7 years), and bilingual. We sought interviewers who would relate comfortably with persons of the socioeconomic, cultural, and age background of the majority of the potential respondents. Selecting interviewers with the language skill that is required is often an appropriate way to select for cultural similarities since language and experience are frequently closely related.

It has been mentioned that minority group members may feel that research participation might increase their vulnerability, a situation that should be minimized as much as possible by researchers (Kelman, 1972). According to Kelman, establishing a sense of anonymity for the respondent minimizes a feeling of vulnerability, thereby strengthening the relationship between the researcher and the ethnic community and strengthening the research endeavor. Applying this to the Chinatown study, it may be easier for a Chinatown respondent to reveal "socially embarrassing" information such as marital discord, mental illness, or a son involved in youth gangs to a Chinese-American interviewer not connected to the social and familial network of the Chinatown community. Thus, in deciding between interviewers who are insiders versus interviewers from outside the community, a sense of anonymity is probably more easily obtained by using interviewers from other communities. Rapport, however, should not be sacrificed for anonymity, and someone from the same community is more likely to have similar experiences and similar world views as the respondent than is an interviewer from outside the community. I have no data on the effect that the interviewers' community of residence plays in establishing rapport and a sense of anonymity, but nevertheless these factors should be considered in survey research in ethnic minority communities.

Determining community attitudes toward the investigated variables. When behavioral pathologies, community problems, personality, or social characteristics of an ethnic minority population are studied, sensitivity to how the data will be used is extremely important. Equally important is determining the community's attitudes toward the variables and procedures to be used in the study. Responses to the study of community problems, psychological or social problems, or personality variables may differ as a function of the individual community, the researcher, and the relationship of the researcher to the community. Understanding the sociopolitical and sociopsychological situation of the population being studied is necessary, as has been pointed out by Warwick and Lininger (1975).

Some persons or communities may feel strongly that such research is needed for the community and that its findings can be useful to the community. Positive attitudes toward such research are likely when members of the community believe that community problems have not been acknowledged or addressed by city, state, and federal agencies and that the larger society has not adequately provided the community with the services, manpower, assistance, or political voice it needs to deal with problems of crime, unemployment, immigration, housing, and stress. Positive attitudes toward research on problems are also more likely when the researchers' perspective or social concern are similar to those of the community.

On the other hand, a minority community is likely to feel negatively predisposed to research on community problems or personality variables if there is reason to believe that data collected on pathology would be used to "blame the victim" or to create damaging consequences to the minority group (Ryan, 1971; Kelman, 1972). Some writers have suggested that research on ethnic minorities should not have a psychological or characterological focus but rather be a study of the situations that impinge on the population (Noblit & Burcart, 1975) or a study of the failure of societal institutions to relate effectively to members of minority groups (Guzman, 1967). Josephson (1970) even cautions against researching any deviant behavior in slums on the grounds that minority communities fear that researchers intend to show how much more "deviant" or "pathological" the ghetto is than other communities. However, the needs and attitudes of ethnic minority communities probably differ. Furthermore, these attitudes will be a function of (1) the researcher's purposes, procedures, attitudes, and relationship to the community, (2) the community's past experiences with research, and (3) the needs of the community and attitudes of the community toward the variables to be studied, the intended outcomes of the study, and the researcher. Lastly, it should be noted that an ethnic minority community like Chinatown does not always "speak with one voice." Attitudes will vary among differing segments of that community, as has been alluded to by Light and Wong (1975).

Assessing and providing benefits to participants and the community. Tanke and Tanke (Chapter 6, other volume) mention that the benefits that accrue from research are usually to the academic discipline through the accumulation of basic knowledge or to society in general, through the practical application of research findings. But benefits need to be considered in a broader way. It is my feeling that benefits to the participant for research participation or as a result of participation have been given little attention. Warwick and Lininger (1975) have warned survey researchers to provide some form or compensation or a more equitable distribution of benefit to survey participants of another culture. Although this statement addresses the issue I now raise, I still find the literature lacking in giving serious consideration to various benefits or remunerations for particular populations.

In laboratory research conducted on undergraduate students, the usual incentive and benefits include course credit, money, or the experience of participating in research. In survey research, the possible benefits can be either abstract or concrete, long-term or immediate, and uncertain or guaranteed. In the Chinatown survey, several possible benefits were considered: they included (1) scientific understanding, (2) social action, (3) short-term companionship, (4) money, (5) data and findings of use to community agencies, and (6) a resource booklet, which contains information about agencies and services available to the participants specialized to their interests, needs, and background.

The pursuit of scientific knowledge in and of itself is probably of little value to most ethnic minority participants other than those who have an intellectual curiosity, with or without an interest in the applied value of such information. The following explanation appeals to knowledge as a potential benefit: "We are conducting this study in order to understand the effect of housing and community conditions on people in Chinatown." Chinatown residents who feel they already understand the variables being studied may see no reason to research or document what to them may be obvious. However, most members of the Chinatown community may feel they understand the problems but feel the importance of documenting these problems, in which case, participation in the study may be meaningful to them.

The value of potential social action or public policy change as an outcome benefit will depend on the degree to which the participant is concerned about the community and the degree to which the participant believes in the effectiveness of social action or the usefulness of research data to create change. As a benefit, social action or policy change is a collective benefit rather than a personal one, and the benefit is conditional since it depends on as yet unknown research findings. The following explanation appeals to social action as a potential benefit of research participation: "We are concerned about the housing and health conditions in Chinatown. The results of our study could lead to constructive improvements for this community."

Interview survey research can serve as short-term companionship to some participants. In the Chinatown study it is most likely that this benefit would serve those elderly who are socially isolated and who would enjoy the company of a younger and interested person inquiring about past experiences and opinions. This benefit is immediate in nature and is largely a function of the qualities of the interviewer as an interested listener.

Monetary remuneration, like other possible benefits to the participants, needs to be assessed in terms of its meaning and value to participants. In the Chinatown study, when comparing money to other possible remunerations such as food or household items, money seemed to be most applicable across differing age, sex, and marital status positions of the potential participants. Even though the money was not necessarily the motive for participation, we expected that most participants would react positively to an offer of monetary remuneration for their time and cooperation. However, one participant in a pretest interview caused us to question our assumption that money would serve as a benefit for all participants. At the close of the interview this participant was given $10, in keeping with the interviewer's promise at the beginning of the interview. When given the money, the respondent reacted negatively, a reaction at variance with her consistently cooperative manner throughout the interview. Apparently, this participant's motives for cooperation included hospitality and friendship. Money implied a business or contractual relationship to her, which altered or negated her original intentions. From this experience we decided to give each respondent a Resource Book with the option of receiving money instead.

If the researcher conducts the study in a manner that involves some collaboration with community agencies, coalitions, or members of such groups and if one of the researcher's purposes is to provide community agencies with data, then providing results to community agencies in a form that they can use and comprehend is an additional possible benefit from research. In our study, contacts with various community agencies and centers have and are being made to determine common areas of interest for inquiry and to determine what variables or questions contained in the study would be of interest to these groups. While nothing has been published about providing specific information to community agencies of research findings relevant to their service delivery or understanding of the community, much has been written to encourage fuller collaboration between the researcher and the community (Cowen, Lorion, & Dorr, 1974; Guzman, 1967; Josephson, 1970; Kelman, 1972; Noblit & Burcart, 1975; Price & Cherniss, 1977; Tyler, 1973).

Since each interviewer will inquire about housing, stress, health, and the family in this study, we decided to expand the role of the interviewer slightly to include that of service referral and information that might be of practical use to the participant. To this end, we compiled a bilingual Resource Booklet for Chinatown residents. The booklet provides information on services on the community, city, state, and federal levels that serve the areas of child care, mental health, health, income maintenance or benefits, legal assistance, employment assistance or job training, housing, recreation, and supplementary education. Most other already existing pamphlets are for agency use and not for resident use. The Resource Booklet will be left with every participant at the close of the interview with the following description: "This resource booklet was compiled and written for people who are interviewed, to provide some useful information about services or procedures in the event that you, a friend or relative may need it at some future time".

It was anticipated that the Resource Booklet would address needs that may arise in the interview process or that the booklet might answer questions a participant might ask during the interview process. For example, if in the process of inquiring about stress, the participant expresses the need for mental health support services, the booklet describes services that would deal with emotional stress and problems. If in the process of being interviewed about the dwelling unit, the participant wonders whether there is any assistance or legal recourse to deal with housing discrimination or unsanitary health conditions, the booklet provides the available departments and procedures that handle this problem.

As a result of strict ethical standards, some researchers have avoided asking "sensitive" questions for fear of causing distress to participants. However, if information is provided for services that can alleviate participant problems, more good can result by studying topics that touch peoples' lives than by avoiding these topics altogether. Benefits to the participants, then, can be made relevant to the variables and purposes of the study itself.

In summary, several types of benefits to participants have been discussed, with examples from our study of crowding in Chinatown. This list of benefits is by no means exhaustive. The intention of the present consideration was to point out that ethical procedures and concerns for the welfare and dignity of participants should include sensitivity to and consideration of what would serve as a benefit to the participant.

Minimizing Feelings of Powerlessness or Embarrassment for the Participant

Kelman (1972) has suggested that the researcher take precautions to counteract the powerlessness of vulnerable participants who serve as research participants. If we assume that the survey participants may be vulnerable by virtue of their ethnicity, age, life circumstances, or by virtue of having fewer choices or opportunities in their lives, we need to consider procedures that will reduce feelings of powerlessness or embarrassment for the participants in the Chinatown study.

First, the Resource Booklet is one procedure for handling possible sensitive thoughts and events that may arise in the process of the interview and may provide hope to the participant that such questions or problems can be assisted through appropriate services and agencies. Second, sensitive procedures should be used that are appropriate to the characteristics of the participants. Take the determination of income, for example. The normal survey procedure for determining individual and family income is to show the participant a flashcard with choices of ranges of income. It is generally held that the flashcard procedure provides more valid responses than asking for income directly. However, the income level of Chinatown residents is low; in 1969 there were twice as many families who made "$6,000 and less" in Core and Residential Chinatown than there were in San Francisco and the largest percentage of residents in these Chinatown areas were in the family income bracket of "$3,999 or less." Knowing this, I wondered whether the flashcard of ranges might cause embarrassment to the Chinatown participants, since the participant would see how low his or her income was compared to the standard income ranges. The ethical dilemma of scientific validity versus participant welfare is raised by this question. One possible solution (True & Tong, personal communication, 1978) involves eliminating the higher income ranges from the flashcard (i.e., "$12,000 or over"), showing the full flashcard to those who say their income is that of the highest category (i.e., "$10,000 or more"), and lowering of the lowest limit of income ranges. This could serve to increase validity by providing greater variance while reducing feelings of embarrassment.

Minimization of powerlessness can be dealt with through selecting interviewers and using semantics, contents and wording of the questionnaire, and procedures of interviewing that convey a respectful and cooperative relationship with the participants. Lastly, any possibilities that questions, procedures, or formats might cause embarrassment or feelings of powerlessness to participants should be investigated through consultation or pretesting. An example of an erroneous assumption on my part concerned questions on specific health ailments taken from the Cornell Health Index. My fear was that a nonmedical person in a nonmedical setting asking personal questions about health ailments may cause embarrassment to participants. Contrary to my expectation, the elderly men who were interviewed in the pretest phase expressed enjoyment over the specific health questions; it made them feel as though someone cared about them.

In summary, consideration needs to be given to procedures that minimize or eliminate potential feelings of powerlessness and embarrassment. Any questions concerning what will or will not create such feelings should, whenever possible, be answered through consultation or through pretesting.

Conclusion

In this chapter ethical dilemmas of conducting research on crowding and its effects on human behavior have been discussed. These dilemmas arise in other areas of social science research as well, particularly research on stressors. The major dilemma raised involves situations of conflict between the researcher's responsibility to society and the responsibility to the participants' welfare. Responsibility to society means that scientifically valid research on socially relevant problems should be conducted. However, laboratory research on crowding may make it impossible to achieve ethical treatment of participants and scientifically valid findings of much useful generalizability. Cultural and scientific validity are ethical issues, since *social injury* may result from the dissemination or application of invalid findings. Social injury results when inappropriate and untested generalizations are made from nonvulnerable participants to vulnerable participants, or from laboratory settings to natural settings, thereby causing harm to a group of people. Social injury may also be a consequence of not using culturally sensitive measures or not making culturally appropriate interpretations. The importance of researching the effects of stressors, such as crowding, on vulnerable participants was discussed with the attendant ethical problem of conducting research on such a population in a laboratory setting.

For both the laboratory and the natural setting, procedures for participant welfare were suggested; these included the use of "participant advocates," debriefing procedures that are specialized to the participants, assessing the effectiveness of debriefing procedures in removing imposed discomfort, assessing the degree of imposed harm on participants, assessing the appropriate setting for ethical and valid research, accommodating the circumstances and needs of the community by addressing problems involved in conducting research in the community and determining community attitudes toward the investigated variables, assessing and providing benefits to the participants and community, and minimizing feelings of powerlessness or embarrassment for participants. Particular issues were raised for the case study of laboratory research on autistic children and for survey research in ethnic minority communities, in this case, Chinatown. At the same time similar themes of ethically valid research procedures and interpretations ran throughout both topic areas.

Researchers should be encouraged to develop sensitive procedures and appropriate methods in appropriate settings for particular problem areas of research and for particular populations. Support for such endeavors should also be encouraged. If

West and Gunn (1978) are correct in stating that there is a current shift toward the investigation of neutral or positive aspects of human behavior in order to avoid having to deal with tightening ethical standards for research, the answer is not to avoid conducting research on difficult or sensitive areas. To avoid conducting research on problem areas would incur on us the wrath of U.S. Senator William Proxmire, who from all evidence opposes federal funding of studies concerned with positive behaviors on the grounds of scientific frivolity and federal funding waste. To avoid conducting research on problem areas would also preclude any gains to society that may result from research on critical problems. The solution lies in conducting scientifically valid research using procedures that are sensitive to the populations studied, conducting research in a setting that is appropriate to the variables studied and to the populations most likely to be affected by the research findings. The struggle to be accountable to society, to vulnerable segments of society, and to the welfare of participants is a difficult one when conducting research on stressor variables, but there are solutions or approaches which make this task less insurmountable.

Acknowledgments. The Chinatown survey was funded by a research grant MH 25522 from the Center for the Study of Developmental Problems and is currently funded by the Center for the Study of Metropolitan Problems of the National Institute of Mental Health. The author wishes to give special thanks to Laurie Kiguchi for her constant support and help. The author also wishes to thank the following people for their editing assistance: Joan E. Sieber, Carols Arce, and Ben Tong; and the following people for their involvement in the Chinatown Pretest: Davis Ja, Tony Lam, David Tong, and Kam Wong.

References

American Institute of Planners Newsletter, January 1967, pp. 2-3.

American Psychological Association, *Ethical principles in the conduct of research with human participants.* Washington, D.C.: American Psychological Association, 1973.

Anderson, E. N. Some Chinese methods of dealing with crowding. *Urban Anthropology*, 1972, *1*, 143-150.

Bartz, W. While psychologists doze on. *American Psychologist*, 1970, *25* 500-503.

Calhoun, J. Population density and social pathology. *Scientific American*, 1962, *206*, 139-148.

Chinatown 1970 census: Population and housing summary and analysis. Prepared by the San Francisco Department of City Planning, August 1972.

Clark, K. *Dark ghetto: Dilemmas of social power.* New York: Harper & Row, 1965.

Cowen, E. L., Lorion, R. P., & Dorr, D. Research in the community cauldron: A case history. *The Canadian Psychologist*, 1974, *15*, 313-325.

Craik, K. Environmental psychology. In *New directions in psychology* (Vol. 4). New York: Hold, Rinehart and Winston, 1970.

Fawcett, J. *Psychology and population.* New Haven, Conn.: The Population Council, 1970.

Guzman, R. Ethics in federally subsidized research—The case of the Mexican American. In Inter-Agency Committee on Mexican American Affairs, 1967. *The Mexican-American: A new focus on opportunity*, Testimony presented at the Cabinet Committee Hearing on Mexican American Affairs, El Paso, Texas, October 26-28, 1967, Washington, D.C., pp. 245-249.

Hutt, C., & Vaizey, J. Differential effects of group density on social behavior. *Nature*, 1966, *209*, 1371-1372.

Josephson, E. Resistance to community surveys. *Social Problems*, 1970, *18*, 117-129.

Katz, I., Robinson, J. M., Epps, E. G., & Waly, P. The influence of race of the experimenter and instructions upon the expression of hostility by Negro boys. *Journal of Social Issues*, 1964, *20*, 54-59.

Kelman, H. C. The rights of the subject in social research: An analysis in terms of relative power and legitimacy. *American Psychologist*, 1972, *27*, 989-1016.

Light, I., & Wong, C. Protest or work: Dilemmas of the tourist industry in American Chinatowns. *American Journal of Sociology*, 1975, *80*, 1342-1368.

Loo, C. Issues of crowding research, vulnerable participants, assessing perceptions, and developmental differences. *Journal of Population*, 1978, *1*, 336-348. (a)

Loo, C. Behavior problem indices: The differential effects of spatial density on low and high scorers. *Environment and Behavior*, 1978, *10*, 489-509. (b)

Noblit, G. W., & Burcart, J. M. Ethics, powerless peoples, and methodologist for the study of trouble. *Humboldt Journal of Social Relations*, 1975, *2*, 20-25.

Price, R. H., & Cherniss, C. Training for a new profession: Research as social action. *Professional Psychology*, 1977, *8*, 222-231.

Ryan, W. *Blaming the victim.* New York: Pantheon, 1971.

Schmitt, R. C. Implications of density in Hong Kong. *American Institute of Planners Journal*, 1963, *29*, 210-217.

Sommer, R. *Personal space.* Englewood Cliffs, N.J.: Prentice-Hall, 1969.

Tyler, L. E. Design for a hopeful psychology. *American Psychologist*, 1973, *28*, 1021-1029.

Warwick, D. P., & Lininger, C. A. *The sample survey: Theory and practice.* New York: McGraw-Hill, 1975.

West, S. G., & Gunn, S. P. Some issues of ethics and social psychology. *American Psychologist*, 1978, *33*, 30-38.

Williams, J. A., Jr. Interviewer-respondent interaction: A study of bias in the information interview. *Sociometry*, 1964, *27*, 338-352.

Wohlwill, J. The emerging discipline of environmental psychology. *American Psychologist*, 1970, *25*, 303-312.

Young, N. Changes in values and strategies among Chinese in Hawaii. *Sociology and Social Research*, 1972, *56*, 228-241.

Chapter 6

Old People Are Not All Alike: Social Class, Ethnicity/Race, and Sex Are Bases for Important Differences

Eleanor K. Levine

Ethical decision making in the social sciences occurs at various levels. The issues we usually consider when thinking about the ethics of social science research deal with questions that arise after the research problem has been defined and the basic methodology developed. However, ethics is also involved in evaluating the underlying premises of social science research. In this chapter, I have chosen to look at ethical premises underlying research on aging. It is hoped that this endeavor will both complement the approaches to ethical decision making employed in the other chapters of this book, and reveal a few ethical problems that do not usually come to light.

The Role of Ethnicity/Race, Social Class and Sex in the Research Literature on Aging: A Study of the Journal of Gerontology

In the professional literature on aging, there is a contradiction between the intent of research—discovery of truths which eventually will assist persons in their journey to and through older adulthood—and the methods used to accomplish this. Social scientists have acknowledged that the rapidly increasing population of older adults is a unique group, possibly requiring special study, attention, and services. But then they use investigative methods that deny the uniqueness of the elderly. Older people are unique not just because they have logged more years since birth, but also because they share a unique combination of demographic characteristics and historical experiences. For example, as compared to the current population of younger adults, this population contains a greater proportion of people with less formal education who have historically different values and work histories. Furthermore, within this group, women greatly outnumber men, Caucasians are disproportionately represented relative to minorities, and there is a correspondingly disproportionate representation of the relatively affluent.[1] These unique characteristics continue to be discarded in research on aging because the paradigm we use ignores them, treating them as though they were extraneous or annoying sources of variability. To the degree that this paradigm distorts the character of the people's lives and to the degree that such distortions result in injustice, the use of this paradigm constitutes an ethical problem.

> Much social science research documents that an individual's beliefs, values, attitudes and behaviors vary according to his or her position in the social structure. Three primary social status locations, or what can be called stratum variables, persistently explain the greatest amount of variation in the attitudes and behaviors of individuals: sex, social class (or socioeconomic status) and ethnicity (racial or national origin group). These stratum variables represent in a short-hand fashion a summary of the life experiences that an individual is likely to encounter by virtue of . . . membership in one social category or another. (Bengston, Kasschau, & Ragan, 1977, p. 331)

If these stratum variables are ignored, we are left with the assumption that all old people are alike because of their chronological age. This erroneous assumption pervades the social science literature on gerontology.

Several years ago, when I became interested in researching perceptual/cognitive change in older people, I tried to construct a grid that might allow me to examine developmental change in relation to factors such as living situation (home versus institution), health, sex, ethnicity/race, and social economic class as indexed by educational level, current or past work status, income, etc. By constructing such a grid, I had hoped to learn how some of these factors correlate with perceptual cognitive change. Specifically, I had hoped to develop some way to determine what, besides chronological age, the common denominator for all older people, might help us to understand development and change.

My efforts resulted in a grid with far more empty than filled cells. That is, the requisite information about living situation, health, sex, ethnicity/race, and socioeconomic was rarely mentioned in the literature on gerontology. When these were mentioned, it was only because those were characteristics of special interest to that

---

[1] The following are some relevant age characteristics of the American population as of 1975:

	Percent 18 to 64	Percent 65+
Men	48	41
Women	52	59
White	83	90
Ethnic/racial minorities	17	10
Not high school graduate	26	63
High school graduate	59	30
College graduate	15	7

Note. Data based on Harris Poll 1975.

particular researcher. It is instructive to look at some representation of this survey. Singled out are the data from nine recent consecutive issues of the *Journal of Gerontology*. What follows is a summary of titles, methods, and results on articles appearing in these nine issues.

Consider first a sampling of actual titles. The following are titles to research papers published in the last fifteen months of the *Journal of Gerontology*, the official publication of the Gerontological Society.[2]

Incentive and practice in the psychomotor performance of the elderly. Grant, E. A., Storandt, M., & Botwinick, J. 1978, *33*, No. 3, pp. 413-415.

Survival after early and normal retirement. James, S. G., McMichael, A. G., & Tyroler, H. A., 1978, *33*, No. 2, pp. 269-278.

Dermatoglyphics and aging. Plato, C. C., 1978, *33*, No. 1, pp. 31-33.

Personality and physiological traits in middle-aged runners and joggers. Hartung, G. H., & Farge, E. J., 1977, *32*, No. 5, pp. 541-548.

Subjective adaptation to loss of the work role: A longitudinal study. George, L. K., & Maddox, X. Z., 1977, *32*, No. 4, pp. 456-462.

Foster placement for the older psychiatric patient. Linn, M. W., & Caffrey, E. M., Jr., 1977, *32*, No. 3, pp. 340-345.

All of these titles prepare the reader to expect general information about aging and the elderly. But, further inspection proves this expectation false. Although not explicitly stated, each article is concerned with a restricted subpopulation of aged subjects. In each instance, the researchers have examined the behavior of only *one* sex, six studied only men and one studied only women. Furthermore, although most of the articles focus on just one race or social class, none says that it refers only to Caucasians or only to middle class or well-educated elderly.[3] Thus, titles are revealing: by noting what information they include and what they exclude, it is possible to discover a research discipline's hidden assumptions and biases.

What's in a Title?

A more detailed content analysis of all article titles found within the past fifteen months of the *Journal of Gerontology* reveals the following: Every article found in Volume 32 (Nos. 1-6) and in Volume 33 (Nos. 1-3) using nonhuman subjects or institutionalized subjects has in its titles reference to the species, e.g., rat, or reference to the residential status of the aged human participants, e.g., institutionalized elderly. However, when the rest of the titles in these same issues are examined, we find that 8% mention that the study was restricted to males, where appropriate, while 80% mentioned that the study was restricted to females, where appropriate.

---

[2] All articles appearing in the *Journal of Gerontology* between January and June 1978 were reviewed. The ones shown are a representative sample titles of papers on human aged subjects.

[3] Valid generalizations about the elderly will be possible only when research reports include specific information about subject selection criteria. However, to simply report the subject selection criteria used by no means vindicates the practice of studying one group only.

When the focus was on sex differences, 100% mentioned this in the title, and all three articles that focused on ethnicity/race mentioned this in their titles. Apparently, rats, the institutionalized, women, and ethnic minorities are unusual enough to require special mention.[4]

The systematic inclusion or exclusion of certain information about sex, ethnicity/race, and social economic class from these journal titles indicates the prevailing research ideology in the field of aging. It is an ideology whose basic assumption is that Caucasian male adult behavior is normative; all else is exceptional or deviant. Thus, it is deemed necessary to mention sex, ethnicity/race, and social economic class when the sample is restricted to women, particular ethnic groups, or when there is a specific focus on sex or ethnic patterns in aging.

What Research Articles Fail to Tell

An examination of the full text of all articles found in these same nine issues of the *Journal of Gerontology* demonstrates the overwhelming absence of information about the social context of the research setting in which the aged subjects participated. It suggests that the social context of the research and of the participating subjects is irrelevant.

A content analysis of the full text of all 95 articles using human subjects shows that the actual research findings refute their own underlying assumptions about the irrelevance of social context. All 95 articles were examined to determine what information about social context was reported. All 95 were scrutinized for the following information:

Subjects: Was information given about the subjects' sex, race/ethnicity, or social economic class?

Investigator: Was information given about the investigator's sex, ethnicity/race, social economic class, or age?

Data Analysis: Were data inspected for sex, ethnicity/race, or social economic class differences or patterns?

Results: Given the appropriate data analysis, were there significant sex, ethnic/race, or social economic class differences or patterns?

When summarized, the content analysis indicated the following demographic data:

Subjects: 85% of the articles provide information about the sex of the participating subjects; 18% indicate the ethnicity/race of subjects; 40% indicate information about the social economic class of subjects. (A very broad criterion was employed in this content analysis: mention of income, occupation, educational level, or the simple assertion of class standing was accepted as a statement of the subjects' class position.)

---

[4] In reality, it is the group of older white men that is unusual. Older women outnumber older men; if we add the number of older minority men, the older white male becomes even less representative. Also, see footnote 1 for demographic characteristics of those 65 years and older.

Investigator: 4% of the articles provide information about the characteristics of the investigators who had direct contact with the subjects.

Data Analysis: 32% analyzed the data for sex differences; 7% analyzed the data for ethnic/race differences; 14% analyzed the data for social economic class differences.

Results: When results were examined the following were noted. Sex: Of the studies in which the data were inspected for sex differences, 64% found them to be a statistically significant variable. (In the one study where sex of interviewer was reported and its effect examined, the interaction was very highly significant.) Ethnicity/Race: Of the 7% of articles in which the data were inspected for ethnic differences or patterns, 86% found ethnicity to be a statistically significant variable.

Overall, the content analysis suggests that sex, social class, and ethnicity/race are virtually ignored in research on the aged. This is unfortunate, for as the survey indicates, these variables often account for a significant proportion of the variability.

In conclusion, these analyses of titles, methods, and results indicate that there is clear bias in the research methods for studying older people. These methods are biased toward treating sex, social economic class, and ethnicity/race as curious sources of variability representing deviations from some true abstract form of older adult behavior, whose standard is the white entrepreneurial male.

Sex, Socioeconomic Class, and Ethnicity/Race Are Not Variations on a Theme, but Are the Themes Themselves

> The aged do not constitute a homogeneous population; in many ways, the old as a group appear to be more varied than younger age strata. Aging does not eradicate sex, race and class distinctions; rather it adds another dimension of social differentiation to the distinctions in middle age. (Bengston, Kasschau, & Ragan, 1977, p. 331)

While on sabbatical for the 1977-78 academic year, I had an opportunity to work at a number of community senior centers. I kept a written log of events, interactions, conversations, and impressions. I have drawn on three examples from the log to illustrate how employing a different paradigm that acknowledges the social realities of aging results in an alternative view of why older people do what they do. Each example is supported by formal data where available.

Informal observations are reported first, since they seem to capture the flavor of the kinds of behavior many of us usually associate with the aged. Often, their misinterpretation provides the intuitive basis for drawing inappropriate causal relationships between chronological age and ability, and for perpetuating stereotypes of the old.

In discussing these observations, both informal and formal, an effort is made to sort out social context from chronological age in accounting for the behavior of old people. In each case it will be shown that it is social class, ethnicity/race, or sex, and not age, that is responsible for the way people act. This is not to say that there are no changes in behavior caused by aging or the processes involved in aging; it is just that these are often not the primary causes of the behavior of older people.

Ranking and Rating

While attempting to assist the county government in assessing the needs of the elderly living in different areas of our county, I distributed a questionnaire to two separate groups of older people gathered together for a weekly discussion session. Although the instructions were on each questionnaire, I repeated them and explained them to make sure they were understood. Each respondent was asked to indicate, by a ranking method, what each perceived to be the most to the least pressing need. The questionnaire instructions read:

> Below we have listed some of the major problem areas that concern and affect the lives of the elderly. Would you list them according to their importance for the older people in your area? (Place #1 along side the most important item and on down to #13 along side the least important.

Four sample items were
Lack of individual and public safety;
Inadequate nutrition;
Lack of adequate housing;
Lack of adequate transportation.

The task was a fairly straightforward one, or so I thought. Since it is the sort of task that I, my colleagues, and our students perform fairly frequently, I thought nothing of it.

Here is what happened. After I had filled out the form myself, I looked around at the others. Much to my surprise, about half the group was finished. Out of curiosity, I glanced at their forms and discovered that approximately half of the participants had assigned the rank of "1" to all or many of the items on the list. After attempting to reinstruct the respondents about the nature of ranking, I began to understand that their strategy actually made as much, if not more, sense than mine. These respondents very clearly stated that all the problems rated "1" were important to them as elderly persons and that they couldn't or wouldn't assign them different rank values. Yes, they did know how to rank order items, but they refused to do so here. Furthermore, they were unwilling to assign a rank of any kind to those items about which they felt unqualified to comment.

In administering the instrument to a second group of older persons, another strategy of the elderly emerged. Now, a number of respondents refused to write anything on the form. Although the forms were anonymous from the county's perspective, and the participants were most eager to verbalize their feelings about each item on the form to the group as a whole, they refused to put any marks on the form.[5]

Having searched the literature on aging, I found a number of studies to verify this suspicion about the role of demographic factors. An excellent example is Drevenstadt (1958), who studied the relationship between age and level of education in performance on the semantic differential scales. Her data clearly show

---

[5] Kahana and Felton (1977) report the same phenomenon. Their interpretation is consistent with that offered here.

that level of education or years of formal education and not age predict scale-checking styles on the semantic differential. Less educated elderly subjects chose fewer scale points in rating items on the scales. Similarly, Kahana and Felton (1977) discuss the relationship between the selective use of 5- and 7-point rating scales and level of formal education among Polish and Jewish aged. Ratings and rankings are often employed in research on the elderly, though social class generally is not taken into account in interpreting the results (e.g., Harris & Associates, Inc., 1975; Gergen & Back, 1966; also consult Glen, 1969, for a review of opinion surveys that fail to account for level of formal education). Since level of education or years of formal schooling is highly correlated with other social class indicators such as occupation and income (see Bengston et al., 1977), the importance of social context to the correct interpretation of the cognitive behavior of older people is affirmed.[6]

Many colleagues, and a number of my associates who have worked with the elderly, suggested two interpretations of my observations on ranking and rating. The most common interpretation was that people get more conservative or cautious with age, and consequently become more cautious in filling out forms. A second interpretation was that older people grew up in a different historical period, hence are not used to filling out forms. However, neither of these interpretations seemed sufficient explanations to me.

It was only after spending half a year working with both community groups that a reasonable explanation for this way of filling out forms occurred to me. The explanation had nothing to do with cautiousness or conservativeness brought about by aging, or historical change; it had to do with socioeconomic class. Almost all of the participants were representatives of the blue-collar working class. Specifically, most had little education beyond high school, and many were not high school graduates. In contrast, a third group of well-educated older persons, representative of the professional class, responded to my request to fill out similar forms just as college graduates respond. All items were carefully ranked from 1 to n, with little apparent concern about leaving a permanent written trace.

Use and Meaning of "You"

If one asks "How do you feel today?", many elderly persons are likely to answer with reference to themselves. For example, they might respond "I'm fine" or "Not too good, today" or with some other self-reference. But should one ask an elderly person "How do you feel about the new tax law?", or "How do you feel about retirement?", there are two ways in which he or she might respond. The individual might either answer with respect to the personal self, e.g., "I feel that . . ." or with respect to the general "you" or general "other": e.g., "Most people feel . . ." or "They say . . ." without divulging his or her own unique personal feelings.

---

[6] Readers interested in pursuing any of the research areas discussed here might wish to consult Riegel (1977) and Bengston et al. (1977) for additional references. Both review data on the historical and social contexts of aging.

Over the course of the year, I discovered that both usages and interpretations of "you," the personal "you" and the general "you," are fairly common among the people at two of the centers at which I worked. What makes this phenomenon so interesting is that although common, it is not universal. I kept a record of who used the personal "you" and who used the general "you" when talking about matters of a serious personal nature, e.g., "How do you feel about retirement?", "What do you think you should do with your time after retirement?", "When you die, how do you want to go?", "How do you feel about living with your family should you find it impossible to care for yourself in the future?"

On examining the record, it appeared that there was a relationship between level of education and occupation, and the preferred usage of "you." Those with college educations and who consequently had held middle class and upper middle class jobs, e.g., as school teachers, nurses, lawyers, and social workers, tended toward the use of the personal "you"; those with less formal education and nonprofessional occupations, e.g., housewives, clerical workers, assemblyline workers, and salesmen, tended toward use of the general "you." With time, it became clear that the particular use and interpretation of "you" was related neither to anxiety about the nature of the question asked, nor to ignorance. All respondents could provide answers in terms of their own personal feelings when I changed the nature of the question or had an intimate friend of theirs lead the discussion. It appears that the use of "you" as "other" in this situation is a way in which the less educated maintain privacy of distance between themselves and the interviewer.

To confirm my suspicion, I collected formal data on the use of "you" in two groups of elderly. Older persons (mean age 66 years, SD = 4.3, 11 men and 26 women, all Caucasians, mean number of years of schooling = 15.4) were compared to a second group of individuals (mean age 64.8 years, SD = 5.1, 9 men and 34 women, all Caucasians, mean number of years of formal schooling = 8.1). There were no appreciable differences between the sexes in years of formal education for either group. I asked two questions, "Would you want to live with your children should you be unable to live independently?" and "What is the best way to prepare for old age?" (This last question does not mention *you*.) Responses were scored in two ways. First, the number of answers containing "I" were counted. Second, three associates who have worked with the elderly rated the answers, indicating whether respondents were talking about themselves or about people in general. All responses were scored blindly. The judges were ignorant of the hypothesis, the particular question asked, and the fact that there were two different groups of subjects represented.

Eighty-two percent of the well-educated group responded with personal "you" interpretations to the first question and 53% gave personal "you" interpretations to the second (which did not contain specific reference to "you"). In the group with less formal education, 36% and 32% provided personal "you" responses to the first and second questions, respectively. Again, all of these interviewed offered personal "you" and then general "you" responses when the questions were reworded and redirected to make only one interpretation at a time possible. These data confirm the informal observations reported above and suggest the importance of separating social context from chronological age.

As an additional check on my hypothesis that it was level of education and not age that motivated the particular interpretation of "you," I compared a group of college students with working persons of the same age. I asked 62 students to provide written but anonymous answers to similar questions. Not one provided a general "you" interpretation even when the question permitted this as a possibility. When I asked the same question of a group of 42 young noncollege educated factory workers (in a plant at lunch time) a different pattern emerged. Again, responses were written and the respondents were asked not to indicate their names on the response sheet. Overall, 72% provided general "you" interpretations; whereas, only 28% provided personal "you" interpretations. No sex differences were observed either in this study or in the study previously described. Since almost all participants were Caucasians, no analyses by ethnicity were performed.

It is clear that these speech styles are not stable class characteristics; rather, they are reasonable adjustments to the perceived nature of the social setting. Well-educated college students are just as likely to switch speech styles when the social situation varies. For example, Holahan (1978) reports that college students switch to the general "you" when their privacy is invaded. With the client's consent, an outsider observed a clinician and college student interacting during a therapy session. When the observer was present, students significantly increased their use of the general "you." Holahan suggested that the switch to the general "you" is a strategy to protect privacy.

One additional account of preferred modes of expression is offered by Riegel and Riegel (1960). To assess dogmatism and rigidity, the Riegels used a set of scales containing some items worded in general stereotyped language and others worded in the first person singular.[7] Depending on the wording of the items and the respondents' age and sex, a different profile for dogmatism and rigidity emerged.[8] When items were worded in stereotyped language, older adults and college students alike responded more rigidly than when items were worded in the first person singular. In addition, whereas developmental increases in dogmatism were observed with

---

[7] Example rigidity items are:

A. In whatever one does, the "tried and true" ways are always the best. (This item reflects general habits and attitudes stated as stereotyped phrases.)

B. I much prefer to eat a familiar dish than something which I do not know at all. (This item refers to a concrete situation and is stated in the first person singular.)

Examples of subscale items for dogmatism are:

A. It is better to be a dead hero than a live coward. (General subscale: This is similar to the first example above. It refers to generalities and is stated in stereotyped language.)

B. I have often observed that strangers were looking at me critically. (Anxiety subscale: Stated in personal "I" and reflecting self-values.)

C. In a heated discussion I generally become so absorbed in what I'm going to say that I forget to listen to what the others are saying. (Intolerance subscale: Stated again in the personal "I" and reflecting self-values.)

[8] A group of 380 German adults over the age of 55 years were compared to a group of 120 German college students between 17 and 19 years of age.

the use of stereotyped language, the reverse was observed with the first person singular. Lastly, older women and older men responded somewhat differently to rigidity and dogmatism items as well as to the wording of these items.

Whether the preference to express oneself through general stereotyped language versus more self-revealing speech indicates a mechanism for maintaining social distance (privacy) is an intriguing question. A reasonable explanation must take into consideration the different social realities that older men and women experience.

Classroom Behavior: Coming to Attention, Sitting Quietly,
and Paying Proper Respect

This last observation has to do with what I consider to be classroom behavior: coming to attention, sitting quietly, and paying proper respect. Such classroom behavior is presumably acquired at school and might make sense within the framework of educational institutions. It is a skill whose performance requires practice (or at least some experience) and the willingness to display it. It is not necessarily a skill possessed or displayed by the participants in the community programs in which I worked.

At scheduled lectures, it was often difficult to assemble the audience, get its attention, minimize neighborly but competing conversation, and keep questions relevant to the presentation and group discussion.

Does this mean, as many of my associates suggest, that the elderly are regressing and becoming childlike, i.e., more egocentric? Does it mean that they are unable to concentrate or attend? Does it mean that their minds are unfocused, wandering from one theme to the next? Or, does it mean that classroom behavior is a skill that ones learns, or that requires practice and makes sense only in certain situations? Does it mean, in the words of one 71-year-old man, that "one of the best things about being older and retired is that you don't have to listen to or take orders from anyone else. You can finally do whatever you want."?

Hurlbut's (1977) recent study on sentence memory supports the second set of interpretations. Sentence memory in young college students (mean age 21.5 years) and elderly participants (mean age 71.9 years) was assessed via a recognition test requiring either semantic memory or verbatim memory. Half the college students (mean number of years of formal education = 14.2) and half the elderly participants (mean number of years of formal schooling = 13.6) participated in the recognition memory test requiring semantic constructive memory or memory for "sense" or "gist." The groups performed equally well. On the verbatim associative memory test, however, the college students (mean years of formal schooling = 14.2) outperformed the group of elderly participants (mean number of years of formal schooling = 12.7) verbatim memory, i.e., word-for-word memory, is an academic skill with little usefulness outside a test-oriented community. It fits the description of classroom behavior, behavior that is adaptive for students or for nonstudents wishing to commit to memory the player name and number association for athletic teams.

By evaluating the social context within which the participants were operating, Hurlbut was able to separate developmental change from social motivation. Failure to have done so would have supported the stereotyped expectation of general cognitive decline with age.

One limitation of the Hurlbut study was that her subjects (both young and old) were overwhelmingly women.[9] It thus becomes difficult to know whether this same pattern would have obtained had male-female comparisons been possible. Although Hurlbut's study does not permit an analysis by sex, there are several other relevant studies on verbal learning and memory among the elderly that do report significant sex differences. Wilkie and Eisendorfer (1977), for example, found an interaction between sex and presentation speed (favoring women) for highly familiar words presented in a serial rote learning taks. Their subjects were 32 women and 32 men aged 60 to 79 years.[10] And Bromley (1958) found sex differences favoring women in the serial learning of a list of nonsense syllables. Bromley's subjects were men and women at three age levels: 27.0, 46.5, and 66.5 years.

These two studies, along with many others which report male-female differences among the aged on verbal learning and memory tasks, emphasize the importance of considering a subject's sex in assessing the performance of elderly persons.

In reviewing past research on verbal learning in the elderly, Wilkie and Eisendorfer point this out very clearly. They say,

> It is generally accepted that rapid pacing in serial rote and paired-associate learning is associated with poorer performance among the aged . . . . For the most part the subjects in these verbal learning studies have been aged men. However, it may not be appropriate to generalize findings on verbal learning in aged men to aged women. (1977, p. 63)

Here is another instance where performance of older persons might have been found deficient had the issue of sex patterns in verbal abilities not been investigated.

Conclusion

The informal and formal observations discussed in this section indicate that we can no longer afford to utilize a paradigm which treats developmental change in isolation from social context. If we do, we run the risk of obscuring alternative explanations of behavior. We run the risk of attributing to age the behaviors that are more properly accounted for otherwise. For example, in the case of classroom behavior, it appears that older persons who have not ever been involved in the academic race for grades and careers are not motivated to play by academic rules. In the "ranking and rating" and "you" examples, it appears that performance is a function of experience related to sex, years, kind of formal schooling, and need for privacy. All older people are not alike. They should not be viewed through a paradigm that assumes they are.

These observations are consistent with the conclusions drawn earlier. A content analysis of articles and their titles appearing in nine consecutive issues of the *Journal*

---

[9] Most of Hurlbut's subjects were women. Each of the two young groups was composed of 13 women and 5 men. One elderly group was composed of 16 women and 2 men, and the second of 15 women and 3 men. Additionally, information on ethnicity is lacking.

[10] Readers are urged to consult Wilkie and Eisendorfer (1977) for additional references to studies showing superior female performance for elderly subjects participating in verbal learning experiences.

of Gerontology was presented to illustrate the extent to which social context is ignored and implicit norms are applied in assessing developmental change associated with aging. An explanation for these is offered in the next section.

Why the Social Context of Aging Has Been Ignored: A Historical View of Underlying Assumptions

> During the course of recent intellectual history, the human being was successfully reduced to an abstract entity within an equally abstract system of traits and abilities. The individual's concrete activities were disregarded, as were his wishes and goals, his questions and doubts. (Riegel, 1977, p. 87)

This was done in the name of "pure" science. The historical failure to recognize the social context within which development and aging occur can be attributed to at least two assumptions underlying the social sciences. First, to foster an air of "hard science" the social sciences drew heavily on models and methods developed in the natural sciences, particularly physics and biology. Later, many of these models and methods proved to be inappropriate not only to the social sciences but to the natural sciences as well. Such models required certain assumptions about the nature of the phenomena studied, the environment in which phenomena occurred and covaried, and the role of the observer. In the name of "science" they legitimized the separation between the observer and the observed, between the environment and the phenomena observed in that environment, and among co-occurring phenomena. As Riegel points out in reviewing the history of gerontological psychology, this model is responsible for the emergence of a sterile view of human behavior.[11] The history of gerontological psychology shows that both general and experimental psychology represent

> the most abstract form of a scientific inquiry. Both individual development and cultural-historical changes are eliminated and thus the human being represents a fictitious point in a developmental-historical vacuum. (Riegel, 1977, p. 72)

A second basic assumption was that the properties of this fictitious human being existing within a developmental-historical vacuum could be isolated, identified, and studied empirically. Concretely, empirical research necessitates the selection of particular phenomena to be investigated and the evolution of appropriate models for doing so. This selection process, i.e., the particular phenomena and the methods chosen, is never neutral! it is guided by what the reseearcher considers to be the important issues at that point in history. The history of ideas up to that date, the prevailing ideology and political-economic structure at that historical time, and the social context of the researcher determine the phenomena to be studied and the methods necessary for doing so.[12] Translated into practice, this has meant histori-

---

[11] Readers are referred to Riegel's, 1977, *History of Gerontological Psychology* for a more lengthy discussion of this.

[12] Readers are urged to consult Buss (1979) and Rose and Rose (1976) for a readable discussion of this issue.

cally that behaviors most consistent with the dominant class structure have been assumed to exemplify human behavior in its purest or most abstract form. The class in power becomes the model for theory building. It should come as no surprise, then, that the adult white entrepreneurial male is the model for normative behavior, and that anything old is a sign of decay in need of replacement. Persons not fitting this model are deviant and thus their relative class position is justified.[13]

As discussed in the first section of this chapter, behavior associated with the white middle and upper middle class male continues to be equated with "normal" adult human behavior. This model for normal adult behavior becomes the yard-stick against which others can be measured and declared deviant. Women, ethnic/racial minority persons, poor persons, and old people who by definition fail the "normal adult behavior test" are considered deviant.

Given these assumptions, it is not surprising to find that research on aging has considered social context to be irrelevant. If the ultimate goal is to describe and justify our society's assumptions about age, then considerations such as social class, ethnicity, and sex become unimportant in research on the aged. They will, therefore, be ignored. But, if that is the goal of social science research, we have before us a serious ethical problem. At issue is the harm done by misrepresenting the complex nature of the population of older adult subjects. Importantly, older adults who willingly serve as subjects are unknowingly jeopardized. By reducing, distorting, and invalidating their life experiences, the paradigm lends support to common stereotypes and myths about them as old people. Also, it undermines efforts to properly assess their life-styles and needs and to design effective services and programs for them.

Evolving a More Equitable View of Aging

Gender, socioeconomic class, and ethnicity/race are more than sociological characteristics of the population of older people. As indicated in the second section, they afford different life experiences and condition different psychological realities that cannot be disregarded. Furthermore, any paradigm that singles out one set of life experiences and its concomitant psychological reality as normative is unethical. It can only lead to inaccurate assessment of, and inappropriate conclusions about, the preferred life-styles, abilities, and needs of older adults. It is particularly harmful to those elderly who already are among the most vulnerable: older women, minorities, and the poor. Obviously, from a practical point of view, it will lead to social programs, policies, and legislation that selectively penalize or ignore a large proportion of the elderly.[14] Let us consider two examples, older women and the minority

---

[13] For an interesting application of this idea to developmental theory, consult Buck-Morss (1973) who traces the history of the relationship between Piaget's theory of cognitive development and the prevailing class structure in European countries. See also Buss (1979).

[14] That older women outnumber men is generally true for most segments of the American population at this time, except for the older population of Chinese and Filipinos. Immigration policy enacted during the late part of the nineteenth century and the early part of the twentieth century excluded the families of Chinese

elderly. It is often expected that one's family or children will look after the elderly. But, what does this imply for women? For them, longevity is a handicap. First, most women outlive their mates by eight years[15] and second, it is infrequently recognized that a large number of older women were never married or were married but were childless; in addition, a large number of older women outlive their children and other family members.[16]

Next, consider eligibility age for pension, social security, or other old age benefits. Given a shorter life span, most minority elderly never reach the eligibility age for receiving old age benefits. Perhaps eligibility age should be separately determined to fit the life expectancies of different subpopulations.

Equally important are the stereotypes and myths about aging which must be challenged. If we ignore the social context of aging, we can never hope to dismantle these myths and stereotypes. Consider the double standard of aging in America. Older women are stereotyped as foolish old bags chattering endlessly about nothing. Where does this stereotype come from? Is it true that women really change so much with age, or is it that the social realities of their lives change? If we focus on the latter, we can develop some alternative explanations to the stereotype. For example, with age, the number of older men declines and the community of older women increases. This means a change in the support network women encounter. With a decline in the community of men which once supported and expected standards of beauty, charm, and social grace, we are left with a community of women who now seem to act inappropriately. That is, the social world that previously supported the (now older) woman's beliefs, attitudes, values, and behaviors has changed in at least two ways. It no longer contains the community of men who encouraged, supported, and expected women to be as they were, and it is now comprised of people who are unable, unprepared, or unwilling to deal with the now inappropriate behavior of the (older) women.

If we do not account for the social and psychological realities that differentiate among people by sex and ethnicity, we will overlook the data critical to appropriate planning at the practical level and critical to explaining our attitudes, myths, and stereotypes about the elderly.

Some Correctives

Given acceptance of the arguments developed throughout this chapter, their resolution is both simple and difficult. It is simply to lay out a few guidelines which, if followed, will begin to change the paradigm. This is done in the paragraphs that fol-

---

and Filipino men. Hence, almost one-half of the older population of Chinese and Filipino males today are single and without families in the United States.

[15] See footnote 1 for demographic characteristics of the population of Americans over 65 years of age.

[16] Consult *The Older Woman: Continuities and Discontinuities* (Louis Harris & Associates, 1978) for more information about older women. One point worth singling out for mention here is that 29% of black women and 20% of white women who reached childbearing years during the great depression were childless. Many of these now are elderly.

low. The difficult part is for social scientists to recognize that the bias inherent in the paradigm is anything but mechanical. Some possible solutions may seem mechanical, but the problem of an unethical paradigm is deeply rooted in a social ideology of male dominance in a class society. The attitudes that this ideology conditions are indeed difficult to change. The simple structural changes suggested below acknowledge this. They are suggestions aimed at introducing an appreciation for the importance of viewing the subject within that context. I hope they will lead to a change in attitude among social scientists. I hope they will do more than add to the list of variables to be accounted for in some mechanical way. Accounting for variables means more than manipulation of a few more parameters. It means finding an honest explanation for variation that pays equal respect to the psychological and social realities of subgroups in our population. It also implies that the research questions we raise must be of relevance and benefit to the community of older women, to the older ethnic/racial minority adults, and to other elderly who are not representative of the normative group of older white males.

The most direct solution is to insist that in addition to chronological age the three social contextual variables (social class, ethnicity/race, and sex) must receive greater attention in research on aging. This means more careful, systematic, and representative selection of subjects, greater attention to these variables in data analyses, and the exercise of greater care in drawing research conclusions and generalizations.

Second, titles of publications should reflect the nature of the sample. If only white males are studied, let the title so indicate.

A third solution requires a new format for research reports; hence, a new journal editorial policy. Research reports should include detailed information about the social context of the research: social class, ethnicity/race, and sex, not only of the aged subjects but of the investigator as well. It is clear that each of these factors greatly influence the sociology and the social psychology of the research situation. Without this information, it is impossible to interpret and compare data.

Fourth, few texts on research methodology in the field of development and aging stress these social factors as important research concerns. Lip service is paid to the description of subject characteristics, but there is almost no concern with describing any properties of the investigator. Texts should reflect the importance of these variables. They should encourage students to include this information in research reports, creating, if necessary, additional subsections in research reports for this purpose. In addition to a subsection on subject characteristics, it is essential to include one on investigator characteristics. By including this information in journal articles and in student reports, the importance of social class, ethnicity/race, and sex to the study of aging will become assimilated gradually into research done by the scientific community.

Fifth, just as new research models and statistical procedures have emerged to account for cohort-historical change in aging research (see Schaie, 1977; Nesselroade, 1977) new research models and statistical models procedures are needed to account for the effects of social context on aging. We need models that go beyond the additive assumptions of analysis of variance. Perhaps these would result from a change in editorial policy which would essentially put a red flag on these social indices.

Lastly, no report should offhandedly justify behavioral or personality differences in terms of sex, ethnicity/race, or socioeconomic class. Research should purposely seek out such differences and explain them with a rigor equal to the explanation of other differences. We can no longer afford to write them off as unexplainable deviations from some group mean.

Summary

The importance of considering social context, social class, ethnicity, and sex in research on aging has been stressed in this chapter. From examining nine consecutive issues of the *Journal on Gerontology*, it is clear that even in 1980, research on aging has continued to ignore the social context within which aging occurs. This failure reflects a pervasive paradigmatic bias toward considering white entrepreneurial adult male behavior as normative and all else as deviant. The foundations for these assumptions were explored.

The informal and formal data reviewed strongly suggest that many behaviors associated with aging can be more parsimonously attributed to an individual's social existence and to the social context of the research situation than to age or to the aging process itself.

Last, although most aged people are victimized by these invalid research procedures, particular subgroups of older people (women, the poor, and ethnic/racial minority people) appear to be most heavily penalized. Correcting this error has implications both for guaranteeing the validity of research on aging and for narrowing the gap between theory and research, on the one hand, and practical application, on the other.

Obviously, changes in research on aging and in its reporting are needed. Not only must research attend to the social context within which aging and aging research occur, it must also employ more appropriate procedures for studying and for describing and reporting the covariates of these social indices. Until some of these changes are instituted, it is the scientific community itself, not an ignorant press or public, that must bear considerable blame for the stereotyping of old people.

References

Bengston, V. L., Kasschau, P. L., & Ragan, P. K. The social impact of social structure on aging individuals. In J. E. Birren & K. W. Schaie (Eds.), *Handbook of the psychology of the aging*. New York: Van Nostrand Reinhold, 1977.

Bromley, D. B. Some effects of age on short-term learning and memory. *Journal of Gerontology*, 1958, *13*, 398-406.

Buck-Morss, S. Socio-economic bias in Piaget's theory and its implications for the cross-cultural controversy. *Human Development*, 1975, *18*, 35-49.

Buss, A. R. *A dialectical psychology*. New York: Irvington, 1979.

Drevenstedt, J. Scale checking styles on the semantic differential among older people. *Journal of Gerontology*, 1958, *13*, 170-173.

Gergen, K. J., & Back, K. W. Communication in the interview and the disengaged respondent. *Public Opinion Quarterly*, 1966, *30*, 385-398.

Glen, N. D. Aging, disengagement and opinionation. *Public Opinion Quarterly*, 1969, *33*, 17-33.

Holahan, C. J. Coping and accommodations as central concepts for bridging environmental and community psychology. Paper presented at Western Psychological Association meeting, San Francisco, April 1978.

Hurlbut, N. L. Adult age differences in sentence memory: An investigation of constructive memory. Paper presented at Gerontological Society meeting, San Francisco, November 1977.

Kahana, E., & Felton, B. J. Social context and personal need: A study of Polish and Jewish aged. *Journal of Social Issues*, 1977, *4*, 56-74.

Nesselroade, J. R. Issues in studying developmental change in adults from a multivariate perspective. In J. E. Birren & K. W. Schaie (Eds.), *Handbook of the psychology of aging*. New York: Van Nostrand Reinhold, 1977.

Riegel, K. F. History of gerontological psychology. In J. E. Birren & K. W. Schaie (Eds.), *Handbook of the psychology of aging*. New York: Van Nostrand Reinhold, 1977.

Riegel, K. F., & Riegel, R. M. A study of changes of attitudes and interests during later years of life. *Vita Humana*, 1960, *3*, 177-206.

Rose, H., & Rose, S. (Eds.). *The political economy of science: Ideology of the natural sciences*. New York: Holmes & Meier, 1976.

Rose, H., & Rose, S. (Eds.). *The radicalization of science: Ideology of the natural science (Critical Social Studies)*. New York: Holmes & Meier, 1976.

Schaie, K. W. Quasi-experimental research designs in the psychology of the aging. In J. E. Birren & K. W. Schaie (Eds.), *Handbook of the psychology of aging*. New York: Van Nostrand Reinhold, 1977.

The myth and reality and aging in America. A study for the National Council on the Aging, Inc. *Louis Harris & Associates, Inc.*, 1975.

The older woman: Continuities and discontinuities. Report of the National Institute on Aging and the National Institute of Mental Health Workshops. September 14-16, 1978. U.S. Department of HEW, Public Health Service, NIH Publication No. 79-1897, October 1979. New York: Van Nostrand Reinhold, 1977. pp. 39-58.

Wilkie, F. L., & Eisendorfer, C. Sex, verbal ability and pacing differences in serial learning. *Journal of Gerontology*, 1977, *32*, 63-67.

Part II

Survey Research and Protection of Privacy and Confidentiality

The major ethical issues that are addressed in Part II, privacy and confidentiality, are most pertinent to survey research but are crucial in other areas of social science research as well. Privacy and confidentiality, in turn, are inextricably related to issues of informed consent and validity of survey findings. The major purposes of this part are to increase awareness of ways in which privacy and confidentiality may be jeopardized and safeguarded in all kinds of social science research, and of ways in which these issues generally relate to issues of validity and consent.

Before considering these problems in detail, let us define privacy and confidentiality. Privacy pertains to persons and confidentiality pertains to data. *Privacy* refers to persons' interest in controlling the flow of information between themselves and others. Persons are said to be able to maintain their privacy when they can control who is privy to information about them and who may intrude into their life. Receiving unwanted information is as much an invasion of privacy as having private information taken. *Confidentiality* is an extension of the concept of privacy which refers to agreements between persons that limit others' access to private information. For example, a research participant may agree to disclose private information to a social scientist if the scientist promises not to allow others to have access to data that can be linked back to the individual subject.

The protection of privacy and confidentiality is a major ethical and legal issue for social scientists. This is so for a number of reasons:

1. Much research in social science takes as its subject that which is private, i.e., that which normally is not intended for others to observe or analyze. Consequently, a major source of risk or harm to participants in this research is psychological, social, or economic harm brought about by disclosure of embarrassing or secret information.
2. The investigator's interest in studying private matters in the lives of others is legally protected only if the investigator is careful to protect the rights of privacy, safety, and self-determination of those who are being studied.

3. It is often scientifically useful to investigators to store data containing unique identifiers (e.g., names and addresses) so that various sources of data on the same set of persons may be merged and analyzed.
4. Research data ordinarily are not immune from subpoena.
5. Recent legislation, including the Freedom of Information Act and the Privacy Act, create additional constraints on the kinds of data that may be gathered and that may be kept confidential.
6. Certain sectors of the population are highly suspicious of the motives of those who gather data or who may obtain access to their data, believing that information they give may be used against them in some way.

These issues are especially pertinent to survey research. Survey research is a method of choice among sociologists and political scientists, and is widely used throughout the social sciences and in fields that employ social science methods, such as epidemiology. In typical survey research, the interviewer asks the respondent some specific questions requiring simple answers, or gives the respondent a questionnaire to answer in writing. Unlike the behavioral researcher, the survey researcher exercises little control over the research setting. Typically, the respondent and interviewer meet for brief encounters on neutral territory or on territory that the respondent controls. For example, they may communicate by phone or mail, or meet in public places or at the respondent's doorstep. Because surveys typically are administered to competent adults who are in a position to understand what is occurring and to refuse to go on with the interview at any point, voluntary informed consent is not the major ethical issue in survey research. Yet, consent is intimately interwoven with the two more major ethical issues, namely, protection of privacy and confidentiality, and validity of the survey.

The validity of survey research rests on the use of a valid sampling procedure. Through the use of one of various valid sampling procedures, the investigator selects persons whose responses would be representative of the larger population to which the findings are to be generalized. Valid sampling procedures allow the scientist to infer what a large group of persons would say although only a small, carefully selected set of persons is interviewed. Thus, once the sample has been drawn, *the investigator must attempt to exercise strict control over the actual selection and interviewing of respondents, making sure to interview those persons who fulfill the assumptions of the sampling model employed*. It is this aspect of rigorous methodology that raises major ethical problems having to do with privacy and confidentiality, and also with consent.

To arrive at a valid sample, the researcher must first learn (from some list, files, or personal communication) who is in the population to be sampled, and draw the appropriate sample of persons from this larger set. This, alone, may breach privacy or confidentiality in various ways as discussed by Hartley in Chapter 8. The interviewer must then contact each person who was selected in the sampling procedure, and persuade each to participate in the interview. The potential respondent is likely to wonder: "How and why was I chosen? Is it in my best interests to participate? How do I know that the information I provide won't be used in ways that will harm me?" The investigator must honestly respond to these concerns by developing a consent statement that identifies the values of participating in the survey and the threats to privacy and confidentiality that actually exist or that the respondent imagines to exist, and the investigator must devise ways to guarantee privacy and confidentiality and to demonstrate these guarantees to the respondent. Thus, the employment of a valid sampling technique may depend on the development of a consent procedure that satisfies respondents' concerns, and this, in turn, may depend on whether the investigator *understands* the issues of privacy and confidentiality that are at stake and knows how to guarantee the protections that the respondent would wish to have.

This set of interrelated problems has caused social scientists to examine their methods and procedures, and to ask questions such as the following: Under what conditions has an investigator the right to obtain private information? How can investigators protect the confidentiality of data? How can investigators persuade research participants that the confidentiality of their data will be protected? If participants are so persuaded, how does this affect their willingness to participate and to provide honest answers?

Questions such as these, in turn, have generated many more specific questions and various approaches have been employed to answer those questions. For example, some social scientists have employed empirical methods to assess what subjects consider as private and to learn under what conditions subjects are willing to disclose private information candidly. Some have developed a range of sampling methods that minimize invasion of privacy without jeopardizing the validity of the sample. Others have sought legal shields or other procedures that protect data from subpoena. Still others have devised statistical and procedural devices for collecting and maintaining data that do not include unique identifiers but that retain scientific usefulness nevertheless. The four chapters in Part II examplify the development of these approaches and present useful concepts and methods for investigators to use in order to protect privacy and confidentiality.

Stated in terms of the humanistic-deterministic distinction discussed in Chapter 1, these social scientists are concerned to reap the values of rigorous methodology and have done so by a combination of humanistic and deterministic methods. By rigorous or humanistic means, the scientist learns the concerns of subjects. This information, in turn, provides a context for developing means of satisfying these concerns and of communicating effectively to subjects that their interests have been protected.

In Chapter 7, Anthony G. Turner reports studies that were performed by the U.S. Bureau of Census, the National Academy of Sciences, and the Institute for Social Research on the relationship between the kinds of confidentiality investigators guarantee and the willingness of respondents to provide personal data. Because of the complex nature of privacy and confidentiality, this set of studies was narrowly focused in order to achieve valid designs, leaving much more research to be done to gain needed understanding of respondents' perceptions of privacy and confidentiality. These studies indicate that the public is concerned about the information sought by both government and private survey researchers and about what happens to this information. Promises of confidentiality do make some difference, but generally are not trusted and the concept of confidentiality is only vaguely understood by the public. Certain sectors of the public and certain kinds of survey questions are particularly prone to misreporting and nonreporting.

Turner perceives a serious need for survey organizations to seek more creative and credible ways to communicate with the public about the purposes of surveys and the protections against disclosure. Mutual trust is needed if a society dependent on valid information about itself is to function effectively. This requires more than development of adequate consent statements; it calls for a more collaborative relationship between survey organizations and public interest groups, and for a public literacy effort via mass media. (See Chapter 7, companion volume, for a discussion of issues connected with the use of the mass media to educate the public about social science processes and products.)

In Chapter 8, Shirley Hartley addresses, directly, issues relating to methods of selecting a valid sample and contacting members of that sample without violating privacy or confidentiality. Hartley sensitizes the reader to a range of related problems that arise in survey research and require ethical decision making. Focusing on sampling procedures including use of population listings, areal sampling, sampling from existing records, and field sampling, Hartley raises such issues as:

1. How to obtain informed consent when full informing would involve possible invasion of privacy through disclosure of a to-be-forgotten fact about the person's past and why they were chosen (e.g., former alcoholism).
2. How to obtain informed consent in such a way that the giving of consent per se does not jeopardize privacy, e.g., as when persons consent to participate in a study of drug pushers.
3. How to get legitimate permission to use lists, and how to incorporate this information appropriately in the individual consent statement.
4. How to maximize the validity of the random sample without using unethical, intrusive, high pressure tactics.
5. How to limit the cost of the research without reducing the benefit of the findings.
6. How to obtain consent for secondary analysis of data and alternatively how to obtain useful information in legitimate ways that do not require informed consent.
7. How inequitable sampling may come about due to economic pressures, scientific fashion, and convenience factors, so that some populations are over- or underresearched and some findings are over- or undergeneralized.
8. How public trust in survey research may be undermined.

In examining these issues, we uncover various decision criteria that the survey researcher uses in ethical decision making: Is the survey procedure too costly, or unlikely to produce the needed information? Does it employ a valid sampling procedure and can that procedure be carried out successfully? Does the consent procedure involve the kind of protection, respectful relationship, and information needed to produce maximum cooperation and to neither deceive nor coerce; what creative adjuncts to the informed consent procedure, e.g., newspaper publicity, are required? Is the sampling procedure inequitable? Is public trust undermined by this survey procedure? Have appropriate steps been taken to determine whether existing data may be obtained for purposes of the current investigation?

Hartley demonstrates that vigilant ethical decision making pays off in terms of valid and useful survey research, good relationships with respondents and with agencies who can provide assistance of various kinds, and public confidence in science.

In Chapter 9, Charles R. Knerr, Jr., discusses the conditions under which subpoena of data is a possible threat to confidentiality and presents case histories of subpoenaed data to sensitize investigators to ways in which this threat may arise. He indicates that the investigator has four major alternatives for dealing with subpoena: to avoid research involving legally sensitive topics, to take no precautions and risk being jailed, to desensitize the research by using design and statistical techniques that minimize the usefulness of the data to legal authorities, or to employ legal mechanisms to avoid compliance with a subpoena. Knerr recommends that investigators consider only the last two alternatives. The last alternative (use of legal mechanisms) is the topic of the remainder of Chapter 9, and the third alternative (use of design and statistical techniques) is the topic of Chapter 10. Knerr describes the various federal and state statutes that protect certain kinds of data from subpoena and advises how this protection may be secured. He also provides advice on steps to take if a subpoena *is* issued. Finally, he strongly recommends that, where possible, the investigator employ statistical or design techniques that minimize the usefulness of the data to legal authorities.

In Chapter 10, Robert F. Boruch and Joe Shelby Cecil present several statistical strategies for preserving privacy in direct inquiry. The purpose of each of these statistical techniques is to eliminate clear linkages between the identity of the respondent and information about the respondent's true condition, while still providing useful, analyzable data. Techniques of these kinds enable investigators who inquire into highly personal matters to acquire information without invading the privacy of the respondent, without creating files that are likely to be stolen or subpoenaed, and without motivating respondents to give untrue responses in order to protect themselves.

Boruch and Cecil present four related classes of statistical strategies for preserving privacy: (1) *contamination methods*, which require each subject to inoculate his or her data with a random error of known characteristics, (2) *randomized response methods*, which require each subject to respond either to the actual survey question or (with a known likelihood of occurrence) to respond to another question to which the mean and variance of the answer for that population is already known, (3) *microaggregation methods*, which involve the compilation of averaged information on small groups of subjects or for small groups of responses, and (4) *balanced incomplete blocks methods*, which involve obtaining differently combined information from different sets of subjects from the same population (e.g., obtaining the *sum* of total number of petty thefts committed and total number of uses of public phones in the last week from one set of subjects, and obtaining the *difference* between these two amounts from another set of subjects). Each of these methods involves the use of simple algebra to compute the unknown values. The benefits and limitations of these methods are discussed in relation to cross-sectional, longitudinal, multisource, and experimental research. Some applications of these methods in various major programs of research are described.

Part II provides useful concepts and methods for those who design and conduct research on sensitive issues, and, it is heuristic in other ways as well. It illustrates that the methods of the social sciences are particularly well suited for investigating and seeking solutions to problems of privacy and confidentiality in research, and it indicates a range of empirical, procedural, and methodological research approaches that can be brought to bear in ethical decision making about these problems. The abstract concept of privacy is difficult to define satisfactorily, and society's increasing concern for protection of the privacy of individuals often seems like a growing impediment to the conduct of research in social science. However, these four chapters indicate that *specific* problems of privacy and confidentiality in research may be rendered understandable and solvable through the use of research techniques such as those illustrated here. The chapters in this part illustrate most forcefully that ethical problem solving is enhanced not by embracing a particular model of social science, but by creatively combining rigorous deterministic approaches with sensitive humanistic approaches, as required to understand and solve a given ethical dilemma.

Chapter 7

What Subjects of Survey Research Believe about Confidentiality

Anthony G. Turner

This chapter discusses the issues of privacy, informed consent, and confidentiality that are faced in the conduct of censuses and surveys. Material is presented from recent studies undertaken by the Bureau of the Census which has had a long tradition of maintaining the confidentiality of individual data it collects. Also, the Bureau has long been sensitive to the type of personal or corporate information it seeks, so that invasion of a respondent's privacy is kept to a minimum. The chapter focuses primarily on privacy and confidentiality factors in the data-collection stage of operations, that is, at the level that is so critical for valid statistical measurement: the raw answers supplied by respondents to questionnaires. Background is provided on why there is increased attention being given to the relationship between survey response and privacy-confidentiality matters. The chapter then describes, in some detail, three studies undertaken by the National Academy of Sciences together with the Census Bureau, and a study commissioned by the Census Bureau and conducted by the Response Analysis Corporation. One of the National Academy of Sciences studies was a nationwide attitude survey, designed to gather some information on citizen perceptions about the Census Bureau plus general attitudes about surveys and how privacy or confidentiality concerns play a role. The second National Academy of Sciences study was an experimental design to determine if varying promises of confidentiality have an effect on the rate of response. Results from a small study conducted in Taylor, Michigan, are also given; this study focused on the validity of response, as opposed to the response rate. The Response Analysis Corporation study was conducted to help make an evaluation of some of the reasons why mail response was comparatively low in a decennial census pretest in Oakland, California.

   A concluding section offers a summary of what these small-scale investigations tell us about privacy and confidentiality vis-à-vis survey research and practice, and what further study needs to be done.

Background and Need for Research on Privacy and Confidentiality

During World War II the Department of War and the Department of State were interested in whether the Bureau of the Census would provide complete lists of all Americans of Japanese ancestry living on the west coast. The Bureau refused to search its decennial records to compile such a list on the grounds that individually identifiable information is absolutely confidential, even when it might have helped another Government agency in times of national emergency (Barabba & Kaplan, 1975). The Bureau's position serves to illustrate several points. The most obvious is that Census Bureau records are unconditionally confidential and may be seen only by officials and sworn employees of the agency. A less obvious point is that, if disclosed improperly, even the relatively innocuous sociodemographic data that the Bureau collects in a decennial census can be used to the detriment of individual citizens (in this case Japanese-Americans). Third, far-reaching implications of the importance of maintaining confidentiality of data collected for research or statistical purposes (as opposed to administrative purposes) is not a new concern for the Census Bureau but dates back several decades.

This episode is but one of many that could be cited where the Bureau has steadfastly upheld the law and refused to release individually identifiable information to others for any purpose whatsoever. The policy of confidentiality has been pursued zealously over the years, for ethical as well as legal reasons. Moreover, it has long been believed that the high level of response the Bureau achieves (usually around 95% or better) in censuses and sample surveys and the accuracy of the data collected are due, in part, to the public's willingness to cooperate by virtue of its perception that the information it supplies to the Census Bureau is treated confidentially (Barabba & Kaplan, 1975). Interviewers and enumerators are trained to stress the confidentiality of a respondent's answers when they seek an interview, and they often use the confidentiality pledge as a sort of special reassurance to convince reluctant respondents to participate.

For sensitive survey questions, Boruch and Cecil discuss in Chapter 10 the statistical techniques that have been developed over the past 15 years for assuring the absolute confidentiality of identifiable records so that not even the interviewer or the data analyst knows what answer an individual respondent gives. But sensitivity is in the eye of the beholder, and especially in a changing society, a question that may seem innocuous today may be regarded as intrusive later. Unfortunately, techniques such as randomized response are not yet practical to use for all the questions that are normally asked in a survey. The more direct methods of inquiry must still be used in the overwhelming majority of survey questioning. Hence, survey researchers must continue to verbally inform and assure respondents of confidentiality pledges or provisions. But how well does a respondent understand the concept and implications of confidentiality when we inform him of this in an interview? Has the word itself become so devalued that it represents a vague and meaningless abstraction to a respondent? How much does he genuinely *believe* in a pledge of confidentiality? Does *what* is asked in the interview matter? Does *who* asks it matter? How do respondents seem to form the ideas they hold about confidentiality guarantees? Does a confidentiality promise really play a big role in gaining citizen consent to be interviewed?

A number of forces have coalesced in the 1970s to make these and related questions (on the invasion of privacy) of great concern to survey research organizations including the Census Bureau, the nation's largest collector of survey information from its citizens. Though the Census Bureau has traditionally practiced the principle of informed consent in conducting its surveys, there was some concern that the explicit requirements of the Privacy Act of 1974 (P.L. 93-579) might lower response rates (Love & Turner, 1975). It has been thought that heightened public consciousness concerning issues of privacy, coupled with such well-publicized government invasions of privacy as the Watergate break-in, may have made respondents more suspicious about surveys. What Frankel (1976) calls the "latent and instinctive human fear of being counted or enumerated" may be scaring people away from the survey or census researcher out of fear that the information given will somehow end up in a central data bank and be used against them in the future. The Census Bureau has had a recent disagreement with the National Archives and Records Service over whether decennial census records should be open to future scholarly research; legislation has been introduced, from time to time, to amend Title 13, U.S. Code (the Bureau's statutory authority making its records confidential) to open the records after 50 years for medical research and after 75 years for genealogical and historical research. (The Census Bureau opposed the bill and it has been defeated.) At a time when the Bureau is under increasing pressure to improve completeness of the 1980 census count over that achieved in the 1970 Decennial Census, particularly with respect to racial and ethnic minority groups, there is institutional concern over the reasons for undercoverage and nonresponse; how much issues of privacy and confidentiality contribute; and, to the extent they do contribute, what can be done to allay the public's fears. Finally, although there is some debate about whether overall response rates are deteriorating among survey organizations (American Statistical Association, 1974; Marquis, 1977; National Academy of Sciences, 1978), there is general agreement that *refusal* rates have been increasing in recent years. Do privacy and confidentiality concerns contribute importantly to these refusals? We make the distinction between overall nonresponse, which includes failure to collect information from people who are not at home, away on vacation, or otherwise not available to participate and persons who are contacted but firmly refuse. Table 7-1 shows, for example, how refusals to the Census Bureau's longest running, continuous survey, the Current Population Survey, have steadily crept up from 1.5% in 1965 to over 2.5% in 1978.

Concepts of Privacy and Confidentiality for Census Surveys

It would be useful to define the concepts of privacy and confidentiality, as used in this chapter. Privacy, as viewed here, is "the right to determine what information about ourselves we are willing to share with others. Confidentiality is the assurance that information provided by a respondent will not be seen by unauthorized individuals nor presented in tabulations in such a form as to permit disclosure of matters which were to be held in confidence. Confidentiality would be less of an issue if people had no desire to keep information private; and if transmission or disclosure

Table 7-1. Average Annual Rate of Refusals to Be Interviewed, Current Population Survey 1965-1977

Year	Refusal rate[a]	Year	Refusal rate[a]
1965	1.5%	1972	1.8
1966	1.6	1973	1.9
1967	1.8	1974	2.0
1968	1.8	1975	2.2
1969	1.8	1976	2.5
1970	1.6	1977	2.5
1971	1.6	1978	2.6

Note. From Beach (1979).

[a]Computed as $\dfrac{\text{(number of households which refused the interview)}}{\text{(number of eligible households in the sample)}} \times 100\%$.

of information were totally suppressed, privacy would scarcely be a matter of concern" (Finkner, 1974).

Current Research

Until recently, virtually no empirical information has been systematically collected on the relationship of privacy and confidentiality concerns to cooperation rates in surveys. The National Opinion Research Center conducted a survey, under a National Science Foundation grant, in 1977 which gave some evidence that item response to sensitive questions, especially sexual activity, increases when less than absolute confidentiality is provided (Singer, 1977).

National Academy of Sciences–Census Bureau Studies

The Census Bureau engaged the Committee on National Statistics of the National Academy of Sciences to convene a multidisciplinary panel of experts to guide some small-scale, exploratory studies to learn "what assurances the public requires, how to effectuate these assurances, and how to convey an understanding of such assurances to people in their capacity as respondents in censuses and surveys" (Martin, 1976). The Response Analysis Corporation was also commissioned by the Bureau to undertake some group interviews with residents of Oakland, California, to obtain some insights on reasons for the poor initial mail response (48%) to the 1977 Oakland Census, which was one of several pretests to the 1980 Decennial Census.

Because so little is known in this area, the approach to these studies has been exploratory, as opposed to confirmatory. The sizes of the research investigations have been extremely limited, especially when viewed against the Census Bureau's usual surveys which typically include tens of thousands of sample units. But equally important, the subject matter (privacy, confidentiality, and reasons for survey participation or nonparticipation) has proved to be multidimensional, elusive, complex, and ambiguous.

The most ambitious project that the Census Bureau has sponsored is with the National Academy of Sciences, resulting in a report entitled *Privacy and Confidentiality as Factors in Survey Response* (National Academy of Sciences, 1979). For the most part, it was undertaken as a methodological exploration to test various methods of investigating how the public perceives the privacy issue, and whether increased interest in privacy and confidentiality affect responses to survey questionnaires. It was expected that promising methodologies would be recommended by the National Academy of Sciences to be used by the Bureau of the Census in larger-scale studies. It turned out, however, that the research designs for the two main substudies of the overall investigation were of sufficient quality that their results were useful not only for methodological testing but for substantive analysis as well.

National survey of attitudes about surveys. One of the substudies was a nationwide attitude survey, based on a probability sample of about 1200 personal interviews with adults 18 or older, conducted in the fall of 1976. The statistical design of the study used the technique of interpenetrating halfsamples. This was done to permit the Bureau of the Census interviewers to conduct half the interviews, while the remaining half was conducted by interviewers from the Survey Research Center, Institute for Social Research of the University of Michigan. Each interviewer identified himself or herself as representing the organization for which he/she worked. The reason for the split auspices approach was that many of the survey questions dealt with topics that a respondent might answer one way if a Census interviewer asked them and another way if a University interviewer asked. There was interest in the extent and nature of biases of the auspices.

The survey form included questions about prior experience with and participation in surveys, reasons for not responding, consequences of participating in previous surveys, choice of survey method (face-to-face, telephone, mail), knowledge about the origin of current data such as the employment statistics, attitudes about which types of organizations are likely to get accurate information from respondents, attitudes about whether a pledge of confidentiality affects the accuracy of reported data, attitudes toward Government in general, attitudes and knowledge about the Census Bureau and its practices with respect to treating information confidentially, plus the usual sociodemographic information. In addition, each respondent, at the completion of the interview, filled out an "interview reaction" form, giving his views on the interview in which he had just participated (how well the purpose was explained; how interesting the survey was; whether any of the questions were easy or hard to answer or caused discomfort; knowledge of whether the interview was voluntary or not; whether it was confidential; and to what extent such factors as auspices, the interviewer's manner and appearance, confidentiality, survey topic, curiosity, and sense of citizenship contributed to willingness to respond).

The survey results did not reflect a high level of citizen trust in surveys. About 20% reported that they felt surveys were a waste of time. About 7% felt survey results could hardly ever be trusted to be right. In particular, respondents think that questions about income are sensitive; such questions make them feel uncomfortable even if they agree to give answers. Forty-one percent felt that hardly anyone reports income accurately in surveys, and 32% felt that a promise of confidentiality would make no difference in the accuracy of income reporting. The most prominent reasons given were that the information is private under any circumstances, or that people will not report accurately no matter what assurances are given because they do not believe the assurances.

Further with respect to the issue of privacy, the survey attempted to develop empirical results by first asking whether the respondent had been contacted recently (within the past 4-5 years) to participate in a survey. For those who had been approached but who had not participated, they were asked why not. Table 7-2 shows the distribution of answers by whether the solicitation was by mail, telephone, or personal visit.

From this distribution we would conclude that the dominant factor affecting nonparticipation in surveys is apathy or lack of interest. If we take the items labeled "objection to approach or content" as reasonable surrogates for privacy concerns, there does not appear to be any substantial evidence that when a respondent refuses a survey it is because he believes the surveys invade his privacy. There is evidence, however, that nonparticipation in *telephone* surveys is due as much to suspicion and distrust as to other reasons.

As for the attitude survey interview itself, respondents indicated answers to the question, "How much did the following have to do with your willingness to be interviewed?" (for this survey). The results are shown in Table 7-3 by the auspices of the collecting organization. A sense of good citizenship and interviewer conduct

Table 7-2. Count of Reasons for Nonparticipation in Most Recent Survey Not Participated in

	Mail	Tele-phone	Personal visit
Total mentions/surveys not participated in	218	154	47
Lack of interest, or inconvenience	165	80	27
Topic uninteresting or inappropriate	43	20	4
General lack of interest, didn't want to bother	62	23	11
Oversight	31	–	–
Too busy	21	23	9
Inconvenient time	–	12	–
Other	8	2	3
Objection to approach or content	36	65	16
Topic objectionable	14	11	7
Questions poor	6	1	–
Method objectionable	1	23	1
Distrust			
In research	2	3	2
Of interviewer	–	26	–
Of sponsor	5	–	1
Dislike of interviewer	–	–	2
Purpose objectionable	8	1	3
Miscellaneous, including no answer and don't know	17	9	4

Note. Derived from National Academy of Sciences (1979), Table 29.

Table 7-3. Factors Affecting Willingness to Be Interviewed in Attitude Survey, by Organization Conducting the Interview (Percent Distribution)

	Sponsorship		Interviewers' appearance and manner		Who could find out		What survey was about		Curiosity about being interviewed		Good citizenship	
	SRC[a]	Census	SRC	Census	SRC	Census	SRC	Census	SRC	Census	SRC	Census
Total	100	100	100	100	100	100	100	100	100	100	100	100
Made me much more willing	20	21	42	41	22	23	21	23	15	17	28	34
Made me somewhat more willing	25	22	30	22	18	20	27	28	23	21	34	33
Made no difference	47	43	22	27	49	44	43	39	54	52	33	24
Made me somewhat less willing	1	2	1	1	2	1	2	1	–	1	–	1
Made me much less willing	–	1	–	–	1	1	1	–	1	–	1	–
Don't know	–	–	–	–	1	–	1	–	–	–	–	–
No answer	7	11	6	10	8	11	6	9	6	8	5	8

Note. From National Academy of Sciences (1979, Table 95).
[a] Survey Research Center, University of Michigan.

thus seemed to rate higher in respondents' opinions about what motivates them to cooperate than sponsorship or confidentiality.

On the matter of confidentiality, some of the citizen perceptions about the Census Bureau itself were interesting. Two-fifths (39%) of the population believed that individual Census records are not held in confidence but are open to other agencies or to the public, while another half (51%) said they didn't know whether the records were open or not. Only 5% believed that Census records are *not* open to the public, are *not* available to other agencies routinely, and are *not* given to other agencies when they really try to obtain them. Thus, the Bureau's responsibility and determination to maintain confidentiality of Census data are not generally believed by the American public. Still, about half believed Census records *should be kept confidential* forever, while the other half thought they should be open for research after a time.

Confidentiality is still apparently a nebulous or abstract concept for many people. From the information supplied on the "Interview Reaction Form" 42% of the respondents did not accurately remember that the interviewer had said the information collected would be kept confidential, even though this had been stated explicitly by the interviewer only minutes before the reaction form was filled out by the respondent. It would seem, therefore, that where we thought there was informed consent, over 40% agreed to the interview without being, in fact, truly cognizant of the confidentiality provision.

National survey of response behavior. The second major substudy of the National Academy of Sciences-Census Bureau collaboration was one designed to test alternative promises of confidentiality. This also was a national probability sample administered by personal interview to a sample of about 2,500 adults in the United States in the fall of 1976. The research design was a controlled experiment utilizing the technique of randomized blocks, wherein approximately 500 clusters of housing units were selected nationwide, each cluster containing exactly five occupied dwellings. Within a cluster, each household was randomly assigned to one of five treatments which varied by the nature of the confidentiality promise which was made. The survey questions that were asked of each household are the typical ones that are found in a decennial census and in many of the Bureau's current surveys. Thus, every respondent was asked to supply the same information; only the stated conditions under which he was asked to do so varied. Depending on the treatment to which a particular respondent was randomly assigned, he was told at the start of the survey interview that the answers he would give would be held confidential forever by the Census Bureau and not given to other agencies or to the public (Treatment A), or they would be held confidential for 75 years (B), or 25 years (C), or no mention of confidentiality was made at all (D), or that his answers might be given to other agencies and to the public (E).

The key statistic of interest in this experiment was the refusal rate and whether it differed by the confidentiality variant. When we discount the refusals that occurred before the interviewer had a chance to read the verbatim statement of confidentiality condition to the respondent (respondents who refused before hearing the statement were presumably not affected by the treatment variation), the refusal rates for the five treatments were A, 1.8%; B, 1.9%; C, 2.3%; D, 2.7%; and E, 2.8%. Nonparametric tests for the significance of the monotonic increase in these rates lead us to the statistical conclusion "that it is improbable that the observed pattern . . . would occur if in fact the underlying rates were the same for all treatments" (Goldfield, Turner, Cowan, & Scott, 1977). In essence, we have statistical evidence that refusals increase with decreasing assurances of confidentiality. The size of the sample used for this study was not large enough, however, to estimate reliably the actual sizes of the refusal differences among the varying treatments. We could not conclude, for example, that there is a statistical difference between the rates for treatments A and B.

But how important is a statement of confidentiality for gaining cooperation? In the research study we found that for all treatments combined, 2.9% of the sample refused prior to hearing the survey conditions that the interviewer was to read, whereas only 2.2%[1] refused afterward. Obviously, there are other factors besides confidentiality condition that make someone refuse a Census Bureau survey, and our evidence does not support the notion that confidentiality concern is the principal motivator. This can be illustrated further by looking at the results in a different light (Table 7-4).

If we combine cases of (1) refusals *before* the statement was read with (2) treatment A cases where the statement was read (the latter representing the group that gets the standard Census pledge) then we have a group of respondents who, we can assume, are not *negatively* affected by the stated confidentiality promise, on the one hand, because they didn't wait to listen to it and, on the other, because the pledge made was the maximum positive reinforcement. This combined group had a refusal rate of 3.2%. For everyone else, that is, those who listened to (or at least were exposed to the interviewer's verbal rendering of) a pledge of confidentiality that was less than perpetual, nonexistent, or not mentioned at all, the refusal rate

Table 7-4. Comparison of Refusal Households by Whether Affected by Confidentiality Pledge

Total eligible households, treatments A-E	4261
(1) Not exposed[a] to confidentiality statement	123
(2) Exposed to statement A[b] and refused	15
Total refusals (1+2)	138
Percent of eligible	3.2%
Total eligible households, treatments B-E only	3379
Exposed to statements B, C, D, or E[c] and refused	80
Percent of eligible	2.4%

[a]Respondent refused before statement on confidentiality was read by interviewer.
[b]Statement A promised confidentiality forever.
[c]Statements B-E promised confidentiality for 75 years, 25 years, not mentioned, and 0 years.

---

[1] Recomputed from Goldfield et al. (1977, page 9, Table 1) so that both figures are on same base.

was 2.4%. What this implies is that those respondents who were inclined to turn down the Census interview had a strong likelihood of doing so *before* rather than *after* being told their answers were not necessarily protected from disclosure to others. In the case of treatment A households, the turndown was in spite of the confidentiality pledge for perpetuity.

Response validity investigation in Taylor, Michigan. The response rates are, of course, only a crude indicator of the degree of cooperation attained in a survey. It is also important to assess the quality or validity of response. A respondent may be reluctant to refuse the interview outright; instead he may consent to the interview but "manage" the information he supplies (Response Analysis Corporation, 1977) by refusing to answer some questions or by purposely misreporting on others. The five-treatment investigation was too small to obtain very much information on whether the confidentiality variants affected item nonresponse. There was some mild evidence that nonresponse to income questions may increase along a continuum from the strongest promise of confidentiality to the weakest.

An examination of the *validity* of response was tested in November 1976 by administering the five-treatment experiment to a small sample of 500 households in an area (Taylor, Michigan) in which the Census Bureau had recently conducted (May 1976) a special census. Thus, census-type information was already available for this community, collected under the standard Bureau guarantee of confidentiality, and we were able to compare the *consistency* of response between the two data collections. In this way, we hoped to be able to tell whether response consistency was affected by the particular treatment the household was assigned to. Again this was largely a methodological test of a procedure and the sample (only 100 cases per treatment) was too small for conclusive analysis.

Response inconsistency between two observations from the same households is to be expected for a variety of reasons, including, of course, actual changes that occur between the two interviews. Inconsistency, per se, is therefore not particularly useful as an indicator of response validity. What would be meaningful, of course, would be an instance where the *degree* of inconsistency tends to be worse for some treatments than for others, or where there is evidence of a linear or monotonic trend in the treatment effects; this is so because all treatment groups were random subsets of the same population.

It is plausible that a lessening of confidentiality assurance would have the following kinds of effects between the two observations. First, if less than total assurance of confidentiality is perceived as a threatening situation to a household respondent, one might expect that the number of persons a respondent reports as household members could be fewer. The lack of a decreasing trend for household size (column 7 of Table 7-5) does not support the expectation. Nor does the joint relationship of the figures in columns 5 and 6 offer any support, for one would expect the households sizes as we go from A to E to diverge increasingly between the Taylor Census and the experiment (with the census being the more stable of the two). Similarly, one might reason that household relationship would be subject to increasing response inconsistency with decreasing assurances of confidentiality; again the figures from column 9 of Table 7-5 deny the hypothesis.

As for income, it is reasonable to speculate that different class intervals of income would more likely be reported if the second observation was solicited with less reassurance than the first. No trend is apparent, however, in the figures of column 10. We could reason, further, that item refusals (NAs) on income would have a tendency to increase in the experimental study with decreasing confidentiality assurance, but that no such trend should be present for the Taylor Census. There is some slight evidence to support this hypothesis, though the trend in the experimental data is not completely monotonic. We can think of no apparent reason why age[2] would be reported differently between the two surveys, irrespective of the confidentiality variant; the data indeed shows no predictable trend.

We would argue that the apparent absence of conclusive patterns in much of the Taylor experimental data may be masked by the very small sample results. A similar study, using a much larger sample size, would be needed to ascertain whether response inconsistency is affected, to any important degree, by the kind of confidentiality pledge. Table 7-5 summarizes what was learned from this investigation. The bulk of the analysis is for "matched" households, that is, the households for which at least one member was identical for the two interviews, since a study of treatment effects would be inappropriate for changed households.

Response Analysis Corporation Study

In preparing for a decennial census, the Bureau conducts a number of trial censuses in the decade preceding the year of the decennial operation to try out various new approaches. One such trial census was conducted in Oakland, California, in 1977. It was essentially a mail operation with personal interview follow-up for nonresponse households. The response rate in the mail portion of the census (prior to personal interview follow-ups) was only 48%, much lower than mail response rates in test censuses conducted during the decade of the 1960s.

Since only about half the citizens of Oakland completed the mail questionnaire and sent it back, the Bureau contracted with the Response Analysis Corporation to conduct some small group interviews with Oaklanders to learn about what might be effective advertising messages for a census. About 100 subjects were chosen for these interviews involving primarily low-income blacks and Hispanic Americans, groups that have traditionally been disproportionately undercounted[3] in censuses. The results, even though not scientifically representative of the attitudes of Oakland residents, are nevertheless interesting and provide some insights that are suggestive for more definitive studies (Response Analysis Corporation, 1977). The focus interviews were designed to learn about attitudes toward the Oakland Census, but issues of privacy and confidentiality emerged as prominent influences in the general dissatisfaction expressed by those interviewed. They seemed to feel, generally, that "government" is too nosy, that census questions are vaguely "too personal" or else

---

[2] Except possibly in the case of someone who might worry that the Census answers might be used by the Social Security Administration to establish or deny benefits.
[3] In 1970, it was estimated that blacks and other nonwhite races were undercounted by over 7% compared to an undercount of about 2% for whites (cf. U.S. Department of Commerce, 1974, 1977).

Table 7-5. Summary Statistics of Matched[a] Households in Five-Treatment

Confidentiality treatment	Total interviewed households	Same[a] household	Different[a] household	Household size for matched households		HH size for identical persons only
				Taylor Census	Experiment	
1	2	3	4	5	6	7
Total	441	388	53	3.34	3.37	3.17
A	91	80	11	3.36	3.30	3.21
B	85	75	10	3.39	3.43	3.16
C	87	78	9	3.29	3.42	3.06
D	92	82	10	3.16	3.24	3.06
E	86	73	13	3.53	3.45	3.38

Note. From Turner (1977).

[a]If at least one member of the address location was determined to be the same person between the two observations, the household "matched" or was the same; otherwise, it was counted as a different household.

[b]Income given for Taylor Census but not answered for experiment.

[c]Income given for experiment but not answered for Taylor.

meaningless and useless, that since government already knows everything about you anyway there is no need for a census, and that there are dangerous risks in reporting certain things accurately. There were pervasive feelings about the need for protecting privacy, and lack of confidence in pledges of confidentiality ("All government information is available to anyone who really wants it or needs it" and "Only a fool takes this confidentiality pledge seriously").

Very few of the subjects in these interviews admitted to having filled out the census forms and mailing them back. They did not perceive the Census Bureau as special or separate from other agencies; they felt nothing is really confidential no matter what is promised. Indeed the notion of confidentiality was confused by some with the concept of anonymity. How can the information be confidential when one's name is on the census form? The use of the individual data in aggregate form was not well understood or appreciated. If the individual answers are really confidential then how can they be used to help that individual? The Response Analysis Corporation report concluded that, for these respondents, suspicion of the government interviewer often is not met with outright refusal; instead, before the respondent gives out information about himself of his affairs he carefully weighs it and selectively reports some things while suppressing the rest. And often he makes sure in his own mind that what he says to one government interviewer is the same thing he told some other government agency, whether accurate or not.

Concluding Remarks

The complex nature of privacy and confidentiality concerns has necessarily forced the research that has been undertaken thus far to be somewhat narrowly focused in order to achieve valid research designs. As a result there remains a host of impor-

Experiment, Taylor, Michigan

Percentage of HHs where		Percentage of matched households where income category was				
Year of birth different for 1 or more identical persons	Relationship to head different for 1 or more identical persons	Different	Higher for experiment	NA[b] for experiment	Higher for Taylor	NA[c] for Taylor
8	9	10	11	12	13	14
28%	8%	50%	17%	14%	9%	10%
30	9	49	19	10	10	10
28	7	52	23	12	4	13
32	10	59	22	14	10	13
24	10	40	12	20	5	4
25	5	52	11	15	18	8

tant issues for which new empirical studies must be designed and carried out. What we have is only a small beginning in the understanding of the roles that privacy and confidentiality play in the taking of surveys.

What do these limited investigations imply for the Census Bureau or for survey research generally? First, much remains to be done to gain a better understanding of these phenomena. The studies so far have all been too small either in scope or in scale to get definitive information about which segments of society are most concerned with or affected by privacy and confidentiality matters in surveys. Methodologically, the results from these small studies may be unduly influenced by interviewer effects. The interviewers' opinions about confidentiality and their appeals to get cooperation in surveys need to be studied further. Also, since we lack empirical information on these topics from past studies, there is no way to measure whether concerns of privacy and confidentiality are greater now than before. Other topics, besides those discussed here, must be researched from an ethical viewpoint as well as from the viewpoint of survey impact. For example, with respect to telephone surveys and privacy-confidentiality concerns, survey practitioners need to know more about the phenomena of party lines and the practice of having supervisors monitor telephone interviews for quality control.

In summary, we *have* learned quite a bit, nevertheless. The public does seem to be concerned about the personal information that government or private research seeks, and what happens to it. As expected from other studies, information such as income is sensitive and subject to misreporting as well as nonreporting. The terms of the promise of confidentiality do have an effect on cooperation rates, even though the concept itself is often only vaguely understood. Citizen trust in confidentiality assurances is at a very low level.

While Knerr (Chapter 9) shows the current hazards to researchers unprotected from investigating agencies, this chapter has demonstrated that even where the researcher is immune (like at the Census Bureau), there is not an obvious spillover to respondents in making them trust a confidentiality pledge unconditionally (witness the finding in which only 5% of our national sample felt that others could not obtain individual respondent records if they really tried). Some observers reasonably argue, however, that the public currently has no compelling reason to fear survey research. Perhaps the high cooperation rates which the Census Bureau obtained in the five-treatment experiment are due to the strong legislation and practice that people know about. If something adverse were to happen to respondents as a result of survey data and this were to become widely known, then survey research that requires high cooperation rates could be in for a disaster.

Evidence has been offered that verbalized guarantees of confidentiality are met with respondent skepticism and outright disbelief. Concern about what information we, as citizens, give out about ourselves, plus apprehension about what may eventually happen to us because of that information, is likely to increase over the years and decades ahead. Survey organizations must now seek better ways to inform the public of the purposes of surveys and censuses and the protections against disclosure. Ways must be found to build mutual trust and understanding between the interviewer and the subject. Without it, fears of evil-producing data banks are likely to grow in a society that is not technically trained to distinguish (or does not wish to distinguish) between information gathered for "research or statistical purposes" and that gathered for purposes of making some administrative decision affecting the individual directly.

References

American Statistical Association. Report on the ASA conference on surveys of human populations. *The American Statistician*, 1974, *28*, 30-34.
Barabba, V. P., & Kaplan, D. L. U.S. census bureau statistical techniques to prevent disclosure—the right to privacy vs. the need to know. Paper presented at the 40th Session of the International Statistical Institute, Warsaw, Poland, 1975.
Beach, M. E. Nonresponse rates on current programs. *Field Methods Research Branch Report*, No. 15, U.S. Bureau of the Census, June 26, 1979 (unpublished).
Finkner, A. L. Privacy and confidentiality discussion. Statement made to the Census Advisory Committee on Small Areas. Washington, D.C., 1974 (unpublished).
Frankel, L. Statistics and people: The statistician's responsibilities. *Journal of the American Statistical Association*, 1976, *71*, 9-16.
Goldfield, E. D., Turner, A. G., Cowan, C. D., & Scott, J. C. Privacy and confidentiality as factors in survey response. *Review of Public Data Use*, No. 4, 1978, *6*, 3-17.
Love, L. T., & Turner, A. G. The census bureau's experience: Respondent availability and response rates. *American Statistical Association Proceedings of the Business and Economic Statistics Section*, Washington, D.C.: American Statistical Association, 1975.
Marquis, K. H. Survey response rates: Some trends, causes and correlates. Paper presented at the Biennial Conference on Health Survey Research Methods, Williamsburg, Virginia, 1977.
Martin, M. E. Report on activities: Committee on national statistics. *The American Statistician*, 1976, *30*, 21-23.

National Academy of Sciences. *Privacy and confidentiality as factors in survey response.* Washington, D.C.: National Academy of Sciences, 1979.

Response Analysis Corporation. Communications themes for the 1980 census. *An exploratory study in Oakland, California.* Princeton, N.J.: Response Analysis Corporation, 1977.

Singer, E. Informed consent. *Consequences for response rate and response quality in social surveys.* New York City: Columbia University, 1977.

Turner, A. G. Tables contained in letter to Edwin Goldfield, National Academy of Sciences, December 15, 1977 (unpublished).

U.S. Department of Commerce, Bureau of the Census, Census of Population and Housing: 1970, Evaluation and Research Program PHC(E)-4. *Estimates of coverage of population by sex, race, and age: Demographic analysis.* Washington, D.C., 1974.

U.S. Department of Commerce, Bureau of the Census, Current Population Reports: Special Studies, Series P-23, No. 65. *Developmental estimates of the coverage of the population of states in the 1970 census: Demographic analysis.* Washington, D.C., 1977.

Chapter 8

Sampling Strategies and the Threat to Privacy

Shirley Foster Hartley

Because of the variation and change in human behavior and social interaction, the need for valid survey research is unending. Whether one is interested in problems of violence and criminal behavior, poverty, physical or mental illness, drug abuse, child rearing, or any of a myriad of other issues that affect human life, valid information is necessary for appropriate action. Too often, public policy has been based in inaccurate knowledge or stereotypes later found to be in error (e.g., immigration policy).

However, there is also an increase in individual and societal concern for the privacy of individuals and for the confidentiality of their data. See, for example, Anthony Turner's empirical data on public response to survey research and to promises of confidentiality, and his discussion of these societal concerns in Chapter 7. People seem to be more skeptical now than in the past of survey research and other activities that involve having information about themselves collected and stored, and having the findings disclosed in some form (aggregated or otherwise) in publications and elsewhere. Researchers, therefore, need to give increased thought to ways of minimizing the intrusions on privacy and confidentiality that may occur in the research process.

Sampling human subjects and the collection of data by mail, telephone, the use of existing records, or personal contact almost always involves some invasion of privacy and some threat to confidentiality. For example, some people may be alarmed merely by the research request. They may fear that the reason for being selected (e.g., previous cancer experience or unwed pregnancy) may become known to family and friends, or the contact may upset unstable persons who fear insensitive questions about matters that even their physician cannot broach with them directly. Notice that privacy is invaded when unwanted information is *given* to the subject as well as when information is taken from or about the subject without consent. For instance, if a researcher exposes subjects to loud and incessant noise or pornographic photographs in order to observe their responses, the subjects' privacy has been violated. So too, the person who is called up and told that the survey is interested in knowing about his or her cancer can claim that privacy is invaded, that he or she did not know of the cancer or did not want to be reminded of that fact. Or, consider the wish of subjects in Milgram's (1974) research, to avoid knowing the level of harm they were capable of inflicting on other human beings! Protecting the privacy of subjects in this broader sense of the word while giving adequate information for informed consent requires a firm ethical commitment and an extremely careful selection of words.

This chapter will detail some of the ways in which sampling procedures may intrude on privacy, violate confidentiality, and raise questions of consent; and it will suggest some of the methods of minimizing the disadvantages accruing from these research procedures. (The issues of informed consent and confidentiality of responses are dealt with in greater detail by several other contributors to this volume, e.g., Boruch and Cecil; Turner; Knerr.) Following a brief example to dramatize the importance of valid sampling, I will review general issues in ethical sample selection that cut across specific techniques of sampling. These include respect for potential subjects, cost/benefit issues, adequate informed consent, nongeneralizable consent, protection of subjects who have violated the law, undersampled categories, and the general issue of building public confidence. Ethical issues related to four specific sampling strategies will then be reviewed. There are ethical dilemmas peculiar to (1) sampling from listings of persons or groups, (2) sampling from geographical areas, (3) sampling from existing records, and (4) sampling in the field or natural settings. These methods are not exhaustive of sampling techniques, nor are the issues reviewed here all-inclusive. Rather, they suggest the types of concerns that researchers will increasingly need to address in the early planning stages of research projects, in order to avoid some of the more glaring violations of ethics that have challenged social scientists in the past. Even if one were not personally concerned with these potential problems, granting agencies and institutional review boards demand that these be considered in the design of the study.

A Case in Point

Sampling is the means by which we learn about the attitudes, desires, and behaviors of human beings. By subdividing people into categories, or "populations" of interest, e.g., adolescents, Mexican-Americans, unmarried mothers, or drug addicts, a representative portion, or *sample*, of that population may be studied. Since no national census can be exhaustive on all types of information (the Census Bureau was empowered merely to count and report on the number of citizens), and since no other research organization has the funds to survey all persons even within subpopulations, some sampling method, for better or worse, is employed in almost all social research. Indeed, everyone uses convenience sampling in making everyday judgments, even though most people are not consciously aware of their sampling procedure. Anyone who knows one or two homosexuals is likely to be ready with an opinion or "theory" about the causes and consequences of that phenomenon for the whole category of persons labeled "homosexual." If the members of a category were homogenous or similar in all important characteristics (as anthropologists have sometimes assumed in studying preliterate tribes), one could learn everything needed from one informant. However, to the extent that the particular person or persons "sampled" are *not* typical of the group, or that the category is very diverse within, reports, judgments, or theories may be not only misleading but grossly harmful to the persons within and outside the category.

An extreme case of misused sampling procedures with deleterious social consequences is found in a classic study of unwed mothers (Young, 1954). The erroneous conclusions of this research influenced social welfare policies for about a quarter of a century. While previous studies, based on a few psychiatric interviews, had concluded that mothers out of wedlock are neurotic, psychotic, or schizoid (e.g., Kasanin and Handschin, 1941), Young purported to sample 100 cases from the files of a home for unwed mothers. To one untrained in sampling, the sample size would seem to be a real improvement over research based on fewer cases. Young, a recognized neo-Freudian, reports finding that these mothers out of wedlock unconsciously wanted the birth and found in the records of these mothers a series of Freudian-type reasons purported to substantiate this view. Incredibly, not one of these mothers was found to be pregnant by accident, even though birth control information and supplies were difficult to obtain or unavailable to young or poor women at the time of the study. The conclusion that these mothers unconsciously wanted children, while consciously denying that they wanted them, can be refuted on the basis of evidence presented in the report itself (see Hartley, 1975, chap. 3). Nevertheless, this false conclusion was used by social workers and their administrators for a period of almost 25 years as justification to deny, refuse, and prevent the discussion of potentially available methods of birth control or reference to Planned Parenthood Clinics on the grounds that such women would not use the information anyway. Thus, an uncomfortable topic could be avoided in dealing with welfare clients. In fact, social workers could be defended as behaving rationally on the basis of what was then judged to be excellent research by a respected investigator. Yet, to use such erroneous conclusions as a basis for social policy and practice was an injustice to clients who might have prevented unwanted births, if they had been given adequate information; and it was an affront to society which bore the often costly results of unwanted births.

The research procedure was clearly an intrusion into the privacy of women whose files were created at a time of their special need, then used for a purpose other than originally intended. The conclusions, whose interpretations the subjects had no opportunity to challenge, were an insult to their intelligence, since the information and means of contraception were often kept from young, unwed, and poor women. The research was also an affront to social scientists. The report is flawed in many respects (Hartley, 1975, chap. 3), but the sampling procedure is particularly at fault in leading to erroneous conclusions. The convenience sample, accessible cases in an agency file, was no better than those cases that might be known by a community member. There was no apparent reason for the number, 100 cases, except that it made percentaging automatic. We were not told specifically how the 100 cases were randomly pulled from a file encompassing some larger number of cases. But, more importantly, there was no consideration given to the fact that women who go to a home for unwed mothers are highly atypical of all such mothers, nor was there any attempt to include unwed mothers from outside of this specific setting. There was no attempt to compare the characteristics of the 100 women sampled (e.g., by their age, race, educational, and familial backgrounds) to the characteristics of unwed mothers nationally to learn whether these women were representative of the entire category to whom generalizations were made. The sampling principle is very clear. If one wants to talk about all members of a category, one must sample from the entire category, not a *specialized* segment of it. Misinformation can be worse than no information. It is no more valid to generalize from a bad sample of 100 than to generalize from a sample of one or two.

Coping with the ever-present dilemma of trying to obtain accurate information, while employing necessarily imperfect sampling techniques, and attempting to respect privacy requires development of sensitivity to each facet of the dilemma and corresponding development of research designs and procedures that at least diminish, if not eliminate, the scientific and moral problems of applied social research. Although the ideal of an equal probability of selection for all elements or possible cases in a population (simple random sampling) is rarely achieved in practice, and may be impossible with populations such as unwed mothers, there are various sampling procedures that are more adequate than the procedure described above (see e.g., Kish, 1965, and Babbie, 1973, for a general discussion of sampling techniques that minimize bias).

In the case of research on unwed mothers, the research of Pauker (1969), Kantner and Zelnick (1972), and Hartley (1975) illustrates some sampling and design strategies that permit more valid inference than was possible from Young's study about the causes of illegitimacy. Pauker compared the ninth grade scores of women who did versus those who did not later become unwed mothers. The ratings on numerous psychological scales did not differ significantly. Kantner and Zelnick (1972, 1973) employed the most adequate sampling strategy yet devised with regard to adolescent pregnancy, much of which occurs out of wedlock. Because they used a national multistage sampling of all females aged 15 through 19, they were able to compare those who did and did not engage in sexual intercourse with respect to levels of knowledge and use of contraception, numbers of conceptions, if any, and resolution in abortion, marriage before birth, or birth of a child before marriage. These studies have destroyed many false stereotypes about unwed mothers and offer excellent detail on the observed differences among young women. While the interviewing procedures employed by Kantner and Zelnick included informed consent, there no doubt was some sense in which the privacy of the respondents was infringed on; yet, long-term benefits of valid research on this important social problem, especially to those at risk, justify some social and emotional costs of the research procedure. Hartley's (1970, 1975) research comparing international levels and trends in illegitimacy indicates that these are systematically patterned in time and space, and are more parsimoneously explained in terms of ongoing social-cultural processes than of the "pathology" of individual mothers.

General Ethical Issues Involved in Sample Selection[1]

The main focus of this chapter is on ethical dilemmas that occur specifically in relation to sampling from lists, from geographical areas, from existing records, and field sampling. However, there are a number of more general ethical issues regarding the location of samples, sample selection, and data collection that cut across sampling techniques, and these merit discussion before proceeding to the ethical dilemmas related to specific sampling strategies.

The first issue involves respect for potential subjects. Most social research is dependent on respondents for their participation and truthfulness. Thus, there is a practical point, as well as a moral point, to treating potential subjects with respect. Yet, valid inference and generalization about the population from which the sample is derived necessitates that a response be obtained from each person or sample unit in the sampling frame; that, in turn, may require that subjects be persuaded, somehow, to respond. In any case the competent interviewer certainly does not make it easy for potential respondents to decline to participate. High pressure salesmanship is sometimes used by interviewers just to get their foot in the door. To some extent, then, the privacy of potential subjects is already disturbed even before data are gathered. The dilemma is how to minimize the intrusion and respectfully gain cooperation without jeopardizing the randomness of the sample.

A highly effective means of minimizing the intrusion and enabling potential respondents to make better informed and more autonomous decisions is o separate temporally the informing or consenting from the actual research participation. For example, the researcher might make an initial contact merely to announce the research and to request an appointment at the convenience of the respondent. This makes it extremely difficult for the potential subject to refuse on the basis of time, since flexibility in meeting the individuals' time schedule almost forces the subject to focus on *when* it would be possible, if not immediately convenient. Yet, this procedure gives the respondent an opportunity to reconsider participating in the survey and to check on the credentials of the investigator, should he or she desire to do so. In research limited to a local community it is possible to inform potential subjects of the nature and importance of the survey through public forums, by sending representatives to discuss the project in local organizations, etc. In areas where fear of strangers may be a problem, articles on the survey, along with photos of the researchers/interviewers may be published in local newspapers or neighborhood pamphlets. Official identification of those making the initial contact is always desirable to enable potential respondents to protect themselves from possible criminals or con artists disguised as researchers.

A second ethical issue relates to cost/benefit considerations. One should attempt to limit the costs of research, without unduly sacrificing the scientific or moral

---

[1] Rather than focus on problems of immoral research activity such as falsification of data, which is dealt with elsewhere (see, e.g., the Code of Ethics of the American Sociological Association), this chapter focuses on those ethical dilemmas of sampling that may arise despite the scientific expertise and good intentions of social researchers.

value of the undertaking, since monies spent needlessly on research could better be allocated to fulfill other legitimate social needs. Often savings can be realized through the use of existing administrative data or through a secondary analysis of existing research data, but these savings must be weighed in relation to potentially lower benefits accruing from data that do not contain precisely the information needed, that offer less than adequate detail, or that were obtained through inadequate procedures. In survey research, the optimization of research value depends largely on the selection of sampling procedures that are scientifically as well as morally acceptable.

A third ethical issue relates to obtaining adequate informed consent from each subject. Potential respondents should be informed of the purpose and procedure of the study and should understand that their participation is voluntary and that no penalties will follow refusal to participate. While there are practical and moral reasons for being entirely open and honest with potential respondents, there may also be practical (scientific) and moral considerations that override the reasons for open and honest disclosure. Some of the practical or scientific reasons can be found in research such as that of Singer (1978) which shows that honestly informed subjects respond with greatest candor. Other practical reasons for openness may be found in Loo's discussion (Chapter 5) of respondents' high level of cooperation when given an opportunity to vent serious concerns to a truly respectful and sympathetic investigator. Scientific or practical reasons for and against limiting disclosure may also be found in Geller (Chapter 2). Major moral reasons for limiting disclosure are those having to do with the way in which full disclosure can invade privacy and cause emotional harm. For example, in a large-scale study of persons successfully treated for childhood cancer, it was deemed important not to inform prospective participants or their spouses that the purpose of the study was to discover whether genetic harm had been caused by treatment of their cancer. It was reasoned that the fact of their childhood cancer may have been unknown to them, forgotten, or hidden from their family. Since the study was particularly interested in the current health of both the respondent and any offspring, an introduction that might arouse fear of (1) lingering cancer in the subject or (2) cancerous possibilities in the children could have been detrimental to all concerned. The problem was resolved by introducing the follow-up survey as one in which respondents were chosen because of their serious childhood disease or hospitalization experience. Only if the respondent asked for more detailed information would the more complete history be revealed (Austin, 1979).

A fourth ethical issue concerns secondary analysis of data. When informed consent has been obtained for one research goal, it cannot be assumed that consent has been obtained for any other uses of the data. Before files of identifiable, privileged information are turned over to a second researcher for purposes other than those for which the data were originally gathered, permission should be obtained from the respondent to transfer those files (Privacy Protection Study Commission, 1977). Yet, there are situations, especially in epidemiology (e.g., Gordis & Gold, 1980) in which the difficulties of obtaining a second consent are virtually insurmountable and the importance of the research would seem to many to override the importance of obtaining a second consent.

The fifth ethical issue concerns the study of persons who have engaged in illegal behavior. No matter what sampling technique is used, the individuals sampled are unlikely to participate unless the willingness and ability of the investigator to protect the privacy of respondents is demonstrated beyond reasonable doubt. Drug pushers, felons, or others who have broken the law are not likely to cooperate in social scientific research if they suspect that they may be identified in any way. The researcher must be willing to put his or her own career on the line, by terminating the study or going to jail rather than reveal information from privileged communications. The investigator must also be wary of ways in which typical procedures might jeopardize the interests of law-breaking subjects. For example, signed consent forms, normally intended to protect the interests of subjects, could actually serve as documentation of admission of criminal behavior in the case of subjects in a study of criminal behavior.

This dilemma has been recognized both by the Commission on the Protection of Human Subjects and by the Department of Health, Education and Welfare in their new proposals for legislation on Human Subjects Research. Both recommend that informed consent not be required when the form itself would put subjects at risk, as by linking the respondent to illegal behavior (Gray, 1979; Fanning, 1979).

In other respects, as well, the researcher must take care to eliminate potential identifiers from all stored data, since the threat of subpoena by local or state prosecutors remains (see Knerr, Chapter 9; King & Spector, 1963).

A sixth ethical issue concerns equity in sampling. Considerations of economy, scientific fashion, and theoretical convenience often dictate sampling strategies that are inequitable. In the sampling of persons, case records, family units, etc., no particular part of the relevant population should be overstudied or understudied. Ideally, sample selection should be random within the population or representative of all of the populations to which the findings are generalized. As mentioned earlier, there are many means of approaching this ideal. It has been pointed out in the report of the National Commission for the Protection of Human Subjects that overstudying of a population is unethical on the grounds that it exploits that population. There is an even broader issue, however, that is particularly relevant to the ethics of survey sampling. As implied earlier, in the discussion of research on unwed mothers, a major implication of over- or undersampling is inappropriate generalization.

In much social scientific research, samples focus on nonappropriate portions of the population of interest, or the sample may exclude important portions of the population. Table 8-1, which was suggested by sociologist Mary-Margaret Franz (personal communication, 1979), illustrates four types of situations in which over- or understudying has undesirable scientific and ethical implications.

In cell A are types of study subjects that have been overresearched and overgeneralized. Although we have learned a great deal from animal studies (Hebb and Thompson, 1968), research on white rats and nonhuman primates has often seemed simpler than focusing directly on the humans we wish to learn about. Similarly, researchers in a university setting have easy access to willing college students for a myriad of social studies. Moreover, social scientists have found it all too tempting and easy to overgeneralize findings on these subject categories to other species and to other adult humans, respectively.

Table 8-1. A Comparison of the Degree of Generalization with Frequency of Research

Degree of generalization	Frequency of research			
	Overresearched		Underresearched	
Overgeneralization	A	White rats; non-human primates; college students	B	Menopausal women; homosexuals, trans-sexuals; criminals
Undergeneralization	C	Unwed mothers; people in poverty; blacks	D	Women

In cell B are underresearched populations from which scientists tend to overgeneralize. For example, while about 15% of menopausal women seek medical relief, the study of them tends to be overgeneralized to menopausal women who do not seek treatment. Psychiatric samples of homosexuals and transsexuals often portray them as representative of the unsampled (typically nonpsychiatric) populations. Prisoners convicted of rape, murder, etc., are taken as representative of those that got away.

In cell C are some examples of categories that are overresearched and undergeneralized. Samples from these populations are often given an aura of uniqueness or noncomparability with the larger human population, and they are thus undergeneralized. For instance, unwed mothers are assumed to be different in ways other than their unwedness, and they are thus not compared to married mothers, e.g., on anxiety measures and monetary concerns. People in poverty are typically assumed by researchers to be different from persons in the middle class in ways other than their financial circumstances, but these assumptions are not empirically tested, leading to the current complaint that this procedure "blames the victim" (Ryan, 1971). The point here is that sampling appropriate comparison groups is necessary if valid and ethical claims are to be made about the nature of categories such as these.

In cell D is the group of humans most frequently underresearched and undergeneralized. Women have historically been left out of most of the research on social stratification, community power structures, delinquency, occupational impact studies, etc., under the assumption that they were different than the relevant (e.g., male) population (Lenski, 1966; Vidich & Bensman, 1958; Harris, 1977). Thus, because it was assumed that women obtained their social status first from their fathers and then from their husbands, there has been little research on the social status of adult women until the last couple of years (Hartley, 1978). Indeed, the first important study on this subject found that wives more often had objectively higher social status than husbands when independently evaluated (Watson and Barth, 1964). Similarly, recent research indicates that occupational participation has just as much of an impact on the intellectual structures and life goals of women as men (Miller, Schooler, Kohn, & Miller, 1979). The assumption that jobs were less central to the lives of women as compared to men forestalled research on the subject. One can validly say what is true for a category or group only when that group has been appropriately included in the sampling procedure rather than controlled out of the study.

A seventh ethical issue concerns the interests of science and society that are served by the way in which the selection and use of a sampling strategy builds public confidence and good will for the process of social research. Each investigator tends to view his or her own research as crucial, but must recognize that without public faith in the value of social research, any and all of our projects are short-lived and ultimately valueless. While concern for scientific validity must guide the choice of sampling procedures, so too must concern for building public confidence and good will for social science.

Ethical Issues Related to Four Specific Sampling Strategies

"Sampling is the use of a *definite procedure* in the selection of a part for the express purpose of obtaining from it descriptions or estimates of certain properties and characteristics of the whole" (Stephan & McCarthy, 1963, p. 23), and there are different ethical dilemmas peculiar to the use of each such procedure. The specific approach chosen depends on the problem to be examined, the monetary, personnel, and time budgets of the principal investigator, and a host of technical considerations (such as the availability of computer resources for the analysis of large-scale samples). While it may seem at first thought that a 100% sample would always be one's first choice, sampling has many advantages over the full population survey. Sampling is advantageous with respect to cost, efficiency, and convenience; on any given budget, a greater amount of detail may be collected, there is reduced opportunity for errors, and more time may be allotted to the collection, processing, and analysis of the data. Sampling less than the whole population also reduces the numbers of persons at risk of an invasion of privacy from the research process.

There is no one best sampling method; each procedure has its advantages and disadvantages. There is usually a preferable method, however, for each problem to be investigated, and thus it is important for the researcher to have enough familiarity with each method to be able to identify the most appropriate sampling tactic for a given purpose.

Some of the ethical dilemmas that social researchers should take into account will be reviewed in relation to each of the following four methods of sample selection: (1) sampling from listings of persons, groups, or organizations, (2) sampling from geographical areas, (3) sampling from existing records, and (4) sampling in the field. These do not exhaust all possible approaches to sampling, for there are various strategies that involve combinations or variations on these methods. However, this discussion will offer some clues as to the ethical issues to be considered when contemplating any of the various sampling procedures. (Related ethical issues concerning sampling and random assignment to experimental and control groups in social experiments are discussed by Ross Conner in Chapter 3.)

Population listings. The category of persons about whom we wish to learn something is defined as a "population." These may be persons in a given city, drug abusers, unwed mothers, students, etc. Or, the population of interest could be *groups* of persons, such as family units, voluntary organizations, hospitals, classrooms, or whole nations.

If it is possible to obtain a complete (or relatively complete) listing of all of the units of the population in which one is interested, sample selection is facilitated. (Other problems of how to contact or interview persons widely dispersed in space may remain.) One may select individual sampling units from a list by means of a table of random numbers or by systematic selection at regular intervals (every kth unit on the list), having begun with a random start. Thus, the researcher who needs a sample of 200 from a list of 30,000 could begin with a randomized (equal probability) choice from the first 150 units and then continue by selecting each 150th unit from then on through the entire list. This approach is almost as acceptable as the more cumbersome use of a table of 100,000 random numbers.

What constitutes the ethical use of such lists? This question has received little attention until recently, since the problem that has tended to bother most social scientists is how to *find* a relevant list, not how to *use* such a list ethically. Since there are different kinds of population lists, the problems that accompany their use vary accordingly. Here, we will examine some problems that arise in connection with sampling membership lists, directory lists, and personally compiled lists, respectively.

In the past, when researchers have been able to obtain listings of members (e.g., church groups, political campaign supporters, professional association members), they seldom stopped to consider whether they would be invading the privacy of the persons listed. However, the research use of listings gathered for membership purposes may indeed be perceived as an invasion of the privacy of persons listed as I recently had personal occasion to learn! I was taken to task by an irate colleague for sampling from a list of members of one of my own professional associations, the American Sociological Association. The research goal was to compare the responses of knowledgeable medical sociologists with those of 2,300 university students on questions regarding reproductive engineering, e.g., sperm banking, in vitro fertilization, sex preselection. (The student sample allowed a before/after follow-up just at the time of the publicity surrounding the birth of the "test-tube" baby, Louise Brown.) Had I submitted greater detail about my project and the comparison intended between the professional and nonprofessional respondents, my use of the listing probably would not have been objectionable to any of those sampled. However, the effective resolution of the dilemma of how much detail is enough remains the subject of future empirical inquiry.

Other sources of population listings that have been widely used in sampling from local areas are city directories and telephone directories. However, since many persons and household units refuse to have their names listed in the phone book, in order to preserve their privacy, random-digit dialing has come into use for telephone sampling. While providing an advantage to the social researcher, this new sampling technique is certainly an invasion of privacy, since there is no longer any way that a person or household can choose to be excluded from this use of their telephone. One may be sympathetic with persons who do not want to be hassled in this way, and yet the research dilemma is clear: to achieve random sampling, these persons must be sampled, despite their desire for privacy. The research team must make the sampling effort, and perhaps the only way to mitigate the intrusion is to politely apologize and respectfully request participation in the study, while respecting individual autonomy and dignity when refusals occur.

A third kind of population listing is the personally compiled list. When there exists no appropriate population listing from which to sample, the researcher may, with some ingenuity and a great deal of perseverance, create a list from which to sample. The compilation of one's own list is often necessary when attempting to study persons who have special interests in privacy, such as those considered deviant in some way or those whose acts may be unlawful. The research of David Graeven (Graeven & Folmer, 1977; Graeven & Schaef, 1978) provides an excellent illustration of the ethical arguments for and against the use of some personally compiled lists. Graeven and Folmer (1977), studying the spread of heroin use among two high school populations, spent months talking with and gaining the trust of both users and pushers, in order to develop a list of students who had ever used heroin, so that an adequate sample might be obtained from among all users at two high schools. Committed to the principle of anonymity, Graeven initially encouraged his fifteen ongoing informants to use numbers that would remind them of the persons, without actually revealing the names of users to the research team. Over a period of time, and especially as the list grew in length, the numbers became increasingly confusing and the names gradually emerged as more appropriate. By that time, the investigator had a reputation for confidentiality and trustworthiness. With the list of persons who had ever used heroin, it was possible to take a sample, stratified by the year of initiation into the drug culture. The results were a valuable contribution to our knowledge of the evolution and diffusion of drug use at the high school level, and the data allowed a series of useful comparisons to be made of the family backgrounds, self-evaluations, etc., of those who continued versus those who discontinued heroin use. The analysis would not have been so highly valued without the excellence of the sampling procedure. Of course, the ethical issues regarding the collection and protection of the names of those engaged in unlawful activities remain. While this particular researcher was, and was perceived to be, unusually trustworthy, can we rely on all investigators to be equally concerned?

Another ethical dilemma posed by Graeven involves payment to subjects. While a small payment for the hours spent in the interview situation was deemed an absolute necessity in moving potential respondents from almost total unwillingness to an eagerness to participate, there is the ethical question of payment to persons who are likely to use the money for illegal activities, such as the purchase of more drugs. While one may rationalize that addicts might obtain money from even more objectionable sources, the question of paying such respondents remains an unresolved issue. Perhaps payment in goods, food, clothing, tickets to sports events, or something else likely to motivate respondents' cooperation would find greater acceptance over the long term.

Areal sampling. One of the most complex sampling procedures is areal cluster sampling. It is useful in large-scale sampling of urban communities, rural areas, and to sample persons and family units within whole nations. To obtain a national sample in a country as large and heterogeneous as the United States, multistage, geographical areal sampling is the most appropriate procedure. The techniques were developed early by the Bureau of the Census and by election pollsters, such as Gallup and Roper, and are used widely by the National Opinion Research Center and other large survey research institutes. There are many variations on the general approach (Babbie, 1973, pp. 118-128). Stage one may begin by sampling from a list of Primary Sampling Units (PSUs). The PSUs are composed of Standard Metropolitan Statistical Areas and nonmetropolitan counties with the United States. Stage two is likely to involve a sample of census enumeration districts within selected PSUs. Stage three usually involves the sampling of blocks within the census tracts. Further stages may involve sampling specific dwelling units (e.g., beginning at the northwest corner and moving south) and finally adults within dwelling units of the blocks sampled. At each stage random, systematic, stratified, or purposive selection procedures may be used. Often at the final stage the selection of specific subjects to be interviewed is designated by quota restrictions; that is, persons of specified ages, income or educational level, marital stauts, etc., must be found.

Because the procedure typically ends up with an interviewer at the door of the potential respondent's dwelling, the problem to be overcome is the almost sacred respect for privacy within one's living quarters—"a man's home is his castle." The interviewer must, like a salesperson, get a "foot in the door." Also, like a salesperson, one needs to convince people to participate. An elderly and/or timid subject is no match for an aggressive interviewer. Further, since the interviewer is often paid on the basis of completed interviews, not time spent explaining the voluntary aspects of informed consent to timid or reluctant persons, the temptation to pressure potential respondents may be overwhelming. The training of interviewers should make a difference in this regard, and most reputable survey organizations spend weeks and even months in the training of survey personnel (Gorden, 1969). Clearly interviewers also need to be compensated for time spent with persons who decline to participate.

One advantage of rigorous areal sampling is that a relatively small sample size (e.g., 1,500) may accurately represent the entire adult population. In effect, then, the privacy of relatively few individuals needs be disturbed in order to gain an understanding of the attitudes, opinions, and reported behaviors of vast numbers of persons.

Sampling from existing records. There are a number of dilemmas, often unrecognized, in the use of records that have been gathered for administrative or human service purposes for the additional purpose of social research. (The misuse of a sample of cases from an agency for unwed mothers has already been discussed.) The potential for misuse seems to grow with the increase in all kinds of record keeping. Yet, our concern for the protection of personal privacy and confidentiality is also increasing. How may we expand the knowledge to be gained from the research use of extant (and thus inexpensive) data at the same time that we protect individuals from exploitation?

One of the primary attributes of complex, advanced societies is the vast array of bureaucratic records kept and processed. Many of these records relate to the private behavior or problems of individual human beings. The proliferation of records often relates to the increased delivery of human services, and their potential use for research purposes offers both a gold mine of information and a threat to the privacy of individuals and the confidentiality of their data.

Consider, for instance, the increase of record keeping about individuals related to health care. We are far removed from the intimate doctor-patient relationship idealized in the past. While 85% of all medical services were of this nature at the beginning of this century, now less than 5% of the providers of medical-care services are private physicians (Freedman, 1975, p. 3). Increased specialization and variety of health services plus private and public health insurance coverage require an increase in record keeping and a legitimate need for the transfer of health information among medical, insurance, and social service agencies. In 1975 alone, Americans made an estimated 1,056,000,000 visits to physicians. Each of these visits probably generated a new medical record or added information to an existing record. Considering that the recommended minimum retention period for a medical record is 10 to 25 years, the accumulation of records seems staggering. Yet, more important to our consideration of the threat to privacy is the fact that many people besides the medical-care providers have access to these records at the same time that the patient has been denied access to his or her own records (Privacy Protection Study Commission, 1977, p. 277). How is it possible to protect the rights of individuals, while facilitating the increase in knowledge potential in the research use of these existing records? The Privacy Commission suggested that the secondary use of medical records "raises the sharpest clash between society's interest in protecting medical confidentiality and its interest in a wide variety of other important functions" (Privacy Protection Study Commission, 1977, p. 281).

The actual sampling of available records has typically been limited mainly by the lack of imagination and ingenuity of the social researcher. Think of the cases on file with social welfare agencies, juvenile court or probation officers, child welfare, adoption agencies, foster care, family counseling centers, and drug addition service centers, in addition to medical records by the millions. Some records are held by local agencies, others by state, and still others by Federal governmental agencies. How can we ethically exploit these records to advance our research goals?

At the one extreme, the research scientist goes to the individual(s) or agency that maintains the records, and those records are turned over to the scientist to do with as he/she pleases. (In some cases this is even permitted by law. For instance, Social Security clerks may now turn over to welfare administrators the names and addresses of missing fathers who are in arrears on their child support payments.) Even if this seems like a good or harmless practice in a particular case, it is a step toward undermining public faith in the confidentiality of records, and a step toward further uses of those data for purposes not originally intended. While we may agree that Social Security records should be used to reinforce paternal responsibility, the use in one case may make it easier to pass legislation allowing less justifiable uses of Social Security data. There are certain kinds of confidence in valued relationships (e.g., physician-patient, government-citizen, public-scientist) that are needed in order for society to transmit information that needs to be communicated (e.g., people may withhold information from their doctors that is necessary for diagnosis of an illness, if the confidentiality of the relationship is questionable). In general, it is poor practice to use records for purposes not originally intended or agreed on as it destroys public trust in the relationships involved.

At the other extreme, the investigator goes to the holder of information of interest and is given nothing at all and no way to obtain the needed data. (For example, the U.S. Department of Agriculture is currently unable to get from the Internal Revenue Service information on who has filed the Farm Tax form.) Under these conditions, an investigator must abandon that research effort, or go to extremely costly and probably less effective ways of obtaining their sample. The basic value problem with this approach is that it causes duplication of effort typically at great expense to the taxpayer, or it causes failure to use existing information for research that would greatly benefit the general public or otherwise satisfy national needs.

There are two midway solutions that seem quite satisfactory but require a lot of cooperation from the record keepers and thus may require that the investigator be prepared to compensate others for their time. These solutions have been used extensively in demographic and epidemiological studies.

One of these solutions is to have the person who holds the files go through them and determine what persons have the characteristics desired for the scientist's sample. For instance, a physician may be asked to find out which of his/her patients have exhibited specific physical or mental symptoms within the last five years. The holder of the files then contacts the patients/clients and asks permission to have a researcher contact them and ask information about whatever the study is covering. Only if the patient consents does the researcher receive the name and phone number for the contact. (Unfortunately unwilling patients/clients may differ systematically from those who are willing to be questioned, thus biasing the sample.)

Another solution is to have the person who holds the files go through and select the appropriate persons and send them each a letter from the researcher (with a cover letter from the record keeper) asking their consent to participate in the study. In this case, it must be made clear to the potential subject and to the investigator that the researcher will not know who received letters, but only who replied to the request. In each of these solutions the wording of both letters should make it entirely clear to the potential subjects that they do not have to cooperate, that they have no obligation to do so, and that failure to cooperate will in no way jeopardize their relationship with the person(s) who holds their files (e.g., their doctor, probation officer, counselor).

These two intermediate solutions are ones that have often been used in local, state, and federal agencies and by researchers working through hospitals, doctors, social service agencies, school districts, etc. Even the Bureau of the Census, which promises confidentiality forever to citizens, will permit the use of these intermediate methods provided that the study is one of national interest and of value to the public and that they control the confidentiality of the responses. Projects funded by the National Institutes of Health or the National Science Foundation are likely to be ones they would cooperate with, but these liaisons are still quite rare. They would probably not cooperate with any strictly commercial research venture.

Sampling from existing records, therefore, in spite of the advantages of time, cost, efficiency, and ability to get at persons with rare attributes, poses a whole series of other problems. How do you ask consent to use files without already having invaded the privacy of knowledge about the records available? One needs to know what sorts of information are contained in case records before asking permission to use them. Often, fortuitous collegial relationships have alerted the investigator to the possibility of using extant data. Without collegial contacts it may be very difficult to learn about available data and research possibilities.

In preparation for seeking out the potential cooperation of agency personnel and subjects, the researcher's ability to imaginatively take on the role of "the other" may be crucial to successful breakthroughs. For scientists connected with a college or university, the submission of their research protocol to the campus Institutional Review Board may be the first of a series of appeals for permission to proceed. These committees are a relatively new form of professional self-discipline; they take seriously their charge to oversee the protection of human subjects (see Tanke and Tanke, Chapter 6, other volume). Committee members may so adamantly challenge the investigator that he or she may be tempted to mislead or outright falsify the procedures and goals of the project in order to obtain approval. Indeed, many of our classic social research studies would not receive confirmation from contemporary Institutional Review Boards. It is wise to draw these colleagues into an advisory role, rather than treat them as adversaries. Asking for their suggestions on the protocol to demonstrate an awareness of potential risk to subjects is often helpful. Even with the approval of the campus committee, one must establish and build relationships with the person(s) who control access to the records of interest.

Gaining access to existing records may take anywhere from a few months to several years. The patience and perseverance of the researcher are crucial. Often the scientist will spend weeks and even months interviewing persons with knowledge of the specific bureaucracy whose help is needed. It is important to be willing to take the time to learn about the psychology of the particular persons with positions in the agency. Who might be threatened and who might find advantage in the intrusion and/or help of the social researcher? Who might resent the possibly higher educational level and/or prestige of the investigator, and who might be more cooperative on the same account? The researcher needs to be aware of, and allow, the variety of attitudes engendered, while seeking a working relationship with agency personnel. It helps to have more than one set of contingency plans, so that an early rejection of the initial proposal need not mean an abandonment of the project. Researchers have noted that top-level bureaucrats typically do not want to take responsibility for giving the signal to go ahead, but they also do not want to say no. The compromise is often a postponement, or referral to one or more committees. They have little immediate gain in helping the investigator, unless the researcher can convince the decision makers that the research could be important to their own work. Even with an okay from the top, the secretarial and clerical staff persons can be the key to actually getting into the files or getting the introductory letters of requests for subject participation out to the potential subjects. In all cases the ability to get the sample involves much more than technical expertise, it involves an understanding of basic human nature and organizational structures. One must be willing to sell the value of the research to everyone involved. On the other hand, if one uses misleading information or false pretenses to gain confidential information, the offense is punishable as criminal behavior (Privacy Protection Study Commission, 1977, p. 16). Whenever we are able to honestly create a winner-winner game in our human relationships, our tasks can be more pleasantly carried through, and often with less time and cost, as well.

Once access to the records has been obtained, it is important that individually identifiable indicators be protected. In most studies, the researcher is only interested in the individual as a carrier of attributes, or characteristics of groups, etc. Individual data are used as major building blocks during the analytic process, but in the final stage both research findings and statistical data are usually presented in aggregate form. The research purpose is to discover and analyze relationships among variables. Therefore, there is no need for the names of individual respondents, except for the initial contacts or in order to obtain permission to use the individual's data for aggregate purposes. It is important to recognize, however, that with small samples, individuals with some unusual characteristic or combination of characteristics may be identifiable by reason of the categorical breakdowns presented for analysis. (If, for instance, one were studying persons seeking help at a mental health facility in a local area, and in record analysis men and women of various occupational or income levels were compared, one might easily identify a woman of high occupation or income, because of the scarcity of persons in that category.) One must eliminate from reporting and analysis those categories that contain few subjects.

The current trend is to disallow use of agency records for research purposes without the specific approval of the subjects. Where an agency is particularly willing and able to cooperate, they may be able to obtain such approval from subjects in the initial stages of collecting data for their own case files. How can the subject, in such an instance, believe that future access to agency benefits may not be contingent on his or her granting permission? It is probably best to make the voluntary nature of subject approval explicit and separated from agency functioning itself. Indeed, the Privacy Protection Study Commission (1977, p. 172) (established by the Privacy Act of 1974) has indicated its concern for the principle of functional separation—the need to separate the use of information about an individual for a research or statistical purpose from its use in arriving at an administrative or other decision about that individual. This principle is not only among the major recommendations of the commission, but, in addition, the commission proposes that researchers using agency records be required to notify individual subjects of such proposed usage. Institutional review processes would aim to protect minors or mentally incompetent persons and those whose consent may be seriously compromised by fear of some loss of benefit or imposition of sanction (e.g., captive populations, such as students, welfare recipients, employees, prison inmates, or hospital patients) (pp. 596-597).

Researchers trained during the years when less stringent ethical norms were prevalent may feel discouraged with the advent of some of these increased concerns and regulations. Yet, it would be foolish to pass up the opportunities available to sample from existing records merely because the preparatory work has increased. We may all be thankful that we are also among those protected by these increased rules regarding privacy and confidentiality.

Another use of existing data for which only the most recent cohorts of social scientists has been trained involves the enormous capabilities of the computer in storing, sharing, and retrieving data. This resource has made it possible for thousands of social scientists to analyze materials and to search for relationships even though they had no part in the initial sampling and gathering of information. While this access to data avoids the ethical problem of individually identifying respondents, there is another danger in the proliferating use of these secondary sources, in general, and data banks, in particular. As Theodore Woolsey, Director of the National Center for Health Statistics, Health Services and Mental Health Administration, Department of Health, Education, and Welfare, warns, "Whenever people become absorbed in problems of storage and retrieval of data in a computerized data bank, they tend to neglect the problems of achieving maximum reliability of the information at the grass roots . . . They seem to overlook all questions of relevance and quality, and they are wildly optimistic about what is really available . . . the existence of . . . information seems to lead to the temptation to use it for purposes for which it is not appropriate, instead of going to the greater expense of gathering appropriate data." (Woolsey, 1970, pp. 1994-1995). Thus, in attempting to *avoid* problems of sampling and data collection, one may be merely neglecting the issues.

Field sampling. Research in the field involves studying human beings in their natural settings. It may include participant or nonparticipant observation and/or in-depth interviewing, and increasingly photographic essays and/or videotape recordings. Just as a professional photographer frames a scene carefully and checks the focus and light meter in order not to waste film, the field researcher plans the selection of samples with both ingenuity and care, lest valuable time, money, and energy be wasted. For example, in his classic study of mental patients, *Asylums*, Goffman (1961) spent a full year working as a medical orderly in order to observe the ways in which patients are treated as nonpersons, and the ways in which they create their own sense of individuality in a depersonalizing situation. How else could an interested researcher have gathered the rich detail evident in this classic without some deception and role playing? The benefit of the research far outweights the ethical problems of deception and invasion of the privacy of patients. Yet, the ethical dilemma implicit in the study of homosexuals by Laud Humphreys, discussed in Chapter 1, cannot be dismissed. Although it is normally considered ethically acceptable to record the audible conversations of persons in public places, because by being in public places and speaking loud enough to be overheard the individual may be assumed to be taking the usual risks of everyday life, Humphreys used deception and role playing in his observations, in following contacts, and in follow-up interviews. The research would certainly not pass a contemporary Committee for the Protection of Human Subjects (Murtha and Seiler, 1979).

The dilemma remains, that is, how to get representative respondents or observational settings *and* protect the privacy and dignity of the subjects. Honest appeals to subjects who have been sampled are only beginning to be attempted. One may appeal to the interest normal human beings have in the process of research and their potential contribution to the enterprise. Some subjects become highly involved in the research itself and in the investigator as a person. One colleague, who spent years studying alcoholics in a series of natural settings, reports that they were not only helpful in finding other subjects for interview (snowball sampling), but they expressed their disappointment when the data gathering phase of the research came to a close. Some of these subjects spontaneously volunteered for follow-up research in the years ahead (Wiseman, 1970). The same investigator, studying the spouses of alcoholics and the relational issues provoked by addiction to liquor, found that wives of alcoholic men were very willing research subjects, but all sampling attempts, including newspaper advertisements, produced very few husbands of women alcoholics who were willing to discuss their situation. Perhaps there is greater stigma for a male spouse, perhaps they are less likely to remain with a wife who drinks excessively, or perhaps they simply do not care about the research effort.

In spousal interviews, an interesting question arises with regard to the problem of third-party privacy. The alcoholic partner has no means of giving informed consent or preventing the spouse's participation, nor is there a means of verifying the accuracy of the respondents' statements about the alcoholic third parties. It is only in the internal consistency of respondents' statements and the similarity of the reports of numerous spouses that truthfulness may be inferred.

Field research often involves the use of "snowball" or chain referral sampling. "The method yields a study sample through referrals made among people who share some characteristic that is of research interest" (Biernacki & Waldorf, 1979, p. 1). This means of selecting a sample is particularly useful when the focus of study is on persons who are deviant in some way. Through omission or glossing over in texts on research methods, one is left with the impression that snowball sampling is a "self-contained and propelled phenomena, in that once it is started, it somehow magically proceeds on its own" (p. 3). Biernacki and Waldorf (1979), however, point out that this is simply not the case; rather the researcher(s) must actively and deliberately develop and control the sample's initiation, progress and termination. They point out a number of problem areas, some of which are pertinent to our ethical considerations. In initiating chain referrals, the investigator must be careful not to be limited to a few cases, since the problem of over- or underrepresentation of persons with certain characteristics (discussed earlier) may occur. For instance, a researcher would not want to end up with predominately white males aged 20 to 24 unless that is the target population. Biernacki and Waldorf's own research is a particularly interesting case study in that their goal was to interview two groups of ex-addicts: 100 who had managed to stop using drugs on their own volition and a comparative group of 100 who had stopped as a result of organized treatment programs. Subjects in both groups were expected to have been nonaddicted for a minimum of 2 years. Initiation and following through on the 100 who had been through formal treatment presented relatively few sampling problems. However, those who had left addiction on their own were more difficult to locate initially, and they were less likely to have knowledge of others for referral. Furthermore, when these persons could be found there was an ethical problem emanating from "the possible suspicions and consequences of the researcher directly contacting individuals whose success in breaking the bond of heroin addiction is related to their ability to hide the facts about their pasts from such persons as employers. In many instances, if the fact of past addiction was made known, it could seriously jeopardize the person's current adjustment" (Biernacki & Waldorf, 1979, p. 14). Whenever possible, another ex-addict may ease the way for an interview by making the referral or initial contact. Thus, one's informants may become de facto research assistants, or locators. In this type of study, the locators may also quell suspicions about the researchers being connected with law enforcement agencies that might somehow obtain the information provided by the respondents to use in unwanted ways.

Another ethical issue in snowball sampling is how far to go in verifying that the subject is an appropriate one for the study. Particularly when the investigators are known to pay respondents for their interview time ($20 in this case), the project office may be deluged with unvouched-for people demanding to be interviewed. Biernacki and Waldorf solved this problem by a strict policy of not immediately interviewing any unsolicited walk-ins. If upon screening they met research criteria, a separate interview appointment would be made at least 1 week in the future. While some currently addicted and therefore unstable persons might be weeded out in this way, a pertinent question remains: How far can or should the investigators go in verifying that subjects in this type of study are really free of addiction? Since lying is said to be endemic among addicts, how may one believe claims of nonaddiction? Can social research personnel require urinalysis of individuals about to be interviewed as a proof of the claim of freedom from addiction? Even if ethically justifiable, what would such a procedure do to the attempt to establish rapport? In this particular case, the investigators used the chain referral system as a means of validating nonaddiction, or they made enough independent contacts to verify the subject as previously but not currently addicted.

Terminating a referral chain before it is naturally exhausted may also involve some ethical problems. When the researchers have solicited respondents and encouraged them to locate others like themselves, it may not be easy to then reject the flow of referrals of one type. It is best to be clear about one's needs with potential locators, and not promise to interview all comers. For instance, Biernacki and Waldorf found, very early in the interviewing process, that they had an overabundance of former addicts who had come through treatment programs and were currently working in similar drug treatment centers. In order to not overly bias the sample with drug abuse counselors, they wisely excluded future respondents from this most readily available source. One can appreciate that it takes resolve to limit referral chains early in the research, when it is not known how many divergent chains of respondents may ultimately be found. The quality of our research, however, is improved by making these difficult decisions.

The newest approach to field research comes out of the theoretical perspective known as "ethnomethodology" (Wallace & Wolf, 1980). The ethnomethodological focus is on the study of the methods common people use to make sense of their everyday activities and the world around them. One of the principle means of "doing ethnomethodology" is to set up an ethnomethodological experiment in which researchers disrupt ordinary activity, or as Garfinkel (1967) suggests, "violate the scene." While some of the experiments and/or assignments mentioned by Garfinkel may seem innocuous, the researcher should consider the ethics involved in disturbing the subjects selected for observations. How may the investigator be certain that violating the scene will not have ominous meanings for the subjects? A poignant example of the type of problem that may be created has been reported by Ruth Wallace (personal communication, 1979). In giving her students Garfinkel's "boarder" assignment an ethical problem inherent in sample selection and the process of violating the scene came to light. The assignment involves the students simply taking from 15 minutes to 1 hour in their own homes imagining that they are boarders and acting out this assumption. They were instructed to conduct themselves in a circumspect and polite fashion. They were to avoid getting personal, to use formal address, and to speak only when spoken to (Garfinkel, 1967, p. 47). One of the students who attempted to complete the boarder assignment happened to be a recently divorced woman with two young children. "The children were so threatened by the shattering of their world at home when the mother began to act out the boarder role that they simply could not handle it, even for fifteen minutes. Though the mother ended the experiment immediately, she said that it took her at least a month to reassure the children that their world was not, in fact, shattered . . ." (Wallace & Wolf, 1980, p. 279). How can we be sure that the violation of trust that accompanies the violation of the scene will not be borne as a psychological and social-interactional burden through life? The risk in this case is surely not worth the benefit to be found in the learning experience.

A final sampling dilemma that needs to be mentioned is the sampling of college students either as survey respondents in the classroom setting or as participants in experimental research settings for classroom credit. Many of these small projects are designed to stimulate the students' experience in a variety of courses in the social sciences. Although we tend to assume the voluntary nature of student participation, the line between volunteering and manipulation or coercion is not a clear one. How is it possible for the student to believe that refusal to participate will not be held against him or her? While it is undoubtedly best to allow alternative student service, the faculty would then need to design two student projects for each one currently suggested.

We are left with difficult or imperfect solutions to many of the ethical dilemmas that are an integral part of the research sampling and data collection process. Basic to any resolution is an increased awareness of the ethical issues that have not always been willingly acknowledged. Putting ourselves in the role of the other, as good social scientists should be able to do, could alert us to some of the potential concerns of subjects and others involved in the research endeavor. Researchers may then be better prepared to anticipate the concerns for dignity and privacy that others hold. The fears and reticence of potential subjects may thus be met more realistically opening the door to a rewarding partnership between the investigator(s) and the subjects of social research. Moreover, the excitement of the scientific approach to the discovery of characteristics of human beings and their interrelationships may henceforth be more widely shared among the research profession, participants in the research process, and the public at large.

Summary

In this chapter a variety of moral and ethical issues related to the sample selection of persons for research purposes have been discussed. The general ethical issues that cut across sampling procedures include respect for potential subjects, considerations of cost/benefit, adequate information for "informed consent," the nongeneralizability of consent, the protection of respondents who may have violated the law, representative versus nonrepresentative samples and problems of generalization, and, finally, the goal of building public confidence.

Dilemmas related to four specific sampling strategies have also been reviewed. Researchers are encouraged to consider the appropriateness of using population or membership lists for research sampling, especially when individuals have no means of indicating that they do not want their privacy disturbed in this way. Sampling from geographical areas often means that an interviewer appears at the doorway of a resident, at times more imposing and difficult to get rid of than the proverbial high-pressure salesman. Finding new ways of encouraging participation in the research endeavor while minimizing the invasion of privacy implied will continue to provide a challenge to conscientious investigators. Sampling from existing records may mean that the invasion of privacy and the problem of confidentiality are not even known to the subject. Therefore, the moral issue of using information about an individual when that person has no means of verifying the accuracy of what is written about him or her and no way to prevent the use of that information is clear-cut, even though those records are tempting to the researcher. Observing people in the field, or in their own space, or questioning them face-to-face at least allows them to withdraw or hide from view anything they do not wish to be generally seen or known. In violating the scene, however, ethnomethodologists often create problems of ethical concern, and this intriguing and easily available research method may be difficult to monitor because of its anti-institutional bias.

In most of these areas of concern, suggestions for resolution of the sampling-research dilemmas have been discussed. It remains for social scientists in the process of working through specific problems to create new and improved means of dealing with the ethical issues. As our awareness of problems increases, new dilemmas will be perceived and these will challenge our thoughtful consideration, reminding us that social research is always in process and never complete.

Acknowledgments. Appreciation for helpful suggestions is extended to Joan E. Sieber, Mary-Margaret Franz, David Graeven, Jacqueline Wiseman, Richard Ames, and Mary Grace Kovar.

References

Austin, D. F., & Werner, S. B. *Epidemiology for the health sciences.* Springfield, Ill.: Thomas, 1979.

Babbie, E. *Survey research methods.* Belmont, Calif.: Wadsworth, 1973.

Biernacki, P., & Waldorf, D. Snowball sampling: problems and techniques of chain referral sampling. Paper presented at the annual meetings of the American Sociological Association, Boston, Mass., August 1979.

Fanning, J. Federal legislation on research with human subjects. Paper presented at the annual meetings of the American Sociological Association, Boston, Mass., August 24, 1979.

Freedman, A. M. Protection of sensitive medical data. In M. A. Jenkins (Ed.), *Patient centered health systems.* Minneapolis, Minn.: Society for Computer Medicine, 1975.

Garfinkel, H. *Studies in ethnomethodology.* Englewood Cliffs, N.J.: Prentice-Hall, 1967.

Goffman, E. *Asylums.* Garden City, N.Y.: Doubleday Anchor, 1961.

Gorden, R. L. *Interviewing: Strategy, techniques, and tactics.* Homewood, Ill.: Dorsey Press, 1969.

Gordis, L., & Gold, E. Privacy, confidentiality, and the use of medical records in research. *Science,* 1980, *207,* 153-156.

Graeven, D. B., & Folmer, W. Experimental heroin users: an epidemiologic and psychosocial approach. *American Journal of Drug and Alcohol Abuse,* 1977, *4*(3) 365-375.

Graeven, D. B., & Schaef, R. D. Family life and levels of involvement in an adolescent heroin epidemic. *The International Journal of the Addictions,* 1978, *13* (5), 747-771.

Gray, B. Current status of key issues regarding social research and human subjects regulations. Paper presented at the annual meetings of the American Sociological Association, Boston, Mass., August 24, 1979.

Harris, A. R. Sex and theories of deviance: Toward a functional theory of deviant type-scripts. *American Sociological Review,* 1977, *42*(1), 3-15.

Hartley, S. F. Standardization procedures in the analysis of cross-national variations in illegitimacy measures. *Journal of Biosocial Science,* 1970, *2,* 95-109.

Hartley, S. F. *Illegitimacy.* Berkeley, Calif.: University of California Press, 1975.

Hartley, S. F. American women as a "minority." *International Journal of Women's Studies,* 1978, *1*(2), 108-132.

Hebb, D. O., & Thompson, W. R. The social significance of animal studies. In G. Lindzey & E. Aronson (Eds.), *The handbook of social psychology.* Reading, Mass.: Addison-Wesley, 1968.

Kantner, J. F., & Zelnik, M. Sexual experience of young unmarried women in the United States. *Family Planning Perspectives,* 1972, *4*(4), 9-18.

Kantner, J. F., & Zelnik, M. Contraception and pregnancy: Experience of young unmarried women in the United States. *Family Planning Perspectives,* 1973, *5*(1), 21-35.

Kasanin, M., & Handschin, S. Psychodynamic factors in illegitimacy. *American Journal of Orthopsychiatry,* 1941, *11,* 66-85.

King, A. J., & Spector, A. J. Ethical and legal aspects of survey research. *American Psychologist,* 1963, *4,* 204-208.

Kish, L. *Survey Sampling.* New York: Wiley, 1965.

Lenski, G. E. *Power and Privilege.* New York: McGraw-Hill, 1966.

Milgram, S. *Obedience to authority: An experimental view.* New York: Harper & Row, 1974.

Miller, J., Schooler, C., Kohn, M. L., & Miller, K. Women and work: The Psychological effects of occupational conditions. *American Journal of Sociology,* 1979, *85*(1), 66-94.

Murtha, J. M., & Seiler, L. H. Institutional review boards: Legal-administrative bases. *ASA Footnotes,* 1979, *7*(6), 5.

Pauker, J. D., Girls pregnant out of wedlock—Pregnant because they are different or different because they are pregnant? In National Council on Illegitimacy, *The double jeopardy, the triple crisis.* New York: National Council on Illegitimacy, 1969.

Privacy Protection Study Commission. *Personal privacy in an information society.* Washington, D.C.: U.S. Government Printing Office, 1977.

Ryan, W. *Blaming the victim.* New York: Pantheon, 1971.

Singer, E. Informed consent: Consequences for response rate and response quality in social surveys. *American Sociological Review,* 1978, *43*, 144-162.

Stephan, F. J., & McCarthy, P. J. *Sampling opinions.* New York: Wiley, 1963.

Vidich, A., & Bensman, J. *Small town in mass society.* Princeton, N.J.: Princeton University Press, 1958.

Wallace, R. A., and Wolf, A. *Contemporary sociological theory.* Englewood Cliffs, N.J.: Prentice-Hall, 1980.

Watson, W. B., & Barth, E. A. T. Questionable assumptions in the theory of social stratification. *Pacific Sociological Review,* 1964, *7*(1), 10-16.

Wiseman, J. *Stations of the lost: The treatment of skid row alcoholics.* Englewood Cliffs, N.J.: Prentice-Hall, 1970.

Woolsey, T. D. Data banks are not the answer: A statistician's viewpoint. *American Journal of Public Health,* 1970, *60*(10), 1991-1995.

Young, L. *Out of Wedlock.* New York: McGraw-Hill, 1954.

Chapter 9

What To Do Before and After a Subpoena of Data Arrives

Charles R. Knerr, Jr.

Social science research frequently is conducted with a routine promise of confidentiality. In conducting attitudinal surveys or personal interviews, and in observing behavioral episodes, researchers often enter into confidential relationships with research participants, occasionally over a prolonged period. (The practice of assuring confidentiality dates to the earliest social research projects. For a review of an early social researcher's difficulties with the practice, see Whyte, 1955, p. 342.) Similarly, in securing information from archival sources or from informants, the information may be held as confidential. In archival research, the confidentiality agreement is typically made between the researcher and those in possession of the research data, and not between the researcher and data subject. Not all investigators pledge confidentiality. Some engage in purely philosophical inquiries (see, e.g., Parsons, 1965). Others depend on public records: legal decisions, census data, and historical materials (see, e.g., Schumpeter, 1964). The exact proportion who enter into confidential relationships is unknown.

As discussed in prior chapters, especially by Turner (Chapter 7) and Hartley (Chapter 8), the respondent's belief in the confidentiality of data is crucial to the obtaining of valid responses in many cases, especially in research on private or criminal aspects of persons' lives, and true confidentiality is essential to the ethical conduct of research. However, most of the methods social scientists employ to keep sensitive data from prying eyes do not suffice when data are subpoenaed.

The Legal Flaw

Researchers can be subpoenaed by judicial authorities, legislative committees, and certain administrative officials, and ordered to disclose confidential information obtained pertaining to research participants. The subpoena can command the disclosure of research records, such as completed protocols, or the researcher's personal testimony (the first form of subpoena is known as *duces tecum*, the latter, *ad testificantum*). Research staff, research assistants and clerical employees, also can be subpoenaed.

A subpoenaed researcher may face a serious ethical dilemma. In order to meet the requirements of a subpoena, a vow might have to be breached and injury to participants might result. On the other hand, the researcher might refuse to obey a subpoena, and serious consequences, such as imprisonment, could result. In certain situations, a choice might have to be made between the imprisonment of the researcher or the imprisonment of the data source.

The legal flaw involves conflicting interests: those of private citizens in preserving private spheres of opinions and behavior, those of researchers in unrestrained research, the interests of public authorities in securing information relevant to public decision making, and the interests of society in securing accurate information about social issues and certain forms of social behavior.

Several legal and ethical questions arise from this situation. At legal issue is the power of public officials to compel the disclosure of confidential scientific data, to fetter the flow of information to the public, and to obstruct social science research. Although social scientists currently do not have the immunity to subpoena that exists for physicians and lawyers, there are certain restricted, poorly understood, and underutilized legal shields that researchers may employ.

The ethical issues connected with the possible subpoena of data are related to the current legal situation. Social scientists are to study significant social phenomena, to produce valid new knowledge, and to do no harm to subjects in the process. Implicit in doing no harm to subjects is the understanding that no promises made to subjects be broken and that subjects' autonomy be respected and protected. Also implicit is the understanding that valid sampling procedures be employed and that procedures be used that maximize the trustworthiness or honesty of the responses obtained from subjects (see Chapters 8 and 10). However, the researcher who conscientiously seeks to study significant social problems and to gather valid data in field settings runs a far greater risk of having data subpoenaed than does the researcher who studies trivial problems or remains in the laboratory setting. Because researchers working in legally sensitive field settings may be vulnerable to subpoena and because there is much confusion about the nature of legal shields for social research, the investigator may be sorely tempted to make harmful compromises. In pursuit of valid data, investigators are likely to make promises of confidentiality that cannot be kept if the data are subpoenaed. Alternatively, the conscientious investigator may warn subjects that the data are vulnerable to subpoena, thereby jeopardizing either the honesty of responses of subjects who remain willing to participate, or the randomness of sampling if some subjects selectively choose not to participate. If data are subpoenaed, subjects may be arrested and convicted, and the subsequent flow of scientific information in certain ways may be curtailed. How may scientists thread their way through this ethical dilemma without jeopardizing one or another interest? To answer this question, it is first useful to review some of the circumstances under which data have been subpoenaed.

The Known Subpoena Incidents

In recent years, various researchers and their staffs have been subpoenaed and ordered to breach pledges of confidentiality. Several researchers have been held in contempt for refusing to comply with a subpoena; at least three researchers have been imprisoned in connection with contempt proceedings.

An economist conducted a study of unemployment patterns among ghetto youth; some 600 youths were interviewed. A final report was released concluding in part that one consequence of high unemployment was that many youthful ghetto residents engage in petty crime. A local government police commission subpoenaed the researcher and a research assistant, and demanded the public disclosure of participant identities. The economist refused to provide this information, on the grounds that anonymity had been promised. Pressures ceased shortly thereafter. (Description of this incident is based on personal interviews with the economist and staff of the police commission, and on documentation provided by interviewees.)

A sexual research institute received a genuine (unstaged) motion picture of a sadomasochistic episode. The supplier of the film inquired whether the institute was interested in securing a copy of the film for research purposes. The director of the institute returned the film and requested a copy. The supplier was subsequently arrested. The director of the sex institute was then subpoenaed to provide all information pertaining to the film. When the director refused, a bench warrant was issued for his arrest. The police never arrested the director, however, and proceedings were later terminated. One of the film participants was convicted of assault. (Description is based on a personal interview with the director of the institute and on documentation provided by the director.)

When an economist studied public utility company decision making, anonymity was promised to all interviewees. The principal investigator and a research assistant were subpoenaed by a party to a civil case, and ordered to disclose all research records and to publicly testify in the trial. The researchers refused and marshalled arguments against compliance with the subpoenas. The court reviewed these arguments and ordered the subpoenas quashed. (Description is based on telephone interviews with attorneys for the economist, and on documentation provided by the attorneys. For a published account of the incident, see "Confidentiality," 1976; "U.S. Court Shields Data," 1976.)

An experimental study was conducted of the behavioral impact of alternative negative income tax policies. A local prosecutor demanded access to the project's research records in order to determine whether any of the subjects had committed welfare fraud. When the researchers refused access, a subpoena was issued; thirteen other subpoenas were later issued. A lengthy legal struggle developed, culminating in the project's sponsor repaying the local government for alleged duplicate payments to welfare recipients (Kershaw & Small 1972).

A sociologist conducted a study of police socialization patterns through participant observation, by attending a police academy and by becoming a patrolman. After completing the research and leaving the police department, the sociologist was subpoenaed by court investigating an alleged act of police brutality witnessed by the sociologist. The subpoena ordered the disclosure of all research files pertaining to the incident and the testimony of the sociologist. The researcher refused, on the grounds that a scholarly right existed not to disclose this information. This assertion was not challenged; pressures ceased shortly thereafter. (Description is based on telephone and personal interviews with the sociologist, and on documentation provided by the sociologist.)

A sociologist conducted an evaluative study of a Federal grant made to a youth gang. An investigating committee of the U.S. Senate issued two subpoenas ordering the disclosure of all research records. Although the researcher was reluctant to provide the files, since anonymity had been promised, no legal protection was believed to exist. The files were disclosed and the research was terminated (Walsh 1969).

Three scholars were subpoenaed by a grand jury investigating the Pentagon Papers affair. The three alleged that the Federal government had engaged in illegal wiretapping against them and that the subpoenas ought to be "quashed" as a result. The court asked the government to respond to this allegation. When attorneys for the Federal government did not respond, the proceedings terminated (Tyler & Kaufman 1972).

A social psychologist conducted a study of the behavior and medical treatment of alleged sex-crime victims. Data were collected through observing the treatment of some 800 alleged victims, and by interviewing victims, police officers, and medical personnel. A local prosecutor demanded a research file pertaining to a subject, for use in a trial. The researcher refused to provide the file, on the grounds that anonymity had been promised to all subjects. When the prosecutor subpoenaed the record and threatened to imprison the social psychologist should the materials not be provided, the record was provided. The prosecutor then subpoenaed three additional research files; each file was released as ordered. (Description is based on a personal interview with the social psychologist, and on documentation provided by the social psychologist.)

A sociologist conducted a participant observation study of police behavior. The sociologist-policeman was subpoenaed to testify before a police board investigating an alleged act of police brutality. The researcher testified as ordered (Kirkham, Note 1).

A murder was committed near a methadone maintenance research and treatment clinic. A witness believed the murderer to be a subject-patient of the clinic. A local prosecutor then subpoenaed the records of the clinic. When the director of the clinic refused to provide the files, he was held in contempt, and fined and sentenced to imprisonment. Lengthy litigation developed, culminating in the upholding of the constitutionality of Federal statutes protecting the records. The subpoena was "quashed" and the contempt proceedings overturned. (Description is based on personal interviews with the director of the clinic, and on documents provided by the interviewee.)[1]

During the conduct of a study of drug users, one of the research participants was arrested for drug use. The research participant served as his own legal counsel in the

[1] For a published account of the incident, see People v. Newman, 298 N.E.2d 641, 32 N.Y.S.2d 379 (1973).

ensuing trial, and secured a subpoena ordering the sociologist to testify at the trial as to the use of drugs by the defendant for religious purposes. The researcher appeared at the trial, but refused to answer questions on Fifth Amendment grounds. The researcher alleged that he might be exposed to criminal proceedings, since criminal behavior had been observed but not reported to the police. The sociologist was not ordered to answer certain questions (Yablonsky, 1967, 1968).

A political scientist was subpoenaed to testify before a grand jury investigating the publishing of the Pentagon Papers, and was asked to divulge sources of research information. When the scholar refused to answer several questions on First Amendment grounds, the grand jury moved to compel disclosure. A court reviewed the claim and ordered the scholar to disclose sources' identities. The scholar again refused, was held in contempt, and was imprisoned for 8 days. (Description is based on personal interviews of the political scientist and others, and on documentation provided by interviewees. For a published account of the incident, see Carroll 1973.)[2]

A research project was conducted involving alleged sex-crime victims. A suspect arrested in connection with an alleged sex-crime secured a subpoena ordering the disclosure of all data pertaining to the alleged victim. The researchers refused, arguing that a Federal statute protected the research files from disclosure. The local (county) judge disagreed, held the researchers in contempt, and ordered the imprisonment of the researchers. The researchers were briefly imprisoned, but were released when the file was disclosed as ordered. (Description is based on a telephone interview with one of the researchers and on documentation provided by the interviewee.)

What To Do Before The Subpoena Arrives

Sound ethical decision making dictates that researchers take precautions to minimize the possibility of legal, social or economic harm to research participants. In regard to the legal flaw, four major alternatives are available:

1. Do not perform research involving legally sensitive research topics, e.g., drug and criminal justice research, or research involving sexual behavior.
2. Take no precautions, but promise research participants that data identifiable to them will never be revealed, and that you will go to jail rather than reveal confidential data.
3. Desensitize the research, e.g., use any of a variety of design and statistical techniques that could serve to minimize the relevance of research data to legal or other authorities.
4. Secure a legal shield that would give the researcher legal arguments to resist a subpoena.

Alternative 1, to completely abandon certain research topics, is not appealing. Society needs better understanding of complex social and behavioral problems. Large amounts of resources, public and private, have been marshaled to address this need. Acquired wisdom about these problems would suffer if the strategy were

---

[2] U.S. v. Popkin, 460 F2d 328 (1972).

widely adopted. Alternative 2, to calmly await the subpoena, is also unappealing (at least to the author). Sound ethical decision making dictates the researchers evaluate the possibility of harm to *themselves* as a consequence of conducting a given research project.

Alternatives 3 and 4 are clearly preferable, to adopt statistical, administrative, and legal remedies to minimize the possibility of harm to participants (see, e.g., Austin & Boruch 1970; Boruch 1970, Boruch 1971a, 1971b, 1971c, 1972a, 1972b, Dalenius 1974, Feige & Watts 1970, pp. 261-271, Greenburg et al. 1969, Horvitz et al. 1967, Manheimer et al. 1972, pp. 205-214, Metraux 1968, Sagarin 1973). In Chapter 7, Turner reports growing distrust of the promises of confidentiality offered by researchers. To counter this distrust, the researcher needs to employ means of data collection and handling that prevent the possibility that data from identified subjects will fall into the wrong hands, and to clearly demonstrate to subjects that such precaution has been taken. An ingenious method of providing this assurance was used by sociologist David Graeven in research on the roles of drug peddlers. Graeven always interviewed his peddler-informants at a downtown location near a U.S. mail pickup box. The informants clearly understood that every interview protocol would be mailed immediately to a Canadian sociologist who would store, analyze, and destroy the raw data outside the reach of a U.S. subpoena. At the close of each interview, Graeven would place the protocol in a stamped, addressed envelope and he and his informant would walk over to the mailbox and deposit the envelope.

Some less dramatic techniques can be equally effective. The criteria of effectiveness include (1) the invulnerability of the method to subpoena, (2) appropriateness of the data yielded by the technique for the intended statistical analysis, and (3) ease with which the technique can be convincingly described or demonstrated to subjects.

The criterion of "understandability to subjects" is sometimes crucial to the validity of the study. The researcher ordinarily is obligated to disclose any reasonable risk to subjects when obtaining informed consent. While the use of privacy-preserving techniques renders the data safe from subpoena, subjects do not know that this is the case unless they are shown that such a technique has been employed. The researcher who neither informs subjects about normal risk of subpoena or about the invulnerability of the method employed may gather invalid data, as well as violate the obligation to disclose risk. Some proportion of the subjects may know that risk of subpoena exists and consequently may falsify their responses, if full disclosure of potential risk of techniques used to make data invulnerable are not communicated clearly.

The balance of this chapter is devoted to Alternative 4, legal mechanisms to avoid compliance with a subpoena.

General Legal Issues

The compulsion of testimony and written records has long been permitted in Anglo-Saxon jurisprudence; the practice dates back perhaps 400 years (for a history of the compulsion of evidence, see Wigmore 1961, Sec. 2100). The general rule adopted over this period is that every shred of evidence applicable to a given case should be brought before court, that judicial authority to compel evidence is supreme, and that refusal to obey could be grounds for punishment.

Jurists have not been eager to assert that their authority is absolute, however. Exceptions to the general rule of evidence have evolved—testimonial exemptions that have been adopted as Constitutional provisions and as legislative enactments (statutes). Among the widely recognized exemptions are the prohibition against involuntary self-incrimination,[3] the exemption regarding evidence secured through unreasonable or illegal search and seizure,[4] and the exemption regarding the public revelation of state secrets (see, e.g., Barker & Fox 1972). A sizable body of law has evolved regarding these and many lesser exemptions (for a review, see Wigmore).

In more recent chronicles of American jurisprudence, a special type of testimonial exemption has evolved, that of "testimonial privilege" for special relationships. Communications between certain individuals have been exempted to varying degrees from the general rule. *Relationships* that have been deemed important to societal functioning include husband-wife, attorney-client, priest-penitent, physician-patient, psychiatrist-patient, accountant-client, journalist-source, among many others (for a listing of these privileges, see Wigmore, Sec. 2290-2339). Several of these relationships have been deemed more important than others, such as husband-wife and attorney-client relationships, and thus are more extensively protected than others. (The husband-wife and attorney-client privileges are recognized by nearly all jurisdictions in the United States under most circumstances.) Nonetheless, none of the relationships is exempted from the general rule in every circumstance, or in every jurisdiction, or in every evidentiary proceeding. Exceptions are made from time to time, by one jurist or another, in one circumstance or another, and by one or both of the parties to a particular relationship. (Outlining *all* of the vagaries of the various testimonial privileges is beyond the purpose of this chapter. For a review, see Wigmore.)

The growth of and the plea for additional testimonial privileges have prompted analysis of the whole practice of exempting the production of certain forms of evidence. Numerous professions have argued in behalf of a testimonial privilege in recent years, including social workers, school guidance counselors, nurses, school teachers, stenographers, college counselors, and public employees, among others. The many relevant articles, books, and reports are too numerous to cite. An influential authority on rules of evidence, Dean Wigmore (Sec. 2285), has argued that for communications between two or more individuals to be exempted from the general rule, the following criteria must be met:

1. The communications must originate in a confidence that they will not be disclosed.
2. This element of confidentiality must be essential to the full and satisfactory maintenance of the relation between the parties.
3. The relation must be one in which the opinion of the community ought to be sedulously fostered.

---

[3] Fifth Amendment, U.S. Constitution.
[4] Fourth Amendment, U.S. Constitution.

4. The injury that would inure to the relation by the disclosure must be greater than the benefit thereby gained for the correct disposal of litigation.

Legislative bodies, jurists, and administrative officials have utilized the above criteria in examining the nature of the researcher-subject relationship. During the 1970s a body of law has evolved protecting certain researcher-subject communications from compelled disclosure. This body of law may be separated into three major currents: Federal statutes, state statutes, and Constitutional common law.

Federal Statutes

In 1970, the Congress enacted a statute which permits the Secretary of the Department of Health, Education, and Welfare (DHEW) to

> authorize persons engaged in research on mental health, including research on the use and effect of alcohol and other psychoactive drugs, to protect the privacy of individuals who are the subject of such research by withholding from all persons not connected with the conduct of such research the names or other identifying characteristics of such individuals. Persons so authorized may not be compelled in any Federal, state, or local civil, criminal, administrative, legislative, or other proceeding to identify such individuals.[5]

A segment of the behavioral and social science research community might be protected by the above statute. When authorized, the "privilege" extends to all proceedings, local, state, and Federal. Coverage is extended to "mental health" research, which is not defined in the statute, but determined by administrative discretion.[6] The researcher need not be sponsored by DHEW[7]; unsponsored reseachers can be authorized by the courts, and held to be constitutional.[8]

The Congress has also empowered the U.S. Attorney General to:

> authorize persons engaged in research to withhold the names and other identifying characteristics of persons who are the subjects of such research. Persons who obtain this authorization may not be compelled in any Federal, state, or local civil, criminal, administrative, legislative, or other proceeding to identify the subjects of research for which such authorization was obtained.[9]

---

[5] 42 U.S.C. 242a(a); Sect. 3 of the Comp. Drug Abuse Prev. and Control Act of 1970, P.L. 91--513, 84 Stat 1271, as amended by the Comp. Alcohol Abuse and Alcoholism Prev., Treat., and Rehab. Act of 1974, P.L. 93-282, 88 Stat. 125.
[6] For administrative regulations regarding this statute, see 40 Federal Register 56692 (4 December 1975).
[7] Applicants must agree to conform to DHEW regulations regarding the protection of human subjects, 46 Code of Federal Regulations 45 (1976).
[8] See People v. Newman, 298 N.E.2d 651, 32 N.Y.S.2d 379 (1973).
[9] 21 U.S.C. 872(c), Sect. 502 of the Comp. Drug Abuse Prev. and Control Act of 1970, P.L. 91-513, 84 Stat. 1271.

Although the above statute appears to provide broad coverage, the statute is embedded within a section pertaining to drug research programs administered by the Department. The statute has been interpreted to apply only to drug research. Other limitations can be noted. Protection is extended to those researchers who have received a specific grant of immunity; administrative review is necessary of pertinent documents provided by applicants.[10] In addition, protection extends only to the identity of a research subject. This leaves open to subpoena other data gathered by the researcher.

The statute does provide some protection. Both testimony and written records are exempted from subpoena. The researcher need not be under grant or contract to a Federal agency. Finally, and most importantly, the statute has been judicially reviewed and held to be constitutional.[11]

Another Federal statute protects research data generated under grant or contract to the Law Enforcement Assistance Administration (LEAA):

> Except as provided by Federal law other than this chapter, no officer or employee of the Federal government, nor any recipient of assistance under the provisions of this chapter shall use or reveal any research of statistical information furnished under this chapter by any person and identifiable to any specific private person for any purpose other than the purpose for which it was obtained in accordance with this chapter. Copies of such information shall be immune from legal process, and shall not, without the consent of the person furnishing such information, be admitted as evidence or used for any purpose in any action suit, or other judicial or administrative proceedings.[12]

The protection afforded by the above statute is very narrow, in that protection is conferred only on those researchers under grant or contract to the LEAA. The protection extends to written records, and not the mental impressions of the researcher. Protection is not afforded against legislative subpoenas. (Only one incident is known of a legislative subpoena demanding research data. For a review of this incident, see Walsh 1969.) Nor is protection extended to information pertaining to the conduct of future crimes.[13] The protection is also limited in that local judicial authorities may hold that Federal law is not controlling, that local law should prevail (see Note 2).

Despite these limitations, the statute may provide protection for a number of researchers, i.e., those under grant or contract to the LEAA. Moreover, all research data are protected, identities and the content or nature of what was learned from or about a research subject, and, in contrast to other Federal researcher statutes,

---

[10] For regulations implementing this statute, see 21 Code of Federal Regulations 1316 (1976).

[11] See People v. Newman, 298 N.E.2d 651 (1973).

[12] 42 U.S.C. 3771(a), Sect. 524(a) of the Crime Control Act of 1973, P.L. 93-83, 87 Stat. 215.

[13] See the regulations implementing this statute, at 41 Federal Register 54845 (15 December 1976).

the immunity is automatically conferred on all LEAA supported researchers. No administrative action is necessary to implement the statute.[14]

Several other Federal statutes protect research data. The Drug Abuse Office and Treatment Act of 1972, amended in 1974, confers a limited immunity on the "records of the identity, diagnosis, prognosis, or treatment of any patient . . . of any drug abuse prevention function. . . ."[15] The immunity is very limited, as a balancing provision has been included in the statute which allows courts to order disclosure where there is "good cause."[16]

The statutes protecting Census data[17] and Social Security data[18] also create immunities for a very narrow segment of the research community, i.e., those employed by the Census Bureau and by the Social Security Administration. University-based research is not protected by these statutes, unless the researcher is formally affiliated with either of the two agencies.

The question of enacting additional Federal protection was recently reviewed by the Privacy Protection Study Commission.[19] Based on information acquired from legal experts, public administrators, and the research community, a recommendation was made to the Congress to extend a testimonial privilege to all Federally supported researchers (U.S. Privacy Protection Study Commission 1977). Whether or not the Congress will enact such a statute remains uncertain as this chapter was written.

State Statutes

State legislators have also reviewed the question of statutory protection for researchers. Of the numerous statutes enacted in recent years, none protects a broad segment of the research community.

State legislatures have enacted statutes protecting research into drug abuse and use. In 1970, the National Conference of Commissioners on Uniform State Laws approved the Uniform Controlled Substances Act, which contained two provisions protecting the identity of research subjects:

> A practitioner engaged in medical practice or research is not required or compelled to furnish the name or identity of a patient or research subject to the (appropriate person or agency), nor may he be compelled in any State or local civil, criminal, administrative, legislative, or other proceedings to furnish the name or identity of an individual that the practitioner is obligated to keep confidential.

---

[14] See the administrative regulations implementing this statute, at 41 Federal Register 54845 (15 December 1976).

[15] 42 U.S.C. 4582, Sect. 333 of the Comp. Alcohol Abuse and Alcoholism Prev., Treat., and Rehab. Act of 1970, P.L. 91-616, 84 Stat. 1848, as amended by Sect. 122 of the Comp. Alcohol and Alcohol Abuse and Alcoholism Prev., Treat., and Rehab. Act Amend. Of 1974, P.L. 93-282, 88 Stat. 125.

[16] 42 U.S.C. 4582, Subsect. b(2)(c).

[17] 13 U.S.C. 8, 9(1970).

[18] 42 U.S.C. 1306 (1970).

[19] Created by the Federal Privacy Act of 1974, P.L. 93-502, 88 Stat. 1896.

The (appropriate person or agency) may authorize persons engaged in research on the use and effects of controlled substances to withhold the names and other identifying characteristics of individuals who are the subjects of the research. Persons who obtain this authorization are not compelled in any civil, criminal, administrative or other proceeding to identify the individuals who are the subjects of research for which the authorization was obtained (see Note 3).

At least 37 states have adopted the model statute, or similar versions. Of these, some 28 states enacted statutes containing one or both of the model law's sections regarding a research privilege (i.e., Arkansas, California, Connecticut, Delaware, Georgia, Hawaii, Idaho, Illinois, Indiana, Iowa, Louisiana, Massachusetts, Michigan, Nevada, New Mexico, New York, North Carolina, North Dakota, Oklahoma, Pennsylvania, South Carolina, Tennessee, Texas, Washington, West Virginia, Wisconsin, and Wyoming).

Drug research is thus protected in more than one-half of the states. However, these statutes vary from state to state. In many states the researcher must formally apply for the "privilege" and meet administrative requirements. None of the drug statutes has been reviewed by judicial authorities, as far as is known.

Several state statutes regarding the licensure of psychologists may serve to protect research data. In Idaho, Indiana, Kansas, Michigan, Utah, and Wyoming, the practice of psychology has been defined to include the measuring of "public opinion" or "research into problems of human behavior."[20] Each of these states also protects psychologist-client communications. Legal ambiguity surrounds these statutes in that several refer to "clients," others to "professional communications." Whether or not a judicial official would recognize the privileged status of communications with *research participants* is problematical. Research data generated by licensed psychologists are presumably protected in each state (the author is forced to use the term "presumably" since no litigation has arisen regarding this question).

Several states protect research whose purpose is to reduce morbidity or mortality: Florida, Georgia, Maryland, Massachusetts, Michigan, Minnesota, and Texas.[21] In these states, the identities of subjects of research studies into the causes, effects, or dispersion of diseases or mental disorders are protected from court-ordered disclosure.

Several of the state newsman shield laws may be interpreted to protect survey researchers. Tennessee's newsman shield law protects "information gatherers," defined as "person(s) engaged in gathering information for publication or broadcast connected with or employed by the news media or press, or who are independently engaged in gathering information for publication...."[22] The statute permits Ten-

---

[20] See, e.g., Idaho Stat. 54-3302(f) (1963); Ind. Stat. 25-33-1-2(c) (1969); Kansas Stat. 74-5301(a) (1967); Mich. 338.1001(b) (1972); Utah Stat. 58-25-4 (1959); Wyoming Stat. 33-343.2(d) (1965).

[21] Florida Stat. 465.01-03 (1974); George Stat. 88-1908-1910 (1966); Maryland Code Art. 134(a) and Maryland Code Courts Art. 5-302 and 10-205; Massachusetts Gen. Laws. C.111 24A (1960); Michigan Comp. Laws 325.131-132; 331.531-533; Minnesota Stat. 144.053 (1955); Texas Civ. Stat. 5547-202 (Vernon's, 1976).

[22] Tenn. Code Ann. 24-113 (1976 Suppl.).

nessee courts to order disclosure in certain situations.[23] Minnesota's newsman shield law extends protection to any "person who is or has been directly engaged in the gathering, procuring, compiling, editing, or publishing of information. . . ."[24] Although researchers might be included within this definition, Minnesota courts may rule otherwise. Alaska's shield law does not define "newsman," leaving the question to the courts.[25] Alaska also extends protection to an undefined group of individuals, "public officials."[26] Researchers under grant or contract would conceivably be protected, as well as researchers employed by Alaska's higher education system. Alaska's courts may interpret the statute narrowly, however.

Several state statutes protect a very narrow range of research data. Montana recognizes a testimonial privilege for researchers studying child mentality.[27] The New Hampshire legislature enacted a statute that empowers the State Commissioner of Health and Welfare to authorize a privilege for "scientific investigators." The statute immunizes from compulsory disclosure:

> all information, records of interviews, written reports, statements, notes, memoranda, or other data procured in connection with such scientific studies and research conducted by the department, or by other persons, agencies, or other organizations so authorized by the commissioner.[28]

The New York legislature enacted a statute protecting records of the Multi-state Information System for Psychiatric Patients, a data bank that is used for research and demonstration purpose.[29] The protection is very narrow, as only data collected and generated by this research project are protected from disclosure proceedings. Researchers under grant or contract to Maryland's Department of Juvenile Services are protected from subpoena.[30]

In summary, many states now protect certain forms of researcher-subject communications from court-ordered disclosure. Available evidence suggests that additional statutes will be enacted over the next several years. The state of Washington is considering the adoption of a criminologist-subject privilege (on file with the author). An expansion of protection is under way.

Constitutional Protection

Several researchers have sought to use the First Amendment to the U.S. Constitution as a shield to resist subpoenas. Their arguments, and those of newsmen, have been based on the maintenance of the free flow of information to the public: in gathering information, it is often necessary to conceal the identities of sources, or to pub-

---

[23] Tenn. Code Ann. 24-115 (1976 Suppl.).

[24] Minn. Stat. Ann. 595.023 (1975 Suppl.).

[25] Alas. Comp. Laws 09.25.150 (1975 Suppl.).

[26] Alas. Comp. Laws 09.25:150 (1976 Suppl.).

[27] Mont. Rev. Code Ann. 93-701-4(6) (1964).

[28] New Hamp. Rev. Code Ann. 126-A:4-a (1973 Rev.).

[29] N.Y. Civ. Rights Law 79-je (McKinney, 1976).

[30] Maryland Code Art. 52A-8 (1966).

lish only part of the information revealed, and that if such confidences are forcibly breached, their sources and the sources of other information gatherers will be unwilling to provide information.[31] In essence, the claimants have argued that the societal interest in the unimpeded flow of information to the public exceeds the interests of prosecutors and other authorities in securing information needed for the disposal of litigation.

Civil Proceedings and the First Amendment

A number of newsmen and researchers have been relieved from complying with subpoenas secured by civil litigants. The leading case is *Baker v. F & F Investment Co.*,[32] in which a journalist was relieved from disclosing information gathered in connection with a newspaper article on discriminatory real estate practices. The court held:

> While we recognize there are cases—few in number to be sure—where First Amendment rights must yield, we are still mindful of the preferred position which the First Amendment occupies in the pantheon of freedom. Accordingly, though a journalist's right to protect confidential sources may not take precedence over the rare and overriding and compelling interest, we are still of the view that there are circumstances, at the very least in civil cases, in which the public's interest in non-disclosure of a journalist's confidential sources outweighs the public and private interest in compelled testimony.[33]

A set of criteria for weighing First Amendment claims in civil litigation was established:

1. Was the subpoenaed witness a party to the litigation?
2. Were other sources of information available?
3. Was disclosure of the identity of a source essential to the orderly administration of justice?
4. Did the identity of the source "go to the heart of" the case?

These criteria have been used on several occasions to quash subpoenas issued to newsmen.[34]

The first researcher claim of a First Amendment based privilege in civil litigation occurred in 1976. In *Richards of Rockford, Inc. v. Pacific Gas and Electric Co.*,[35] two subpoenas seeking testimony and research notes were issued to an economist and a research assistant studying public utility decision making. The economist and the research assistant argued that:

---

[31] Based upon the arguments in Branzburg v. Hayes, 408 U.S. 665 (1972).
[32] 470 F.2d 778 (1st. Cir. 1972), cert. den. 411 U.S. 896 (1973).
[33] 470 F.2d 778, at 783.
[34] Loadholtz v. Fields, 389 F. Supp. 1299 (D.C. Fla. 1975); Apicella v. McNeil, 66 F.R.D. 78 (E.D.N.Y. 1975).
[35] D.C.N.Cal. No. C-74-0578-CBR (1976).

1. They were not parties to the action and had no interest in the outcome.
2. There was no showing that alternative sources of information had been exhausted by the plaintiff.
3. There was no public interest represented in behalf of disclosure.
4. There was no showing that the testimony sought went to the "heart of the dispute."[36]

The *Richards* court held that while the issues in the case did not rise to that of Constitutional status, the facts of the case warranted quashing both subpoenas.[37] The decision is the first known upholding of a researcher's claim of a First Amendment right to protect confidential research sources.

Criminal Proceedings

Judicial authorities have not supported First Amendment claims advanced in connection with *criminal* litigation. The leading case for academic researchers is *Popkin v. U.S.*[38] In refusing to answer several questions posed by a grand jury investigating the release and dissemination of the Pentagon Papers, Popkin argued that the government must show a strong need for requiring questions to be answered, or else all scholarly research would be threatened. (Description is based on an unofficial transcript of Popkin's testimony, provided to the author by Popkin.) The courts declined to support Popkin's arguments. When Popkin persisted in refusing to answer certain questions, he was held in contempt and imprisoned. (For a detailed analysis of the incident, see Carroll, 1973.)

The controlling First Amendment case is not *Popkin*, but *Branzburg v. Hayes.*[39] In this case, three newsmen petitioned the Supreme Court to quash subpoenas; all three argued that the burden resulting from compelling reporters to disclose confidential information exceeded the public interest in disclosure. The court did not support their arguments. A majority held that the interest in securing incriminating evidence outweighed that of assuring the reporting of crimes. In post-*Branzburg* decisions, the courts have consistently held that reporters must disclose confidential information, when ordered to do so in criminal proceedings.[40]

---

[36] Memorandum of Points and Authorities in Opposition to Plaintiff's Motion For Order Compelling Production of Documents Pursuant to Subpoena, Richards of Rockford, Inc. v. Pacific Gas & Electric Co., 17 February 1976, at p. 16.

[37] Memorandum of Opinion, Richards of Rockford, Inc., v. Pacific Gas & Elect. Co., No. C-74-0578 CBR, at pp. 3-4.

[38] 460 F.2d 328 (1st. Cir. 1972); cert. den. 411 U.S. 909 (1973).

[39] 408 U.S. 665 (1972).

[40] See Bursey v. United States, 466 F.2d 1059 (9th Cir. 1972); Lightman v. State, 15 MD. App. 713, 294 A.2d 149, aff'd per curiam, 266 Md. 550, 295 A.2d 212 (1972), cert. den., 411 U.S. 951 (1973); People v. Dan, 41 App. Div. 2d 687 (N.Y. 1973); United States v. Liddy, 354 F. Suppl. 208 (D.C.D.C. 1972); In re WBAI-FM v. Proskin, 42 App. Div. 5 (N.Y. 1973); State v. St. Peter, 315 A. 2d 274 (Vt. 1974); Brown v. Commonwealth, 204 S.E. 2d 249 (Va. 1974); In re Farr, 36 Cal. App. 3d 577, 11 Cal. Rptr. 649 (1974); Lewis v. United States, 517 F.2d 236 (9th Cir. 1975), 501 F.2d 418 (9th Cir. 1974); Morgan v. States, 325 F.2d 40 (Fla. App. 1975).

Summary and Overview

A body of law has evolved regarding the legal status of researcher-subject communications. Whether the privileged status of such data is enlarged or contracted, or remains stable, will largely depend on the research community's willingness to pursue the question. Of course, the willingness of judicial and legislative authorities to answer Wigmore's criteria in an affirmative fashion is crucial. No amount of empirical evidence can be brought to bear on the issue in any persuasive fashion.

At the individual researcher level, the best strategy may well be to take whatever statistical and administrative strategies deemed appropriate to the research question, and to secure an available testimonial privilege. In the event a subpoena is issued, the researcher should consult university legal counsels, the sponsor (if any), the relevant professional association(s), and consider retaining personal legal counsel. The alternatives faced by subpoenaed researchers are great: harm to the research participant versus harm to the researcher.

Reference Notes

1. Kirkham, G., *The criminologist as police officer: A participant-observation study.* Paper presented at the annual meeting of the American Society of Criminology, New York, 1973.
2. This issue arose in a Colorado case, where a judge imprisoned two researchers for refusing to disclose confidential research data. The Attorney General of Colorado later ordered the conviction overturned and the record expunged. Thus, no reference can be given. However, documentation of the incident is available in the files of the author, and will be supplied upon request.
3. *Handbook of the National Conference of Commissioners on Uniform State Laws* (1970), Subsect. 504(c), 508(d).

References

Austin, A. W., & Boruch, R. F. A "link" system for assuring confidentiality of research data in longitudinal studies. *American Educational Research Journal,* 1970, *7*, 615-624.

Barker, C. M., & Fox, M. H. *Classified files: The yellowing pages.* New York: Twentieth Century Fund, 1972.

Boruch, R. F. Assuring confidentiality of responses in social research: A note on strategies. *The American Sociologist,* 1971, *6*, 308-311. (a)

Boruch, R. F. Educational research and the confidentiality of education: A case study. *Sociology of Education,* 1971, *44*, 59-85. (b)

Boruch, R. F. Maintaining confidentiality of data in educational research: A systematic analysis. *American Psychologist,* 1971, *26*, 413-430. (c)

Boruch, R. F. Relations among statistical methods for assuring confidentiality of social research data. *Social Science Research,* 1972, *1*, 403-414. (a)

Boruch, R. F. Strategies for eliciting and merging confidential social research data. *Policy Sciences,* 1972, *3*, 275-297. (b)

Carroll, J. D. Confidentiality of social science research sources and data: The Popkin incident. *PS* (American Political Science Association), 1973, *6*, 268-280.

Confidentiality: Court declares researcher can protect resources. *Science*, 1976, *173*, 467-470.

Dalenius, T. The invasion of privacy problem and statistics production: An overview. *Sartyck Ur Statistick Tidskrift*, 1974, *3*, 213-225.

Feige, E. L., & Watts, H. W. Protection of privacy through microaggregation. In R. L. Bisco (Ed.), *Data bases, computers, and the social sciences.* New York: Wiley-Interscience, 1970.

Greenberg, B. G., et al. The unrelated question randomized response model: A theoretical framework. *Journal of the American Statistical Association*, 1969, *64*, 502-539.

Horvitz, D. G., et al. The unrelated question randomized response model. *1967 Social Statistics Section Proceeding of the American Statistical Association*, 1967, pp. 65-72.

Kershaw, D. N., & Small, J. C. Data confidentiality and privacy: Lessons from the New Jersey negative income tax experiment. *Public Policy*, 1972, *20*, 257-280.

Manheimer, D. I., et al. Technical and ethical considerations in data collection. In S. Einstein & S. Allen (Eds.), *Proceedings of the First International Conference on Student Drug Surveys.* Farmington, New York: Baywood, 1972.

Metraux, R. Study program in human health and the ecology of man—China: Measures taken for the protection of confidentiality in an interdisciplinary study of health and cultural adaptation based on retrospective life histories. *Daedalus*, 1968, *98*, 379-381.

Parsons, T. *Theories of society.* New York: Free Press, 1965.

Sagarin, E. The research setting and the right not to be researched. *Social Problems*, 1973, *21*, 52-64.

Schumpeter, J. A. *Business cycles* (Rev. ed.). New York: McGraw-Hill, 1964.

Tyler, R. M., & Kaufman, D. The public scholar and the First Amendment: A Compelling need for compelling testimony? *George Washington Law Review*, 1972, *40*, 995-1023.

U.S. court shields data of scholar. *New York Times*, June 13, 1976, p. 29.

U.S. Privacy Protection Study Commission, *Personal privacy in an information society.* Washington, D.C.: U.S. Government Printing Office, 1977.

Walsh, J. Antipoverty r & d: Chicago debacle suggest pitfalls facing O.E.O. *Science*, 1969, *165*, 1243-1245.

Whyte, W. F. *Street corner society.* Chicago: University of Chicago Press: 1955.

Wigmore, J. H. *Evidence in trials in common law* (Vol. 8). Boston: Little, Brown, 1961.

Yablonsky, L. Universities: Risks of research. *Time*, December 22, 1967, p. 40.

Yablonsky, L. The problems of deviant research. *Criminologica*, 1968, *6*, 10-13.

Chapter 10

Statistical Strategies for Preserving Privacy in Direct Inquiry

Robert F. Boruch and Joe Shelby Cecil

A remarkable variety of statistical methods has been developed to preserve the confidentiality of an individual's response to a social researcher's inquiry. They have been designed to eliminate a clear linkage between a respondent's identity and information about his true condition, without seriously undermining the researcher's ability to analyze resultant research data.

Most of these methods are appropriate for eliciting discrete bits of information during face-to-face interviews and in more impersonal settings. They result in research records that are not susceptible to either direct disclosure or exact deductive disclosure. The methods do, however, impose some constraints on the research design, they can increase the costs of data collection and analysis, and they may prevent some kinds of data analysis entirely.

In the following pages, the *simpler* strategies and some new variations on them are presented first for cross-sectional research. Their benefits and limitations are discussed in connection with four basic research designs: cross-sectional, longitudinal, multisource, and experimental.

Cross-Sectional Research

Four related classes of strategies can be used for research based on a cross-sectional design. The first three, contamination methods, randomized response, and Balanced Incomplete Block (BIB) approaches, can be applied to direct interview situations and to telephone or mail surveys. The fourth, microaggregation, is more appropriate for mail surveys and other impersonal methods of eliciting information, but some variations can be applied in direct interview settings. Each class is, in principle, applicable to longitudinal, experimental, and other research designs.

Contamination Methods

We begin with this approach partly because it is simple, though less efficient than other methods. The contamination method requires that each respondent inoculate his or her response with a random error. The *general* character of the error is controlled by the researcher so that while it is impossible to tell whether any particular response is accurate, it is still possible to estimate important statistical parameters from a *large* sample of respondents (see Boruch, 1972, and Warner, 1965).

To be specific, suppose we would like to estimate the proportion of students in a large sample who have used a particular drug. The question "Have you tried cocaine?" is presented to the respondent along with the choice of permissible responses: e.g., Yes or No. The respondent is instructed not to answer the question directly but to use a randomization device to determine whether he will give a true or false response. If a die is used, the respondent is asked to answer falsely if, for example, a one shows, regardless of his true behavior. If 2, 3, . . ., 6 show, he would be required to answer truthfully with a Yes or No response. The respondent does *not* inform the researcher which number actually turns up on the die. He or she merely answers Yes or No in accord with the instructions. Under these conditions, 1/6 of all responses will be false. The researcher cannot know which particular responses are true or false. Give these known parameters for error, it is easy to compute the proportion who have actually tried the drug.

$$\hat{\pi}_m = (\hat{P}_y - \phi_p)/(1 - \phi_p - \phi_n) \qquad \phi_p + \phi_n < 1, \phi_p < \hat{P}_y$$

where $\hat{P}_y$ = observed proportion of Yes responses, and

$\phi_p = \phi_n = 1/6$ (in this example) = specified probability of false positive and false negative responses

So, for example, the researcher who finds that 40% $(\hat{P}_p)$ of his respondents say Yes under this scheme will estimate that in fact about 35% $(\hat{\pi}_m)$ have tried cocaine.

In preserving confidentiality, the method has an obvious benefit: There is no clear linkage between an identified individual's response and his true state. He may or may not have used cocaine, regardless of the fact that his recorded response is Yes. It is not a very difficult strategy to implement, judging from pilot studies. Moreover, the researcher can obtain valid estimates of the true proportion of respondents who have used cocaine or have some other potentially stigmatizing characteristic. This is true *provided* that the respondent adheres faithfully to the procedure. Some studies designed to estimate adherence rate and to assess the consequences of failure of the method have been discussed in Boruch and Cecil (1979).

The contamination method does have some important disadvantages. Since they are similar to those incurred in the randomized response methods, they are discussed following the description of these more efficient techniques.

Randomized Response Methods

There are two general classes of randomized techniques: the related question asked, invented by Stanley Warner (1965, 1971), and the unrelated question technique, suggested by Walt Simmons and extended creatively by Greenburg, Horvitz, and

Abernathy (1974) at North Carolina, and by Bourke and Dalenius (1973, 1974) in Sweden. Although these techniques are related to the contamination method just described, they are distinctive and can usually be made more efficient.

In a simple variant of the unrelated question technique, the researcher presents each respondent with two questions. Assume that the first question is of primary interest to the researcher and is likely to generate a social or legal risk to the respondent should disclosure occur, e.g., "Did you read a pornographic magazine last month?" The second question, answerable in the same Yes-No format as the stigmatizing question, must be innocuous, e.g., "Did you use a public telephone last week?" For the simple analysis, responses to the latter *must* be statistically unrelated to responses to the stigmatizing item. That is, there must be no inherent relation between people's reading a pornographic magazine and their weekly use of a public telephone. The respondent is then instructed to select one of the questions randomly and to answer it truthfully without revealing which item was chosen. In using a die as a randomization device, the researcher specifies that (say) a one indicates the first question must be answered, and 2, 3, . . ., 6 indicates that the second question should be answered. Again, the researcher is not shown the result of the die throw. Given the probabilities of choosing both questions, 1/6 and 5/6, respectively, in this example, the observed proportion of Yes responses (P_y) is equal to

$$\hat{P}_y = 1/6\,\hat{\pi} + 5/6\,\hat{P}_m$$

where $\hat{\pi}$ equals the proportion of people who did read a pornographic magazine and $\hat{P}_m$ is the proportion of people who used a public telephone the previous week. We can obtain an estimate of $\hat{P}_m$ from an independent survey sample, and knowing $\hat{P}_m$ and $\hat{P}_y$ we can solve for $\hat{\pi}$.

Where confidentiality of response is important, a major benefit of the randomized response methods is that even in interviews, there is no clear linkage between an identified individual's response and his actual condition. Indeed, the researcher cannot know which question was answered, much less what the true response is to either question. Despite this, the data analyst can estimate proportions that reflect incidence of an embarrassing characteristic in the population.

The feasibility of these techniques and their limitations have been demonstrated in research on fertility control, illegal drug use, racial attitudes, and other sensitive topics. For example, in the North Carolina Abortion Study and the Taiwan Fertility Control Study, valid information about abortions appears to have been obtained without subjecting respondents to any serious depreciation of privacy or to sociolegal threats (Greenberg et al., 1969; Chi, Chow, & Rider, 1972). Other studies of the effectiveness of the methods in obtaining data on drug usage (Brown & Harding, 1973), marijuana usage (Boruch & Endruweit, 1973), and other topics (Campbell & Joiner, 1973) have also yielded promising results. Randomized response methods can probably be adapted well to mail surveys, but Brown and Harding's study is the only one we have been able to locate. Because the methods can be applied in face-to-face interview situations, they eliminate the problem of how sampling validity can be appraised, a difficulty in using some of the procedural methods described earlier. To assure validity of response and the respondent's adherence to the strategy special side studies can be developed. Bourke and Dalenius (1974), for example, show how one can use side studies to estimate lie parameters, and they specify conditions under which precision can be maximized, given that some respondents fail to follow instructions.

A final benefit of the randomized response methods is that they are quite flexible. A wide range of techniques has been developed for dichotomous response categories (e.g., Yes or No), for multichotomous responses (Yes, No, Do not know), and for continuous responses (e.g., number of antisocial acts: 0, 1, 2, 3, or more). Like the contamination methods, they can be used in conjunction with questions that are completely direct; i.e., in the same interview, some questions are answered under the randomized response paradigm, while others are answered directly.

Limitations, Costs, and Vulnerability

Neither contamination methods nor randomized response methods have been adapted to narrative responses and it is not at all clear that is possible. Nor are the techniques appropriate for situations in which actual behavior of the research participant must be observed. Though they are applicable in principle to telephone surveys, we have found no demonstrations of their feasibility in these settings.

The costs attached to applying either the contamination method or the randomized response method can be grouped into two broad categories: those that are primarily statistical in nature and those that depend on the social-psychological character of the research. Considering statistical matters, it should be intuitively clear that all these methods introduce some random noise to the research data. This additional noise implies a loss of precision in estimates of statistical parameters of the population such as mean (including proportions) and variance. Consequently, larger samples are necessary to make confident judgments about interesting properties of the population. Work is proceeding rapidly, however, on developing more efficient variations on these techniques. In some of the most thorough work to date, Greenberg, Horvitz, and Abernathy (1974), for instance, found that more recently developed types of randomized response approach generally yield more precise results, followed in order of efficiency by extended versions of the contamination method, and older versions of the randomized response techniques. Their standard of comparison was data simulated for situations in which the clearly identified respondent is asked a sensitive question directly and lies at some known level in responding.

The social psychology of the interview process is rather complex, especially if the topics of inquiry are sensitive or controversial. It is reasonable to expect novel statistical methods to complicate the interview process further and to have unwanted side effects. An obvious complication is simple confusion in the interview. In using one variation of the randomized response method, for example, researchers at the Illinois Institute of Technology Research Institute and The Chicago Crime Commission (1971) elicited what appears to be valid information on crime in Illinois but noted that errors did occur due to the respondent's misunderstanding instructions or failing to implement the procedure correctly, and due to awkward handling of the interview by the interviewer. A more serious difficulty is that the respondent may fail to follow the researcher's instructions because the strategies provoke rather than reduce suspicion, or because the instructions create confusion which the respondent is unwilling or unable to articulate. The hostility or indifference that can characterize *any* method of inquiry can of course jeopardize the usefulness of these special methods as well as ordinary methods of inquiry. Experimental tests by Chi and colleagues (1972) suggest that these kinds of problems will *not* always obtain. They have found, for example, that women are more willing to admit that they have had abortions under the randomized response paradigm (relative to direct questioning) and that female respondents in this fertility control research are not unduly suspicious of or confused by the method. Other empirical investigations, however, suggest that certain classes of respondents in other types of research will have different reactions. For example, pilot studies on servicemen's use of marijuana led us to conclude that a respondent's adherence to instructions in the randomized response method is a function of the military rank of the respondent and other variables (Brown & Harding, 1973). Social-psychological theory is *in*sufficient for predicting adherence to instructions and reactions to the novel statistical methods of inquiry in general, but it is sufficient to guide construction of pilot studies for testing and validating these methods in the field.

Microaggregation of Sample and of Response

Microaggregation methods have been suggested by Feige and Watts (1970, 1972) as a device for assuring confidentiality of archival data. These methods are also potentially useful for eliciting information directly from individuals in survey situations.

To understand the procedure, consider its original application to proprietary records on call reports and income of commercial banks. The records are maintained by a centralized data archive, which is prohibited from releasing anything but statistical summaries of information contained in the records. More specifically, even anonymous individual records cannot be released for outside statistical analysis. The Feige and Watts view is that, to permit sophisticated outside analysis of the data, the archive could create and release statistical data on aggregates of records rather than unit records. So, for example, 1,000 sets of three records each might be constructed from a sample of 3,000 records. The 1,000 records would contain averaged information on call reports, assets, liabilities, and so forth, of three banks within each aggregate. The archive can supply these aggregate records to *any* outside analyst without breaching legal regulations against disclosure of sets of anonymous unit records.

The benefit of the technique then is that the risk of deductive disclosure stemming from the release of unit data can be deduced considerably and eliminated for practical purposes. Yet the outside researcher can compute meaningful descriptive statistics to characterize the data. In particular, if the criteria for aggregation are proper, the researcher can develop sophisticated statistical models for the data, estimate each model's parameters, and make inferences about the likely effect of changes in these parameters (changes in policy) on data collected in the future.

Whether and how well the outsider can do various analyses depends largely on the way in which records are aggregated. For the cost of aggregation is that imprecision and (possibly) bias are introduced to the analysis. Clearly, if we obtain only means for each aggregate, we lose information on banks within aggregates. Any aggregation reduces effective sample size, and so estimates of statistical parameters in linear regression models, for example, will be susceptible to relatively high sample-to-sample variation. For example, the ratio of variance of a slope estimator based on aggregated data relative to variance of the estimate for disaggregated data increases with increasing variance within aggregate. The resultant uncertainty about parameters can be crucial to the research and various strategies have been developed to minimize this unavoidable inefficiency. One general class of strategies involves setting up rules for aggregation which reduce imprecision but avoid systematic biases. One must choose aggregation criteria that are independent of the error variance of the statistical model. Doing so is difficult at best, and if unit record data are not available at some stage for testing biases induced by aggregation rules, it may be impossible. Feige and Watts, for example, have had to develop crude rules for aggregation by empirically comparing statistics based on disaggregated data statistics computed from aggregated data on the same sample of banks. Searching for aggregation criteria that do not undermine precision and accuracy of analysis is not an easy task, and for this reason, microaggregation is likely to be more useful for panel studies than for one-time-only research.

We can also propose some approaches to the problem of assuring confidentiality in direct inquiry, based on the microaggregation technique. The first variant is a straightforward generalization of the banking example: microaggregation of members of a target sample in a cross-sectional study. The second variant involves microaggregation of each respondent's reply to inquiry rather than microaggregation of individuals.

To make the first approach concrete, consider the problem of eliciting information on legal problems of a population of 2,000 physicians. We might randomly allocate them into 100 aggregates of 20 individuals each, then designate one representative per aggregate to receive anonymous responses, to average them, and to provide resultant group means (on age, number of malpractice suits of a particular type, etc.) to the researcher. Responses of anonymous individuals might sometimes be supplied directly to the researcher, of course. But with reference to confidentiality, the benefit of microaggregation is that the possibility of deductive disclosure by the outside researcher can be eliminated. Confidentiality of unit records is maintained with respect to the designated representative only if collateral information cannot be used to discover the identity of a respondent.

The aggregates can be determined by a formal lottery set up by the researcher, or through natural (nearly) random processes. Membership in an aggregate can be determined by birth date, birth month, or week of birth, for example. Naturally occurring groups may also serve as aggregates *provided* that there is no unspecifiable relation between the grouping criteria and the sampling error underlying the model used to analyze the data. In a study of malpractice suits against physicians, for example, using age as the criterion for aggregation is likely to yield biased estimates of parameters for unit level data since incidence of malpractice cases is correlated with age. Some variable such as birth month of a friend of the physician, degree of liking for a particular food, or some other unverifiable, innocuous, and unrelated criteria would be more appropriate. The most appropriate criterion, one that reduces imprecision relative to random grouping and induces no bias, often cannot be specified beforehand. But side studies on unit level records may be helpful in discovering such variables. More generally, if good aggregation criteria are known to coincide with natural groupings (police departments in studies of policemen, youth gangs in studies of delinquency, etc.) then microaggregation methods may be exploited for making inferences about unit level phenomena from aggregate data.

Unlike aggregation of individuals, response aggregation is relevant to both direct interviews or to mail surveys. In this case, one searches for a set of questions to which numerical answers can be supplied and elicits an aggregate response to all questions rather than specific responses to each individual question. For example, in a study of petty theft we might present each respondent the following questions and response categories:

How often did you engage in petty theft last month? Not at all *3*. Once *1*. More than once *0*.

How often did you use the telephone last week? More than average *-1*. Same as average *0*. Less than average *1*.

How much candy did you eat last week? Less than average *-1*. Same as average *0*. More than average *1*.

An individual's response to the interviewer is the *sum* of the numeric values corresponding to each individual question. If the respondent reports the number 1, for example, it could mean that he has engaged in petty theft, used the telephone less than he usually does, or eaten more candy than he usually does. For any reasonable application of this approach, some of the questions must be innocuous. The implicit assumptions underlying the simplest variation is that responses to the innocuous questions are unverifiable and have a known or estimable mean. Insofar as responses to the last items average to zero, for example, and are random and independent, the technique is not different analytically from the contamination method mentioned earlier (i.e., responses to the last two are random noise). More generally, the mean level of telephone use and of candy consumption can be estimated from an independent sample in which responses are supplied separately to each question.

There are, of course, a great many difficulties in applying the response aggregation approach: respondents may be suspicious; they may not add correctly; they may not understand the process; etc. Further, the approach is not particularly efficient as presented here. Better variations on the strategy are possible, and these are presented in the section on Aggregation of Response and BIB Designs.

With respect to confidentiality, microaggregation of respondents or of responses has the benefit of reducing direct and deductive disclosures of identifiable information to the researcher. Even if the researcher knows the identity of individuals within aggregate, the threat of exact deductive disclosure is negligible if the aggregate is large. Microaggregation of individual respondents appears most appropriate for situations in which respondents will not or cannot cooperate directly with an outside researcher but an intermediary (the representative) is available. For a cross-sectional study, neither the representative of the aggregate nor the researcher needs to know the identify of other members except for side studies. The statistical costs of using microaggregates rather than individual response as a basis for data collection and analysis are similar to those encountered in the contamination and randomized response methods. It is an inefficient technique in the sense that larger samples are necessary to achieve the levels of confidence obtained in analysis of individuals rather than groups. Unless one is very careful in their use, however, the technique can lead to crucial biases in estimates of parameters, e.g., using as a basis for aggregation some variable that is correlated with error in a regression application with result in biased estimates of parameters that describe unit level phenomena.

The statistical technology available for analyzing microaggregated data is well developed in some respects, notably for simple linear models. But even that technology may not be useful if the aggregation process has produced data that cannot be analyzed under more complex models and cannot be disaggregated. Moreover, unless the same functional model used to generate aggregates is also used to analyze the data, new analyses (models) may produce misleading results. Of course, checking the validity of sampling within aggregate and validity of reporting within aggregate is impossible unless the social researcher conducts a side study on small subsamples within the larger target group. Linking aggregate data with aggregated records from other data files on the same individuals is possible only if clear identification of each individual within each aggregate is available.

Aggregation of Response and BIB Designs

Consider a situation in which the researcher presents an individual with two questions, each answerable with a numerical response. For simplicity, let one question be innocuous and the other sensitive. He then enjoins the interviewee *not* to furnish a response to each individual item but rather to add up the numerical value corresponding to each response and to furnish that total value to the researcher. So, for example, the respondent may add the number of times he used the telephone during the previous week (say, 3) to the number of times he engaged in petty theft (say, 1). The total, 4, is the only response supplied to the researcher. If the researcher proceeds in exactly the same way for each respondent in a random sample of some target population, he can compute the average numerical answer to his questions, $\overline{Y}_1$. That average can easily be described in terms of a single equation in two unknowns. If the average response is 5, for example, we have $\overline{Y}_1 = 5 = \overline{X}_1 + \overline{X}_2$ where $\overline{X}_1$ represents the (unobserved) average incidence of telephone use and $\overline{X}_2$ represents the (unobserved) average incidence of theft. We are of course interested in determining the numerical values of $\overline{X}_1$ and $\overline{X}_2$ but this equation is insufficient for doing so. In order to obtain estimates of the rates of telephone use and theft, the researcher simply takes a *second* random sample from the population and asks each respondent in the sample to subtract (rather than add) numerical values for his responses. He might obtain an average response of 1 from such a procedure, and this average can then be described in terms of a second independent equation in two unknowns:

$$\overline{Y}_2 = 1 = \overline{X}_1 - \overline{X}_2$$

The two equations based on the two independent samples are sufficient for estimating values of $\overline{X}_1$ and $\overline{X}_2$:

$$\overline{X}_1 = (\overline{Y}_1 + \overline{Y}_2)/2 = 3, \text{ and}$$

$$\overline{X}_2 = 2$$

That is, the average weekly incidence of telephone use in the sample at hand is 3; members of the sample engage in petty theft about twice a week.

One additional problem deserves our attention: estimation of variances and covariances for the responses to questions. Variances can be computed as

$$\text{Var}(X_1^1) = \tfrac{1}{4}\text{Var}(\overline{Y}_A + \overline{Y}_B)$$
$$\text{Var}(X_2) = \tfrac{1}{4}\text{Var}(\overline{Y}_A - \overline{Y}_B)$$

and the covariance between $\overline{X}_1$ and $\overline{X}_2$ can be estimated using:

$$\text{Cov}(\overline{X}_1, \overline{X}_2) = \tfrac{1}{4}[\text{Var}(\overline{Y}_A) - \text{Var}(\overline{Y}_B)]$$

Judith Miller of George Washington University was kind enough to clarify the mathematics for me in a letter and to point out some *possible* merits in the technique. Calculation of the estimates is a bit more direct than randomized response methods, and because the traits about which one asks need not be independent, selecting questions is less difficult. Estimating means for subgroups, which can be difficult under the randomized response method, is less difficult for this approach. However, this method appears not to have been tested in the field and so its acceptability and flaws are not so well understood.

The problem of assuring that sample estimates of population parameters (means, proportions, etc.) are as precise as possible is not a simple one. There are a wide variety of ways in which we can combine questions (e.g., prescribing weighted responses, using random numbers as weights, using 1's, 0's, and –1's as weights) but few of them would be optimal. Most of the work in enumerating good combinations, however, has already been done in another context: statistical design of experiments.

Raghavarao and Federer (1973), for example, have pointed out that here we can capitalize on a 30-year-old source of information about combining arrangements of elements: weighing designs and more specifically, balanced incomplete block (BIB) designs. One can adopt these designs to the current applications by recognizing the following design parameters:

1. Total number of questions.
2. Number of subsamples available.
3. Number of questions asked of each member of a subsample.
4. Number of times a given pair of questions is administered to the same subsample.
5. Number of respondents per subsample.

Once the parameters are specified by the researcher, optimal combinations of items can be taken from standardized tables. For more information on the construction and use of these tables for BIB designs, see Kempthorne (1952).

The major benefits of this response aggregation technique are that it preserves the confidentiality of responses to individual items (since only an identifiable sum is acquired) and does not depreciate privacy, yet it yields information useful to the researcher, i.e., an unbiased, sample estimate of the incidence of telephone use and petty theft in the population. Moreover, the technique is simple to understand for both the interviewer and the interviewee. It does not carry even the mild "shell game" flavor of the more complicated methods described earlier. It requires little algebra to compute estimates of incidence of sensitive characteristics of the sample and only a bit more technical information to compute properties of the estimates. The method may be used with simple dichotomous responses (Yes or No) as well as with continuous responses (e.g., 1, 2, . . ., 10). Naturally, care must be taken to assure that every question does not have a potentially stigmatizing and verifiable response, but this is a mechanical problem, resolved by identifying innocuous and unverifiable questions beforehand and by judiciously combining questions. Finally, the technique can be used with any reasonable number of questions and subsamples of respondents. Reasonableness is also determined by the way in which design parameters, enumerated above, can be manipulated.

Longitudinal Research

The worth of the statistical strategies in longitudinal research must be judged in terms of the purpose of that research: tracking average development of individuals over time. The crucial issues here are needs for linkage of individual records collected over time, assurance of confidentiality, and the precision and accuracy of statistics based on the resultant data.

Mechanical linkage of records accumulated periodically under many of the statistical strategies is simple, since clear identification is always coupled to a response to inquiry. This operational simplicity is crucial where the procedural approaches to assuring confidentiality are not feasible and where it is difficult to maintain contact with a target group. The opportunity to use either interviews or mail as a device for eliciting information is an advantage over most of the procedural techniques. Microaggregation methods present no problem in this regard provided that individual members of each aggregate remain constant.

That confidentiality of identifiable records can be assured is clear. Despite the linkage between the response and the identifier, the individual's state cannot be inferred by the interviewer or (from the record) by anyone including the data analyst. Furthermore, since the methods can be focused on a single question or cluster of questions, one does have the opportunity to use more direct methods for collecting information about more innocuous characteristics of the respondent.

The main costs of using these statistical methods are that data analyses *may* result in less precise estimates of population parameters of interest to us. At the core of the precision problem is the fact that the methods reduce effective sample size. This reduction means that we will be less certain of the actual magnitude of any detected relation.

Suppose for example, that there is no change in relative incidence of illegal methadone usage in a target group of 100 individuals for two points in time. We may suspect, however, that there are no consistent users, e.g., individuals using methadone at one time are different from those using it the next. Suppose that in fact there is actually strong consistency in the data. Our ability to detect that consistency can be reduced dramatically depending on the induced error. Under certain conditions, a contamination rate of .35 will reduce the effective sample size to 75; an error rate of .167 will reduce it to only 20. Upper and lower limits on the probable size of the relationship will increase accordingly. The theoretical framework for estimating damaging effects on power of statistical tests is given by Assakul and Proctor (1967). Actions such as increasing sample size are the only available mechanisms for partial accommodation of the induced error.

Systematic biases in estimates of important population parameters may also obtain depending on the particular strategy and on the particular parameter being estimated. For example, simple product moment correlations between repeated measures of continuous characteristics will decrease in absolute value with the contamination method and can increase artificially with microaggregation. Since the error rate parameters in the contamination approach are fixed by the analyst, it will be possible to adjust sample statistics upward or downward to reflect the induced bias. In fact, with population data, adjustment of biases may well involve well known techniques (e.g., correction for attenuation). But the problems of adjusting the estimates will not in general be straightforward. We can rely on a substantial literature in mental test score theory and theory of measurement in censuses to accommodate adjustment problems in the simpler models. In general, the problems in this context have been better explicated for contaminated data than for microaggregated data.

Research Using Multiple Data Sources

The statistical devices for assuring confidentiality permit one to couple clear identification of the interviewee with the response. Consequently, there are no mechanical problems in linking research records so obtained with other identifiable records maintained on the same individuals. Moreover, because the research record cannot inform one about the state of the particular individual, there is no direct threat of disclosure associated with supplying that record to an agency for linkage with archival records. It must be made clear, however, that the records are not informative in order to avoid naive efforts to appropriate them for nonresearch purposes.

To assure confidentiality of the archival record (vis-à-vis the researcher) in a linkage with research records, both the procedural and statistical strategies must be used. For example, the linked records returned to the data analyst through an insulated data bank arrangement can be inoculated by computer with small amounts of controlled random error, processed through a simulated randomized response paradigm, or microaggregated. These processes reduce the possibility of deductive disclosure of the archival records. In fact, the microaggregation methods mentioned earlier were developed for application to data archives (on banks) and generalizing the techniques to multiple data sources is a natural step.

The joint use of procedural and statistical techniques in linking records provides a stronger assurance of confidentiality than the use of procedural methods alone. They can eliminate any possibility of exact deductive disclosure in this context. However, because the statistical methods do denigrate effective sample size, and may introduce some systematic biases into analyses of linked data, their use must be carefully planned beforehand. That planning and the technical expertise required will of course increase the monetary cost of linkage. The primary criterion for judging whether the methods can be adopted at all is the availability of technical knowledge to accommodate imprecision and bias and logistical support necessary for the procedures. Campbell, Boruch, Schwartz, and Steinberg (1975) provide detailed advice on combining statistical and procedural methods for assuring confidentiality of individual records when multiple data sets must be linked for research purposes.

Experimental Studies

The main objective of an experimental test of a social program is to obtain a fair estimate of the program's effect in a way that permits us to quantify the reliability of the estimate. This usually involves comparing the mean differences between responses of persons to alternative programs. Sensitive outcome variables here may include incidence of drug usage, theft or cheating, violation of medical standards, etc., in programs designed to reduce incidence of these phenomena. Detecting program effects is usually difficult since social programs are often weak to begin with, and outcome variables that reflect the program's effect are often susceptible to uncontrollable measurement error.

Using the statistical strategies may help to ameliorate the problem of natural error in response to the extent that they eliminate threats of disclosure and embarrassment usually associated with a respondent's providing sensitive information about himself. Because single individual records reveal nothing about the exact state of the individual on whom the record is maintained, confidentiality is assured. They do substitute controllable error for the uncontrollable, however; and insofar as the controllable error is large, the overall quality of the data may be reduced relative to direct questioning. Tests of program effects based on such data may then be unnecessarily pessimistic. That is, the analyst will fail to detect program effects not because they are absent but because the methods used to assure confidentiality also denigrate the quality of the data intolerably. How the power of statistical tests is affected by the use of the statistical strategies requires both theoretical and empirical work.

To illustrate the problem, consider a simple experiment in which we compare quality of medical care rendered by physicians and nurse-practitioners to two equivalent groups of patients with a particular disease. The observations may be simple, e.g., judges' ratings on whether care rendered by a particular individual was good, unremarkable, or poor. Judges may prefer to remain completely anonymous to avoid embarrassment or libel suits. Identifiers may be used with one of the statistical methods described earlier to assure confidentiality of response. Because either method depreciates effective sample size, our ability to detect a difference between the proportion of physicians rendering good care and the corresponding proportions for nurse-practitioners is weakened. A failure to detect a true difference would be critical here since we may erroneously adopt the nurse-practitioner program under the assumption that failure to find a difference means that no difference exists.

In general, any true difference between proportions will be reduced by error in classification, induced or otherwise. We will fail to learn about differences if they occur. Formal statistical tests are biased with respect to what they might be if there were differences but there were no errors. Because the character of the induced inefficiency is known, however, it is possible to anticipate reduction in empirical inquiry. It is possible to anticipate reduction in the power of statistical tests applied to the data. Doing so is not an easy task even for expert statisticians, but we can rely on work done already by Assakul and Proctor (1967) and others. It is clear that to increase power in such situations, one must increase size of the program effect, reduce the level of (usually uncontrolled) error in the observations, or reduce the contamination deliberately introduced to the system, or increase sample size. The first two actions may be difficult if not impossible. The third action must be taken, and we have good methods for accomplishing this. The last, increasing sample size, will be costly.

Recent Research and Development: Randomized Response

During the 1970s, work on statistical methods for assuring privacy expanded dramatically, stimulated by professional eagerness to meet public interest with scientific needs, and by the challenge of working on interesting problems. In the following remarks, we outline some of the advanced work conducted in the United States, Sweden, and elsewhere. Most of the research concerns randomized response methods.

1. Variations on the Randomized Response Methods
2. Randomization Devices: Use in the Field
3. Choice of an Innocuous Question
4. Pilot Study, Side Study, and Adherence Checks

Variations on the Randomized Response Methods

For the practicing researcher, a useful catalogue for these methods can be based on the type of response elicited, and on the methods' special functions and operating characteristics. So we adhere to a conventional response typology: dichotomous; discrete, continuous and polytomous; and continuous. Within each type, special functions, such as improving efficiency, or special operating characteristics, such as the use of single or multiple samples, provide additional dimensions for a typology. For the mathematical statistician, the more useful and interesting basis for cataloguing involves unifying mathematics.

Dichotomous response: Single sample, single trial. In each of the dichotomous response variants, the objective is to estimate the proportion of individuals in two mutually exclusive and exhaustive categories: the proportion of those who are type A, π_A, and the proportion of those who are not of type A, $1 - \pi_A$. A physical randomization device (cards, dice, spinner, etc.) must be used to generate the random choice, and odds on a choice are fixed beforehand.

Warner's (1965) method is the remarkable precedent. The interviewer presents two statements to each respondent: "I am a member of A"; I am *not* a member of A." The respondent is then asked to respond (saying True or False) to the first statement with probability ϕ_W and to the second statement with probability $1 - \phi_W$. The respondent may be instructed, for example, to cast a die and to react to the first question if a one turns up: $\phi_W = 1/6$. A response to the second statement is made if $2, 3, \ldots, 6$ turn up on the die.

Boruch's (1972) contamination method requires that the respondent be presented with only one question "Are you a member of A?" He or she is then told to respond faithfully with probability ϕ_P and to say No if he or she is A with probability ϕ_N. Small sample results are reported in the reference.

Lanke (1976) and Drane (1975) proposed a single sample variation of the unrelated question approach which requires the interviewer to present a question "Are you a member of A?" and a statement "Say Yes." The respondent chooses the question with probability ϕ_L and the statement with probability $1 - \phi_L$. The variation is simple, and can be very efficient in the sense of reducing variance of the estimate of π_A to a bare minimum. The tactic is a special case of a model invented by Simmons (1970) and can be regarded as a special case of the contamination method. It has been successfully field tested by Reaser, Hartsock, and Hoehn (1975) in studies of attitudes of U.S. Army officers.

In the single sample variations of the Simmons (1970) and Greenberg et al. (1969) approaches, the respondent is presented with a sensitive question: "Are you a member of A?", for which a proportion must be estimated, with probability ϕ_S. A second, innocuous question, presented with probability $1 - \phi_S$, concerns a trait B whose relative frequence in the population, π_B, is known.

In Ericksson's (1973) device three options are presented to each respondent in the sample: "Are you a member of A?"; "Say Yes"; and "Say No." The choice is determined by a randomization device so that the probability of answering the question is ϕ_2, the probability of saying Yes is ϕ_2, and the probability of reacting to the No statement is $\phi_3 = 1 - \phi_1 - \phi_2$. Test results for a small sample are given in the author's dissertation.

In Swensson's (1975, 1976) strategy, rather than respond to one of two statements, the individual responds to a single question involving several attributes: "Do you belong to A or B?" where A is sensitive and B is not. In the simplest case, the traits A and B are stochastically independent and the population parameter $P(A_2)$, concerning the proportion who have trait B, is known. The minor variations include asking whether the individual belongs to A or not to B, and asking whether the respondent belongs to:

$$A \text{ and } B \qquad \text{or } \overline{A} \text{ and } \overline{B}$$

The first two variations give equal efficiency under equal levels of protection, $P(A_1 /$ Yes), the third is least efficient.

Dichotomous response: Multisample. Simmons (1970) and Greenberg et al. (1969) have produced an unrelated question model based on the original randomized response idea. In it, the interviewer presents two questions to each respondent: "Are you a member of A?"; "Are you a member of B?" In the first of *two* independent samples of individuals, each respondent chooses the question randomly with probability ϕ_1 specified by the researcher. The second question is chosen with probability $1 - \phi_1$. In a second sample, the probabilities are altered to ϕ_2 and $1 - \phi_2$, respectively. The traits A and B must be independent for simple application. The variation often yields more efficient estimators of the incidence of the sensitive trait than the Warner approach. When the relative incidence of the innocuous trait, π_B, is known for the population, then the technique is notably more efficient. Field test results from an abortion study are reported in the references.

Folsom, Greenberg, Horvitz, and Abernathy (1973) developed a variation, suggested by D. T. Campbell, to increase statistical efficiency of the original unrelated-question randomized response method. In the first of two independent samples, respondents are asked to use a randomization device to choose between two questions: "Are you a member of A?" and "Are you a member of B?"; they are asked to respond directly to a third question: "Are you a member of C?" A is sensitive; B and C are not. In the second sample, respondents choose randomly between questions concerning A and C, and they are asked to respond directly to the question about B. The use of two innocuous questions, B and C, in this instance, permits a more precise estimate of the incidence of the sensitive characteristic A, when population parameters for the alternative innocuous items π_B and π_C are unknown. A field test, concerning alcohol consumption, is reported in the paper. The occurrence of A, B, and C in the population must be independent in simpler applications. Again, the motive for the invention of the method is to lay out a novel alternative which would require smaller sample size than the original Warner approach to obtain precise estimates of π_A.

These two sample variants can be reduced to one sample variations if the parameter associated with traits B and C are known or can be fixed. They may be known, for example, from published census statistics on the population at hand. They may be fixed by using as trait B, for example, in the Greenberg et al. variant, the statement "Say 'Yes.' " Or, it may be fixed by using an additional randomization device, a second flip of a coin, etc., to determine the response to the second item. The two sample approach is likely to be useful only where information about the relative frequency of the auxiliary traits, B, C, etc., is unavailable and is itself useful. The unrelated question technique is a risky approach if the assumption of independence of traits A and B is untenable: estimates of π_A will then be biased if the regular formulas are used.

Multiproportion and discrete quantitative response. The basic problem is to establish a reasonable idea of the proportion of people who are of type 1, type 2, and so on.

Abul-Ela, Greenberg, and Horvitz (1967) formalize the problem in estimating the proportion of individuals in each of π-related but mutually exclusive categories: $\pi(A_1)$, $\pi(A_2)$, . . . , $\pi(A_\pi)$. In their approach, $\pi - 1$ independent samples must be taken. In the first sample, any given individual is asked to respond Yes or No (True or False) to one of the π statements bearing on group membership. The statement is randomly chosen. The probability of reacting to the statement regarding A_1 in the first sample is ϕ_{11}, the probability for A_2 is ϕ_{12}, etc. In the second sample, the proportions are fixed at different values: ϕ_{21}, ϕ_{22}, . . . , ϕ_{2k}. For each sample, i, the sum of the probabilities must be 1.00:

$$\sum_{j=1}^{k} \phi_{ij} = 1$$

and so on, down to the $k - 1$ sample. Field test results from a study of pregnancy and abortion are given in the reference.

Warner's (1976) proposal is an extension of his contamination approach. In estimating proportions for three mutually exclusive categories, for example, one constructs six sets of three statements; each set contains a permutation of assignment of the following form:

> If you're a member of A_i; report A_j
> If you're a member of A_j, report A_k
> If you're a member of A_k, report A_i

where $i, j, k = 1, 2, 3$, and $i = j, f, k$. The odds on a respondent selecting any three statement set $\phi_1, \phi_2, \ldots, \phi_6$ are fixed by the researcher and constrained so that $\Sigma\phi = 1.00$.

In the Bourke and Dalenius (1973) variation, the problem is again to estimate the proportion of individuals in mutually exclusive and exhaustive categories A_1, $A_2, \ldots, A_k$. The solution is a single sample variation on the Abul-Ela et al. model just described. Each member of a target sample is told to select one of three cards, each containing questions about A; probability of selecting each card is prescribed by the researcher ($\phi_1, \phi_2, \ldots, \phi_k$). Each card contains k numbered statements; ϕ_1 of the cards enumerate as follows: $1 = A_1, 2 = A_2, \ldots, k = A_k$; ϕ_2 of the cards enumerate in a different pattern: $1 = A_2, 2 = A_3, 3 = A_4$. The respondent, having selected a card, then just declares the number of the statement corresponding to his or her status. The pattern is fixed and conforms to a Latin square.

Bourke's (1974a, b, c) systematic extensions of this work involve a half dozen novel designs based on an unrelated question framework similar to that used in the original Simmons (1970) and Greenberg et al. (1969) approaches. They require only one sample but some variations require two or more stages of randomization. In the simplest case, for example, the respondent reacts to one of two sets of questions, the set being selected randomly. One set concerns the attributes $A_1, A_2, \ldots,$ A_k and the respondent merely indicates which number corresponds to his status. The second set of questions refers to an unrelated set of categories $B_1, B_2, \ldots, B_k$ and if that set is chosen randomly, the respondent again merely reports a number.

The Liu, Chow, and Mosley (1975) variation is appropriate for discrete quantitative data or categorical data. The interviewer presents the respondent with a long-necked bottle containing colored or numbered beads, the color of each bead corresponding to a group: color 1 indicates group A_1, color 2 indicates group A_2, etc. The neck of the bottle is graduated so that the beads fall into a single line and the order of the beads from 1 to m is evident from markings on the neck. The respondent is asked: If you are a member of A_1, indicate the position in the neck which your bead occupies: first from bottom, second from bottom, and so on. The interviewer is not allowed to see the bottle's neck during the process. Estimates of the proportion of a sample of size N belonging to exclusive categories $A_1, A_2, \ldots, A_k$ are obtained from the observed proportion of designations of each bottleneck position P_y, and the preselected probability of each color of bead falling into the bottleneck position, ϕ. The probability of the ith color bead $(i - 1, 2, \ldots, k)$ falling first into the jth position in the bottleneck $(j - 1, 2, \ldots, m)$ is computable from information about the total number of beads, and the number of beads of each color, m_i. A small-sample, physical feasibility test is described in the paper. The method is complicated; its merit lies in its novelty and the fact that split samples need not be used.

Continuous quantitative response. Greenberg, Kuebler, Abernathy, and Horvitz (1971) cast the problem in terms of estimating the population parameters of a continuous variable, e.g., mean number of abortions. In the original variant, two independent samples are required. Within a sample, any given individual is presented the first (sensitive) question with probability ϕ_1 and the second question with probability $1 - \phi_1$, the choice of question being made randomly. The questions should be answerable using a numerical response: e.g., How many pornographic magazines have you bought this week (Z_A)? How many times did you compliment someone this week (Z_B)? The mathematics have been worked out for the simplest case, in which traits A and B are unrelated in the population. Members of second, independent samples are asked the same questions, but with probabilities ϕ_2 and $1 - \phi_2$, to provide sufficient information for estimating mean levels of the traits, μ_A and μ_B, and variances.

As in other two sample variations, the second sample is unnecessary and the procedure is more efficient when population parameters for the innocuous question are known. Three other simple variations on the theme have been proposed. In the first, proposed by Poole (1974), each respondent is asked to add the numerical responses to each question $(Z = Z_A + Z_B)$ and to provide that information to the interviewer. This is itself a simple variant on the microaggregated response tactics discussed earlier. A second tactic involves multiplying numerical values of response; the respondent reports only $Z = Z_A \cdot Z_B$. Pollock and Bek's (1976) analysis suggests that the additive response model can be set up to be more efficient than the single sample randomized response method for $\phi < .7$. Recall that values of $\phi > .7$ in the randomized response approach generally yield better efficiency relative to direct questions. The multiplicative model's efficiency is difficult to assay since it requires good guesses about the mean and variance of the sensitive trait being examined.

In Eriksson's (1973) single-sample variant, the options presented to each individual are: "To what degree do you possess the trait A_1?"; and "Say that you possess the trait to the degree A_j." The probability associated with the question is fixed at ϕ. The probability of reacting to a specific statement about level A_1, level A_2, etc., is fixed at $\phi_1, \phi_2, \ldots, \phi_J$, so that

$$\sum_{j=1}^{J} \phi_j = 1 - \phi$$

The randomization device suggested is a deck of cards: ϕ of them concern the question; ϕ_1 of them concern a statement about level A_1; ϕ_2 concern A_2; and so on. Each respondent selects a card from a completed, shuffled deck, and responds accordingly. Used in a single sample, the technique permits one to estimate the mean and variance of the level of trait A, and it permits one to estimate the proportion of individuals at each level $A_1, A_2, \ldots, A_k$.

Other variations on those methods have been developed to accommodate the researcher's need for establishing relations among variables. They are described below in the section on estimating relations.

Randomization Devices: Use in the Field

Whether any of the randomized response procedures is effective depends partly on the way a random choice is generated. It is reasonable then to examine a few standards for evaluating randomization devices.

Physical characteristics of the randomization device will influence the duration, convenience, and complexity of an interview. Contemporary research suggests that a variety of devices are acceptable at least insofar as they present no remarkable handling problems. Barth and Sandler's (1976) repondents flip coins. Locander, Sudman, and Bradburn (1976) use little boxes containing colored beads, an adaption of devices used earlier by Greenberg et al. (1969). Chi, Chow, and Rider (1972) shake a bag of colored stones; Abul-Ela et al. (1967) and Brown and Harding (1973) shuffle cards. Reaser et al. (1975) use a paper target containing numbers in randomly assigned positions; the respondent, to whom the questionnaire and target is mailed, pokes the target with a pencil without looking at it. In a few instances, telephone numbers whose statistical properties are established *beforehand* have been used, e.g., by Goodstadt and Gruson (1975).

The respondent's perception of or attitude toward a randomization device may be a bit more important, but again, no major problems have been reported. Most devices can be built to conform with local culture: Chi et al.'s (1972) black and white stones, used in Taiwan, are similar to those used in the game of Go; dice and coin flipping are familiar in many if not most societies. Such devices have some face validity for the respondent in that they appear to generate random choices. A few respondents in any given sample are likely to announce their suspicion that the dice are fixed, that the cards are marked, and so on, but the reported incidence of these is very low. Some respondents are amused, e.g., "My first reaction to the little colored balls is to eat a few." Whether those minority reactions actually influence a respondent's behavior much is unknown.

The statistical properties of numbers generated by various randomization devices have not received much attention. Cards are usually assumed to be shuffled well, bead bags are assumed to be shaken vigorously, and so on. Greenberg's work on bead boxes is an exception; they have attempted to construct a simple device with demonstrable ability to generate numbers with fixed properties. The Reaser et al. (1975) tests is another interesting exception. They find that numbers picked blindly by a respondent from their randomly unnumbered paper target are distributed more uniformly than the numbers obtained in die throws. However, no other properties of the obtained numbers are reported. That the assumption of randomness in some instances may not always be warranted is clear from other social endeavors in which randomization procedures have been found wanting. The early military draft lotteries of the early 1960s, for example, were not random selections as they were advertised to be.

Using "naturally occurring" numbers as a basis of randomization poses more serious difficulties. For example, one might ask a respondent to use the fifth digit of an unnamed friend's telephone number as the basis for making a random choice, under the *assumption* that the distribution of the numbers is uniform. Contrary to some expectations, however, the distribution of the numbers appearing in any given position (digit) of a telephone number is often not uniform. Even the fifth digit, which is often most immune to manipulation, does not contain numbers which are uniform in distribution for the telephone directories we've examined. Similarly, many naturally occurring serial numbers have sticky subsets, i.e., pairs or triplets go together more often than one would expect on the basis of chance alone. Paul Lavrakas (1975) confirmed what we'd expect, for example, in asking people to "think of ten random numbers." The numbers so generated deviated considerably from a uniform distribution (people favor numbers ending in zero), and numbers can be predicted imperfectly from numbers appearing earlier in a sequence, from numbers in the sequence, phone numbers, and from addresses of the individuals in the study. On the other hand, when the properties of a population of such numbers are well understood or a large enough sample can be taken to specify their properties well, naturally occurring numbers can be a more convenient randomization device. Goodstadt and Gruson (1975), for example, counted the incidence of numbers 0, 1, . . . , 9 appearing as the last digit of telephone numbers in a large sample, developed a reasonable statistical characterization of the numbers, then successfully used that characterization as a basis for estimating incidence of drug abuse from randomized responses. The idea can be adapted in an obvious way to digits in social security numbers, serial numbers on paper money, lottery tickets, credit cards, and so on.

Choice of an Innocuous Question

The general class of unrelated question randomized response methods, developed by Horvitz and others, requires that a second question, dealing with a nonsensitive trait, be used as a foil for the question about a sensitive trait. The usefulness of any such question depends heavily on:

1. Relations between the occurrence of each trait in the target population.
2. The trait's attractiveness versus its innocuousness.
3. The trait's potential use in deductive disclosure.

All of the methods discussed here, and the mathematics underlying each, involve the assumption that the prevalence of the sensitive trait is not related to the presence of the nonsensitive one. They are supposed to be stochastically independent. It is possible, of course, to generate methods that permit an association, but they will be more complex than current methods. To guarantee the independent traits, one could exploit birthdates (Is your mother's birthday in April?), telephone numbers (Is the fifth digit of a friend's number "2"?), and other traits that intuition tells us are independent of the sensitive one. That a choice based on the intuition can be risky is clear, however. Shimizu and Bonham (1978), for example, used this non-sensitive question in one of their studies: "This time last year, did you live in a different county or state than this one?" The main question dealt with abortion. It is not unreasonable to argue that the likelihood of abortion is indeed related to migration behavior; middle income families, who incidentally move across county lines often, may find it easier or cheaper, etc., to have an abortion than low income families who incidentally do not move across county lines very often. A second risk in exploiting intuitively appealing nonsensitive traits is tied to memory. Shimizu and Bonham (1978), for example, also used "Was your mother born in April?" as others have done for their nonsensitive question. They had the good sense to do a side study on a subsample and discovered that just over 8% of the group admitted that they could not recollect the month, a problem that has cropped up in other tests of confidentiality assurance. If the impact of memory failure is random, the problem is negligible. But it is a bit more likely to be systematic and, if so, it will exercise systematic effects on estimates of the incidence of the sensitive trait. That influence too might be negligible, but we simply do not know enough about it. Where the evidence is ambiguous, or the issue crucial, we think it best to adopt one of the randomized response techniques that require no auxiliary unrelated question.

The second concern is that a respondent's view of the nonsensitive question's attractiveness may influence cooperation. Suppose the sensitive question bears on reading pornography and the nonsensitive one bears on having eaten a bar of candy. The negative affect associated with the sensitive question may override the neutrality of the second, and the respondent may say No regardless of what he or she is instructed to do. And so for example, Zdep and Rhodes (1976) stress that the "innocuous" item should involve an attractive or socially desirable trait. Their pilot tests and experimental results, using attendance at PTA meetings as the foil for their questions on punishing children, seem to bear that out. The symmetrical randomized response approaches, e.g., Warner's related question and the Bourke inventions, constitute a logical circumvention of the problem, but it is not clear to us that respondents attach the same emotional value to Yes and No. We know of no direct research on this topic.

Finally, the topic of the innocuous question may lend itself to deductive disclosure of other information. Consider the question about whether the respondent's mother's month of birth is April, used in the abortion study cited earlier. If it is possible for the interviewer to determine mother's birth month for the particular respondent, as it usually is in principle if not in practice, then deductive disclosure is possible. A Yes response implies the respondent had an abortion, if it is determined later that her mother's birthday was in August. A No response would imply having no abortion, if it is determined that the birth month is April. A Yes is "safe" only for children of April's child. It is reasonable also to expect that some respondents will recognize the problem, as they have in other research. We are aware of no studies of randomized response which address the problem.

Pilot Study, Side Study, and Adherence Checks

The statistical strategies may be used for at least one of two purposes: (1) to assure that the respondent's privacy is sustained, and (2) to sustain privacy and so encourage more accurate responses. Regardless of the objective, it is essential that the quality of data obtained under the models be examined.

That is, even if simple protection of privacy in an innocuous survey is the main objective, the data generated under the statistical methods may be suspect. Respondents who are confused by the method will fail to adhere to instructions. For the more sensitive inquiries or more difficult-to-reach target populations, the validity of the data resulting from the method must also be examined, just as are data resulting from the use of methods of inquiry that rely on procedural or law-based protection.

Adherence checks can be emplaced at several points in the measurement stream: before, during, or after the main survey. For example, if one purpose is to assure that more accurate responses will be elicited, then presurvey study of "normal" rates of providing sensitive information and presurvey study of willingness to provide information under the novel methods are warranted. Such a study might, for instance, involve asking each identified member of a subsample of the target population the questions directly, then asking a second subsample to respond anonymously. The difference between rates of admitting of sensitive information under the two conditions can be regarded as a range within which the statistical models can produce an effect, i.e., produce more accurate responses. When no difference appears between the subsamples, we think it is unlikely that the statistical methods will produce any remarkable results. But their use may still be justified on the fundamental grounds that they protect privacy and permit follow-up.

Results of exploratory pilot tests are rarely presented in published reports on use of these protection methods. However, Zdep and Rhodes (1977) provide some advice based on their presurvey research on the use of the Greenberg et al. (1969) unrelated question technique. They observe that to increase the effectiveness of the method, they had to employ an unrelated question that involved a socially desirable trait rather than a mental one; instruct the respondents orally before any questionnaires and descriptive material were provided; establish upper bounds on the amount of information provided, so as not to confuse respondents; and use a randomization device and selection probability with face validity for the sake of reducing respondent apprehension. The Zdep and Rhodes survey that followed their pilot test suggest that one can obtain notably higher cooperation by using the randomized response method rather than using direct questions and sealed envelope returns in research on corporal punishment of children.

Any discrepancy between anonymous respondents and clearly identified respondents in the pilot study can serve as a parameter in designing the randomized response method to be used in the main survey, e.g., in selecting probability for responding to each question in the unrelated question approach (Horvitz, Greenberg, & Abernathy, 1975). Base rates on mean level of distortion in response, relative to some standard, are also often available from prior research. The relevant literature has been enumerated by, among others, the U.S. Bureau of the Census (1974). More convenient synthesis and tabulated data have been produced by Sudman and Bradburn (1974). Far too few of these products exist, however, and fewer still will bear directly on the target sample at hand.

During the main survey, side studies can usually be mounted to secure some evidence on quality of the data collected under the novel statistical model. Having chosen a model for use with the main sample, one might adopt one or more of the following approaches. First, a subsample may be held aside and asked to answer questions directly and with full identification. The difference between response rates for this subsample and the rate for the main sample will be an indicator of respondent confusion, induced sensitivity to questions, and so on, if the inquiries are generally innocuous. If the inquiries concern sensitive information, the comparison will reflect these factors as well as the trust induced by the novel method. If the statistical method induces more candid responses, the rate of affirming embarrassing characteristics can often be expected to be higher in the main sample than in the side sample in which respondents provide information directly. So for example, Zdep and Rhodes (1976) found in their studies that the rate of admitting child abuse under a randomized response approach was notably higher than admissions under nominally anonymous conditions: 15% vs. 3-4%. On the other hand, some target groups asked to provide direct information may tend to exaggerate their sensitive characteristics, e.g., college students and construction gangs when invited to discuss their beer consumption. Then a difference between main sample results and side sample results will be an indicator of the novel method's ability to reduce inflated responses.

Second, a subsample may be held aside and asked to respond anonymously to a questionnaire by mail or telephone. To the extent that rates of affirming innocuous traits differ between the main sample and this subsample, then there may be problems in implementing the novel statistical method of inquiry. For sensitive traits, the finding that there is no difference would enhance our belief that the statistical method yields results as accurate as an anonymous questionnaire would. A notable difference may suggest that the new method is far from perfect but still better than the anonymous approach.

Finally, it is possible at times to compare data yielded by the statistical methods on subsets of questions against data known to be very accurate. For example, Locander et al. (1976) compare willingness to admit bankruptcy and other *presumably* sensitive characteristics and willingness to affirm voter registration and other desirable traits under a randomized response model when population data were available from public records. They found that the Greenberg et al. (1969) method was not particularly effective in reducing overreporting of traits like having registered to vote and carrying a library card, relative to more conventional methods of identified inquiry. On the other hand, verifiable distortion rate was lowest under the randomized response when questions about bankruptcy and drunk driving were asked, especially relative to self-administered questionnaires.

Quality assessment devices may also be employed after application of a statistical method in a main survey. At a minimum, some questions should be put to respondents asking about their reactions to the method and, for the sake of comparisons, at least some of those questions ought to conform to similar questions used after other similar surveys. Greenberg, Horvitz, and others have found questions about respondents' trust or belief in the method helpful, though interpreting those responses is difficult. Their practice of asking identified respondents questions about their attitude toward the method, following its use, has the merit of being direct. But the disadvantage is that it involves a potentially sensitive question: expressed reactions may be negative, whatever the respondents' actual behavior under the statistical method, because the respondent would like to exhibit intelligent skepticism. The approach assumes that individuals who were covertly unwilling to adhere to the instructions under the statistical method would, when in a more familiar process, be willing to imply nonadherence.

Acknowledgments. Background research on this topic has been supported by the National Science Foundation. This is an excerpt from Boruch and Cecil (1979).

References

Abul-Ela, A., Greenberg, B. G., & Horvitz, D. G. A multiproportions randomized response model. *Journal of American Statistical Association*, 1967, *62*, 990-1008.

Assakul, K., & Proctor, C. H. Testing independence in two way contingency tables with data subject to misclassification. *Psychometrika*, 1967, *32*, 67-76.

Barth, J. T., & Sandler, H. M. Evaluation of the randomized response technique in a drinking survey. *Journal of Studies on Alcohol*, 1976, *37*(5), 690-693.

Boruch, R. F. Relations among statistical methods for assuring confidentiality of data. *Social Science Research*, 1972, *1*, 403-414.

Boruch, R. F., & Cecil, J. S. *Methods of assuring confidentiality in social science research*. Philadelphia: University of Pennsylvania Press, 1979.

Boruch, R. F., & Endruweit, G. Mathematische methoden zur sicherdung der vertraulichkeit und anonymitat von forschunosdaten. *Zeitschrift fur Soziologie*, 1973, *2*(3), 227-238.

Bourke, P. D. Multiproportions randomized response using the unrelated question technique. Confidentiality in Surveys Report No. 74, Department of Statistics, University of Stockholm, Stockholm, 1974a.

Bourke, P. D. Symmetry of response in randomized response designs. Confidence in Surveys Report No. 75, Department of Statistics, University of Stockholm, Stockholm, 1974b.

Bourke, P. D. Vector response in randomized response designs. Confidence in Surveys Report No. 76, Department of Statistics, University of Stockholm, Stockholm, 1974c.

Bourke, P. D., & Dalenius, T. Multi-proportions randomized response using single sample, Forskningsporjektet, Fel I Undersokningar, Rapport Nr 68, Stockholms Universitet, Statistika Institutionen, Stockholm 23, (December) 1973.

Bourke, P. D., & Dalenius, T. Randomized response with lying. Forskningsprojktet Fel I Undersokningar, Rapport Nr 71, Stockholms Universitet, Statistika Institutionen, Stockholm 23, (January) 1974.

Brown, G. H., & Harding, F. D. A comparison of methods of studying illicit drug usage. *HUMRO Technical Report 73-9*, Arlington, Va.: Human Resources Research Organization, 1973.

Campbell, D. T., Boruch, R. F., Schwartz, R. D., & Steinberg, J. Confidentiality preserving modes of access to files and to interfile exchange for useful statistical analysis. Appendix A In A. M. Rivlin (Ed.), National Academy of Sciences, The Committee on Federal Agency Evaluation Policy. *Protecting individual privacy in evaluation research.* Washington, D.C.: NAS, 1975.

Campbell, C., & Joiner, B. L. How to get the answer without being sure you've asked the question. *American Statistician*, 1973, 27, 229-231.

Chi, I. C., Chow, L. P., & Rider, R. V. The randomized response technique as used in the Taiwan Outcome of Pregnancy Study. *Studies in Population Planning*, 1972, 3, 265-269.

Drane, W. Randomized response to more than one question. *Proceedings of the American Statistical Association: Social Statistics Section,* Washington, D.C.: ASA, 1975.

Eriksson, S. A. Randomized interviews for sensitive questions. Doctoral dissertation, University Institute Statistics, University of Gothenburg, Gothenburg, Sweden, 1973.

Feige, E. L., & Watts, H. W. Protection of privacy through microaggregation. In R. L. Biscoe (Ed.), *Data bases, computers and the social sciences.* New York: Wiley, 1970.

Feige, E. L., & Watts, H. W. An investigation of the consequences of partial aggregation of microeconomic data. *Econometrica*, 1972, 40(2), 343-360.

Folsom, R. E., Greenberg, B. G., Horvitz, D. G. & Abernathy, J. R. Two alternate questions randomized response model for human surveys. *Journal of the American Statistical Association*, 1973, 68, 525-530.

Goodstadt, M. S., & Gruson, V. The randomized response technique: A test on drug use. *Journal of the American Statistical Association*, 1975, 70, 814-818.

Greenberg, B. G., Abul-Ela, A. A., Simmons, W. R., & Horvitz, D. G. The unrelated question randomized response model: Theoretical framework. *Journal of the American Statistical Association*, 1969, *64*, 520-539.

Greenberg, B. G., Horvitz, D. G., & Abernathy, J. R. A comparison of randomized response designs. In F. Proschan & R. J. Serfling, *Reliability and Biometry*. Phila.: SIAM 1974, 787-815.

Greenberg, B. G., Kuebler, R. R., Abernathy, J. R., & Horvitz, D. G. Application of the randomized response technique in obtaining quantitative data. *Journal of the American Statistical Association*, 1971, *66*, 243-250.

Horvitz, D. G., Greenberg, B. G., & Abernathy, J. R. Recent developments in randomized response designs. In J. N. Srivastata (Ed.), *A survey of statistical design and linear models*. Amsterdam: North-Holland, 1975.

Illinois Institute of Technology Research Institute and The Chicago Crime Commission. *A study of organized crime in Illinois*. Chicago: IIT Research Institute, 1971.

Kempthorne, O. *The design and analysis of experiments*. New York: Wiley, 1952.

Lanke, J. On the degree of protection in randomized interviews. *International Statistical Review*, 1976, *44*(2), 197-203.

Lavrakas, P. J. A randomized response technique for assuring confidentiality of data in a group survey situation. Research Memo. Psychology Department, Loyola University, Chicago, 1975.

Liu, P. T., Chow, L. P., & Mosley, W. H. Use of the randomized response technique with a new randomizing device. *Journal of the American Statistical Association*, 1975, *70*(350), 324-332.

Locander, W., Sudman, S., & Bradburn, N. An investigation of interview method, threat, and response distortion. *Journal of the American Statistical Association*, 1976, *71*(354), 269-275.

Pollock, K. H., & Bek, Y. A comparison of three randomized response models for quantitative data. *Journal of the American Statistical Association*, 1976, *71*, 884-886.

Poole, W. K. Estimation of the distribution function of a continuous type random variable through randomized response. *Journal of the American Statistical Association*, 1974, *69*, 1002-1005.

Raghavarao, D., & Federer, W. T. Application of BIB designs as an alternative to the randomized response method in survey sampling. Mineo Series, Biometrics Unit, Cornell University, Ithaca, N.Y., 1973.

Reaser, J. M., Hartsock, S., & Hoehn, A. J. A test of the forced alternative random response questionnaire technique. *HUMRO Technical Report 75-9*, Arlington, Va.: Human Resources Research Organization, 1975.

Simmons, W. R. Response to randomized inquiries: A technique for reducing bias. *Administrative applications conference transactions: American society for quality control*, 1970, *1*(10), 4-13.

Shimizu, I. M., & Bonham, G. S. Randomized response technique in a national survey. *Journal of the American Statistical Association*, 1978, *73*(31), 35-39.

Sudman, S., & Bradburn, N. M. *Response effects in surveys: A review and synthesis.* Chicago: Aldine, 1974.

Swensson, B. Combined independent questions: I. Confidentiality in Surveys Report No. 7, Department of Statistics, University of Stockholm, Stockholm, November 14, 1975.

Swensson, B. Combined independent questions: II. Confidentiality in Surveys Report No. 11, Department of Statistics, University of Stockholm, Stockholm, May 10, 1976.

U.S. Bureau of the Census. *Indexes to survey methodology literature* (Technical Paper No. 34). Washington, D.C.: U.S. Government Printing Office, 1974.

Warner, S. L. Randomized response: A survey technique for eliminating evasive answer bias. *Journal of the American Statistical Association*, 1965, *60*, 63-69.

Warner, S. L. The linear randomized responsive model. *Journal of the American Statistical Association*, 1971, *66*, 884-888.

Warner, S. L. Optimal randomized response models. *International Statistical Review*, 1976, *44*, 205-212.

Zdep, S. M., & Rhodes, I. N. Making the randomized response technique work. *Public Opinion Quarterly*, 1977, *41*, 531-537.

Author Index

(Italics denote entries from the companion volume, *The Ethics of Social Research: Fieldwork, Regulation, and Publication*)

Subject Index

(Italics denote entries from the companion volume, *The Ethics of Social Research: Fieldwork, Regulation, and Publication*)

The Ethics of Social Research
Fieldwork, Regulation, and Publication
(Companion volume to The Ethics of Social Research: Surveys and Experiments)

Contents